Late Ch'ing Imperial Robe with the Twelve Symbols (rear).
(Courtesy of the Walters Gallery, Baltimore.)

CHINA'S DRAGON ROBES

BY

SCHUYLER CAMMANN

UNIVERSITY MUSEUM, PHILADELPHIA

ART MEDIA RESOURCES LTD. CHICAGO

ART MEDIA *SCHOLARLY REPRINTS* SERIES

Copyright@ 1952 by The Ronald Press Company
This ART MEDIA RESOURCES, LTD edition is a republication of the first edition originally published by
Ronald Press Company in 1952. In this present edition a number of errors have been electronically corrected.

ISBN 1-588-86000-0
Library of Congress Catalog Card Number:LC52-9462
ART MEDIA RESOURCES, LTD.
1507 South Michigan Avenue,Chicago,IL 60605 USA
Tel:(312)663-5351 Fax:(312)663-5177
Email:info@artmediaresources.com
Web:www.artmediaresources.com

To My Wife
with gratitude

Foreword

MANY examples of Ch'ing Dynasty dragon robes have found their way into Western museums, notably the Metropolitan Museum in New York City, the Minneapolis Institute of Arts, the Chicago Art Institute, and the Royal Ontario Museum of Archaeology in Toronto, as well as into numerous private collections. These robes are popularly referred to by a variety of ambiguous and inappropriate names such as "mandarin coats," "ceremonial robes," and even "Chinese kimonos." Very few actual facts about them have been published. The scanty material which has appeared, in exhibition catalogues, etc., has been largely devoted to describing them as examples of fine textile work, without giving any proper conception of their evolution, their function in their own times, and their place in Far Eastern culture in general.

I have attempted to provide some of this neglected material, believing that the story of the evolution of the dragon robe and its further development in the Ch'ing Dynasty can help to give a fuller understanding of later Chinese history and culture. In preparation for this I have investigated the histories of various Chinese dynasties, particularly T'ang to Ch'ing, their dynastic statutes, and the available references in contemporary records, as indicated in the bibliography. In addition, evidence has been sought in the robes themselves and in contemporary portraits, both in this country and in China.

Thanks are due to Dr. Chou I-liang, formerly a fellow student in the Harvard Graduate School, and Mr. Joseph Wang of the Library of Congress, for their help in solving problems of translation, as well as the librarians of the Chinese and Japanese libraries at Harvard and Columbia Universities, and the Library of Congress, who have been very generous in their cooperation. I am also grateful to Mr. Laurence Sickman of the Nelson Gallery, Miss H. E. Fernald of Toronto, and the curators of a number of other museums throughout the country who have given generously of their time and experience. Thanks are also due to a number of private collectors who have made their robes available for study, notably Dr. and Mrs. D. Clifford Martin of Port Washington, L. I., and Mr. and Mrs. Walter Beck of New York City. I gratefully acknowledge the kindness of Mr. G. E. Wingfield Digby of the Victoria and Albert Museum, who furnished several of the photographs, and the generosity of Joseph Wang and John L. Bishop who did the fine calligraphy and excellent sketches of the principal symbols found on the robes. Last, but by no means least, my wife, Marcia de F. Cammann, deserves boundless gratitude for many hours of proofreading, numerous fine suggestions, and her constant patience and encouragement.

Parts of Chapters 5 and 6 have already appeared in an article for *Oriental Art,* in England, and portions of Chapters 4 and 11 have been published in *Artibus Asiae,* in Switzerland; while most of Chapter 9 formed an article for *T'oung Pao,* in Holland. However, most of this material is making its first public appearance in the United States.

SCHUYLER VAN R. CAMMANN

Philadelphia
    September, 1951

CONTENTS

PAGE

Foreword   V

Part I

DRAGON ROBES PROPER

CHAPTER

1 The Early History of Dragon Robes   3
2 Ming Dragon Robes   10
3 Manchu Dragon Robes: Early Laws and General History   20
4 Early Ch'ing Dragon Robes: Evolution of the Patterns   35
5 Later Ch'ing Dragon Robes: the Laws of 1759   50
6 Later Ch'ing Dragon Robes: Problems of Dating   58
7 Women's Dragon Robes and Dragon Jackets   69
8 The Symbols on the Dragon Robes   77
9 The Making of Dragon Robes: Techniques and Dyes   108

Part II

RELATED ROBES

10 Unofficial Dragon-Figured Robes   127
11 Ch'ing Court Robes for Men   135
12 Women's Court Robes and Court Vests   146
13 The Robes of the Taiping Rebels   152
14 Dragon Robes in Other Lands   157
15 Summary   176

Bibliography of the Principal Oriental Sources   187
Appendices   189
Glossary   201
Index   219

PART I

DRAGON ROBES PROPER

1

The Early History of Dragon Robes

BY simplest definition, a "dragon robe" is a long garment that was worn by courtiers and officials of the later dynasties in China, on which the principal pattern consisted of dragons. Such decoration was especially popular in the Ch'ing Dynasty (1644-1911), when the dragon became practically the symbol of China, eventually appearing on most Chinese coins and medals, and even on the national flag. During this period, almost all the court and official robes were figured with dragons, but the term "dragon robe" [1] was restricted to a specific type of semiformal robe. It is the latter which will occupy our chief attention in the following pages.

Although robes with dragon patterns reached their height of popularity in the Ch'ing Dynasty, they had enjoyed a comparatively long history before that. But they cannot claim any real antiquity. Some scholars have thought that they must be very old because of occasional references in the old Chinese classics to something called a "dragon garment." However, this term referred merely to the upper coat of the sacrificial costume worn by the rulers of China and their highest officials, [2] and not to the full robe. Furthermore, the decoration on these consisted of a combination of the Twelve Sym-

---

[1] In the Ch'ing Dynasty two terms were used for "dragon robe," depending on the number of claws on the dragons. Those with five-clawed dragons were called *lung-p'ao,* while those with four-clawed dragons were called *mang-p'ao.* (The characters for these and other Oriental words and phrases are given in the glossary.) In the records of previous dynasties one sometimes finds references to "dragon garments," *lung-i* or *mang-i.* But the term *lung-i* was also sometimes used for other types of clothing worn by the Chinese emperors, because the ruler of China was figuratively called "the Dragon," hence the word dragon was used to qualify any of his possessions, as in the familiar expression "dragon throne."

[2] See Note 1. The proper name for the Emperor's upper ceremonial robe was *kun.*

bols,[3] and although dragons did occur among these, they were small
and relatively unobtrusive, forming a comparatively insignificant part
of the whole pattern. Therefore these sacrificial coats were not true
dragon robes.[4]

The first reliable reference to dragons as the principal design on
robes dates from the T'ang Dynasty (618-908). In 694, during the
reign of the notorious Empress Wu, the Court gave out embroidered
robes for presentation to officials above the third rank, with patterns
on them according to the station of the recipient, and the princes
received robes with coiled dragons, or deer, on them.[5] It is important to note that these robes with coiled dragons were presentation
robes, because the later dragon robes were often bestowed by the
Emperor on favored individuals. This seems to mark the beginning
of that tradition.

We cannot say whether or not the Emperors of the T'ang wore
dragon robes, as the laws of this dynasty do not mention such robes
for the Emperor's use. The Palace Museum in Peking has a pair of
portraits supposed to represent the first two T'ang Emperors, in
which they are shown wearing robes with large dragon medallions
on them.[6] However, the dragons themselves are painted in Yüan or
Ming style and have too many claws—the dragons of the T'ang regu-

[3] These were called the *shih-erh chang*. For a detailed description of these
symbols, how they were used, and their significance, see Chapters 2, 5, and 8,
Section B.

[4] Both Couvreur and Legge, in their translations of the *Li chi*, spoke of this
upper robe—here called *chüan* (Giles, no. 3146) instead of *kun*—as a "dragon-
figured robe." However, such a translation is completely unwarranted, since it
gives an inaccurate picture of the garment. See Couvreur, *Li Ki* I, p. 732, and Legge,
Li Ki II (Sacred Books of the East Series, Vol. 28), p. 32. De Visser quotes these
two references to indicate the importance of the dragon at an early period in China,
but since this was merely a robe with many symbols, among which the dragons
occupied a subordinate position, the quotations did not prove what he hoped they
did. See M. W. de Visser, *The Dragon in China and Japan* (Amsterdam, 1913),
p. 100.

Legge again mistranslates *kun*, calling it a "dragon robe," in *Li Ki* I, p. 434 and
II, p. 247. Then, in translating the Book of Poetry, he also refers to this ceremonial
robe, here called *hsüan kun*, as "a dark-colored robe with dragons on it"—the same
misleading description. See Legge, *Chinese Classics* IV, Part 2 (*She King*), pp. 402,
547. See also Chapter 8, Note 42, below.

[5] *T'ang hui-yao* 32.2.

[6] Illustrated in the *Ku-kung chou-k'an* No. 110 (Nov. 14, 1931), p. 1, and No. 111
(Nov. 21, 1931), p. 1; as well as in *Chung-kuo li-tai ti-hou-hsiang*.

larly had only three [7]—so these paintings are undoubtedly very late and useless as evidence.

We find no further mention of dragon robes until the tenth century, when the first Emperor of the Sung Dynasty (960-1279) presented an imperial robe with coiled dragons worked in pearls to one of his officers, Tung Ch'iu-hui.[8] This seems to be the only reference to the presentation of a dragon robe in this dynasty, but the fact that it is called "imperial" suggests that it represented a type usually worn by the Emperor. Meanwhile, a passage on the Emperor's clothing in the Sung Dynastic History speaks of a deep crimson robe brocaded with clouds and dragons in stripes of red and gold,[9] and the Dynastic Statutes mention a robe of this description as part of the Emperor's "carriage-riding costume." [10] Furthermore, in the year 1111 dragon patterns were forbidden to all subjects, along with brocades of gold wire, etc.[11] This law, apparently the first of its kind in China proper, indicates that at this time the use of dragons on robes had been made a prerogative of the Emperor and Empress, unless they wished to bestow them as marks of special favor.

None of the surviving portraits of the Sung Emperors shows a robe with a dragon pattern, so we cannot see how the dragons were disposed on the robes of that period. However, we do know that they were probably three-clawed dragons with horns curling upward at the tips, like those of the T'ang (although the four-clawed dragon had begun to appear in later Sung art), for this three-clawed type is shown, figured among clouds, on the collars and robe borders in several portraits of the Sung Empresses.[12] Furthermore, we cannot tell if the Sung had yet developed the bold patterns that characterized

[7] For T'ang examples (not on clothing) see S. Cammann, "A Rare T'ang Mirror," *Art Quarterly,* Vol. 9 (1946), No. 2, figs. 4 and 5.

[8] *Shan-t'ang szŭ-k'ao* Supplement 44.6b. This describes the robe as *yü chên-chu pan-lung i,* but in Tung's biography (*Sung shih* 273.20b) the word *yü* is omitted.

[9] *Sung hui-yao kao, tsê* 45 (*ch.* 5514) *yü-fu* 5.14.

[10] *Sung shih* 151.14, *ch'êng-yü-fu.*

[11] *Sung hui-yao kao, tsê* 44 (*ch.* 19, 815) *yü-fu* 4.7b.

[12] See the portraits of the Empresses Ying Tsung and Shên Tsung of the Northern Sung Dynasty in *Chung-kuo li-tai ti-hou-hsiang.* It is possible that these are not the originals, but they seem to have faithful reproductions of the original costume details. However, the second portrait of the former is a much later painting of Yüan or Ming date, and the artist has added extra claws to the dragons on her collar.

the later dragon robes. We can only assume, in the light of other art productions of the period, that the Sung Emperors probably preferred small and subtle patterns.

Probably it was one of the foreign peoples of the North who developed the use of large, bold dragon designs on the robes. For, in the meantime, dragon robes had apparently captured the fancy of the Tartar rulers of North China and Manchuria. In 1077, the Khitan Emperor of the Liao Dynasty (947-1125) passed a law that officials and common people could not wear clothes of silk or brocade with the sun or moon, mountains or dragons, patterned on them.[13] Thus, dragon patterns must have been a monopoly of the Emperor, and perhaps his highest princes.

Moreover, in 1140 the Ju-chên tribe, which had succeeded the Khitans and formed the Chin Dynasty (1122-1234), issued a series of sumptuary laws, one of which refers to imperial dragon-figured robes. This edict states that if members of the Imperial Family and collateral relatives had been presented with imperial yellow robes proper to the Emperor, having dragon patterns and cloud collars with the sun and moon, they must exchange them for others.[14] This not only indicates that the Chin Emperors were wearing dragon robes, but also informs us that they had occasionally bestowed them on their noble relatives.

It is interesting to read that the Chin dragon robes had "cloud collars," *yün-chien,* for this convention—or survivals of it—reappears on many of the dragon robes of succeeding dynasties. The cloud collar was a form of decoration consisting of four triangular or heart-shaped lobes, projecting down the chest and down the back, and extending out on the shoulders. Sometimes it was actually a detached collar, but in this case, as was common at that period, it was woven into the robe as part of the design.[15] The cloud collars were

---

[13] *Liao shih* 23.7. This was the first law against wearing dragons in China, as far as we know, but an earlier law in Korea (1043) had prohibited the wearing of robes with brocaded or embroidered dragons or "phoenixes." (*TPMHPK* 80.3.)

[14] *Chin shih* 43.11.

[15] The use of detachable cloud collars in more recent times, by Chinese brides and lama priests, will be discussed in later chapters. The history of the cloud collar

variously decorated and, judging from this passage, that on the Chin Emperor's robe was figured with the sun and moon, probably as symbols of his power.[16]

The Mongols of the Yüan Dynasty (1260-1368) inherited the tradition of dragon robes from both the Sung and the Tartar dynasties of the North, and they apparently made it an established institution, though our evidence for this is rather scattered. In 1271, several years before Khubilai Khan actually assumed the throne of China, he forbade the use of silk or satin woven with the sun or moon, dragons or tigers;[17] while a woodcut of Khubilai in a Ming encyclopaedia, which was probably taken from a Yüan portrait, shows this famous ruler wearing a robe with dragons on each shoulder, extending over onto the chest and back of the robe.[18]

The Yüan sumptuary laws are full of foreign words for fabrics, etc., rather awkwardly transcribed, which make especially difficult reading, but they describe robes worn by the later Emperors, of various colors with *lung* dragons woven in gold.[19] One of these laws expressly forbids officials to wear the *lung,* and defines this creature as having five claws and two horns.[20] The appended definition implies that the five-clawed dragon was confined to the Emperor and his princes, but that lesser nobles and officials could wear the four-clawed dragon, which later dynasties called a *mang.* In fact, a Ming scholar definitely asserts that the four-clawed dragon

---

in general and its significance are discussed by the writer in "The Symbolism of the Cloud Collar Motif," *Art Bulletin,* Vol. 33 (1951).

[16] Incidentally, these figures of the sun and moon enhance the fundamental cosmic symbolism of the whole collar. For the form of the cloud collar as a whole reflects ancient cosmic symbolism involving the four directions, etc., as noted in *ibid.*

[17] *Yüan shih* 10.6. This is an especially valuable reference as it shows that the dragon was an imperial monopoly among the Mongols even before they completed the conquest of China. Furthermore, since this law was made before the Mongol emperors had adopted the Chinese sacrificial costume—on which the sun and moon were included among the Twelve Symbols, and therefore forbidden to others—it indicates that the sun and moon in themselves must have had special significance for the non-Chinese peoples of the North. This, then, might also explain the Liao and Chin references to the sun and moon as particularly restricted symbols.

[18] *San-tsai t'u-hui, jen-wu* 1.24.

[19] *Yüan shih* 78.10; *Hsin Yüan-shih* 95.2b. See also Chapter 9 for a brief description of the fabrics used.

[20] *Yüan tien-chang* 29.2b.

was generally used in the Yüan by officials of all ranks.[21] These five-clawed dragons (and perhaps the four-clawed ones as well) were probably themselves of foreign origin, Khitan, Ju-chên, or Mongol; since, as we have seen, the traditional Chinese dragon had only three claws.

Although the literary evidence makes it clear that the Mongols wore dragons on their robes, nothing is said about how they were displayed. Furthermore, pictorial evidence from Chinese paintings of the period is also very scanty. We know of only one contemporary portrait showing a Yüan-style dragon robe, and that dates from the end of the dynasty, apparently showing a rather late development.[22]

Fortunately, however, we can get some evidence from the Persian miniatures of the period, for the Mongol rulers of Persia seem to have worn the same type of costume as their relatives, the rulers of China. For example, some illustrations in a rare Yüan book preserved in the Palace Museum at Peking depict the Mongol officials of China wearing long, tightly belted robes with very long sleeves, or robes of similar cut with short sleeves, worn over long-sleeved under robes [23]—exactly the same styles that are shown in the miniatures of contemporary Persia, which picture the Mongols there.[24] But, whereas the Yüan artist in the book cited did not bother with the details of the decoration on the robes, the Persian painters have rendered them in great detail. Some of the robes had allover patterns, presumably in brocade, but more often the decoration was limited to certain areas. The decoration on the upper part

[21] Ch'iu Hsün, in *Ta-hsüeh yen-i-pu* (1488), quoted in *T'u-shu chi-ch'êng, li-pu* 330. (1st) 19b.

[22] Worn by Li Chên (1303-1378), brother-in-law of the first Ming Emperor. The portrait shows him as a relatively young man, so it must have been painted considerably before the fall of Yüan and the founding of the Ming—at which time he would have been about sixty-six. The portrait is reproduced in the Li Family History (see Bibliography), no pagination.

[23] The *Shih-lin kuang-chi*. See two of the illustrations reproduced in *Ku-kung chou-k'an*, No. 358 (June 13, 1934), p. 4; and No. 359 (June 30, 1934), p. 4.

[24] See the illustrations in E. Blochet, *Histoire des Mongols de Fadl Allah Rashīd ed Dīn*, E. J. W. Gibb Memorial, Vol. 18.2 (Leyden and London, 1911), esp. pl. 4, p. 41. These Mongol styles also continued on into the fifteenth century in Persia, and can be seen at their best in the miniature paintings of the Timurid period.

of the robe was usually confined to a cloud collar; patches on the shoulders (as shown in the picture of Khubilai Khan, mentioned above); or on squares on chest and back, and sometimes on the shoulders as well. The same design was usually repeated on a narrow strip across the skirt at the knees, or slightly below them. (See Plate 1.)

Only one of these miniatures shows a dragon pattern on the robes; this depicts two "Chinese princes" (of the Yüan) with dragons in squares on the backs of their robes, presumably repeating a similar design on the front.[25] But we can assume that the dragons on Yüan robes in China were displayed at the same places as the Persian ones, on cloud collars and strips across the skirts as well as in squares, because, as we shall see, the patterns on the Ming dragon robes preserve survivals of all these usages.

The late Yüan portrait of an official wearing a dragon robe, to which we previously referred,[26] shows some interesting variations. The robe is of the long-sleeved type, and shows two principal dragons. The head of the first is on the chest of the robe, and its body loops out and back over the left shoulder, while the second dragon must be similarly disposed on the back of the robe, for its tail is seen emerging over the right shoulder. (Note the similar arrangement of the upper dragons in Plate 2, left.) Thus the combined pattern of the two dragons forms a composition in the form of four lobes, on the chest and back and out on the shoulders, as if to fit within the confines of a cloud collar, although the characteristic outer border of the latter has been omitted. The rest of the robe, including the sleeves, has an allover diaper pattern made by countless very small dragons in medallions.

This was no doubt only one of many Yüan types. For if the T'ang and Sung had invented the idea of dragon patterns, it seems to have been the Yüan that first developed their use on a large scale, and thus the Mongol Dynasty was responsible for making dragon robes an important element in the court and official costume of later China.

[25] *Ibid.*, pl. 1.
[26] See Note 22, above.

2

Ming Dragon Robes

IN the Ming Dynasty (1368-1644), the ultraconservative and nationalistic Chinese Court did everything possible to get away from the foreign influence of the Mongols. As a result of this, in preparing the detailed regulations for Ming costume, the Board of Rites stressed the return to the old Chinese customs of the Han and T'ang, when China was ruled by strong native dynasties.[1] The new official robes were traditionally Chinese in cut, with wide flowing sleeves and very full skirts, slit at the sides. Instead of being tightly girt with Mongol-style belts, they were worn with stiff and clumsy hoop-belts that stood out quite far in front, and were intended primarily to display jeweled plaques indicating the wearers' rank. In short, though these robes must have presented an impressive and dignified appearance, they were impractical for anything but a quiet life at court. (Plate 2 shows the general cut of these robes.)

This trend away from foreign innovations may have prevented dragon robes from becoming part of the prescribed official costume of Ming, but they did not drop out altogether. A portrait of the first Ming Emperor, said to have been painted by a contemporary, and now in a French collection, shows him wearing one.[2] The robe is yellow, with two principal dragons on the upper portion, arranged like those of the late Yüan portrait referred to above, the only difference being that their heads are facing instead of being shown in profile; while below, a pair of dragons form a horizontal band of decoration across the skirt, recalling the horizontal strip on the Yüan robes.

[1] *Ming shih* 67.1b, 5.
[2] O. Siren, *History of Later Chinese Painting* 1, pl. 10. This painting is (or was) in the Collection of M. Halphen, in Paris.

Unfortunately this is not a very finished portrait, and we cannot assume that the robe is painted in full detail.[3] The interesting thing is that the Emperor is shown in this type of robe with the principal dragons looping over the shoulders, for the later Ming Emperors were never painted in such robes, though they probably had them. Also the heads of the two main dragons are facing. This latter feature demonstrates the early origin of the Ming tradition that the principal dragons on the Emperor's dragon robes—and later, on those of his most favored courtiers as well—should be shown facing, while those of all other nobles and officials entitled to wear dragon robes should be in profile.

For some reason, the Ming laws for costume never mention dragon robes of this type, though, as we shall see, they became very common. However, they do mention some with dragon medallions, for the tradition of dragon medallion robes, which may have died out during the Yüan, was revived in 1405. In that year, it was officially announced that the informal robes of the Emperor should be yellow, with four coiled-dragon medallions, woven in gold, on chest and back and on each shoulder;[4] while the Heir Apparent, first- and second-degree princes, and sons of first-degree princes, should wear red robes, with the same four dragon medallions in gold.[5]

These medallion robes, unlike the other form of robe with the larger dragons, apparently were not differentiated by having facing dragons for the Emperor and dragons in profile for those beneath him. At least this was not done during the first half of the dynasty, for portraits of some of the earlier emperors show them wearing four dragons in profile.

The first marked variation from the pattern of four medallions on the imperial robes came with the Hsüan-tê Emperor (1426-35).

---

[3] The face, for example, is little more than a caricature, even though the Hung Wu Emperor is said to have been notoriously ugly, and the attempted perspective of the throne is very bad, so we can conclude that this was only intended as a crude sketch-portrait.

[4] *Ming shih* 66.6.

[5] *Ibid.*, 66.12.

His portrait, preserved in the Palace Museum in Peking, shows him wearing a robe with twelve large medallions, each having a pair of dragons; the usual four on chest, back, and shoulders; four more on the skirt, at front and back, and on either side; and one on the front and back of each broad sleeve.[6]

The final step in the basic development of the Ming imperial dragon robe apparently came in the second reign of the Emperor Ying-tsung, after he returned from captivity among the Mongols. His robes and those of his successors continued the tradition of the twelve dragon medallions, twelve being a complete and auspicious number. However, only eight of them appeared on the outer robe; the other four being figured on an under robe. The upper part of the outer robe had the usual four dragon medallions, on chest, back, and shoulders, with two on the front of the skirt and two on the back, placed vertically, one above the other; while four more, also arranged vertically in pairs, were displayed at the sides of the under skirt, projecting through slits at the sides of the outer robe.[7]

In addition, he and the later emperors wore the Twelve Symbols, which had appeared since ancient times on the Emperor of China's sacrificial robes, and now were being used for the first time on less formal dress. The sun disc was woven on the left shoulder, and the moon disc on the right. The constellation of seven stars appeared above the mountain, which was placed over the main dragon on the back,[8] and the pheasants were arranged in pairs on each sleeve. (The dragon as a separate symbol seems to have been omitted from this set, because dragons were already shown on the robe.) On each side of the front and the rear panels of the skirt were arranged the rest: a sacrificial cup, water weed, grains of millet set out in a medallion, flames, the sacrificial axe, and the *fŭ* symbol.[9] (See Plate 3.)

---

[6] *Chung-kuo li-tai ti-hou-hsiang* (no pagination).

[7] *Ibid.*

[8] The *Ming shih* (66.2b), describing another form of Twelve-Symbol robe, explains that the stars were placed with the mountain on the back of the robe. Note that the Ming used all seven stars of the constellation, while the Ch'ing imperial robes used only three.

[9] For fuller descriptions and interpretations of the Twelve Symbols, see Chapter 8.

The only changes in the fundamental pattern of this type of imperial dragon robe in the further course of the Ming, judging from portraits of the emperors, was that the background material was sometimes of cloud-figured satin instead of being solid-colored dark silk, and at the very end of the dynasty there were slight differences in the disposition of the Twelve Symbols.[10]

Another form of imperial dragon robe, for less formal occasions, was devised in 1528 by order of the Chia-ching Emperor. The Emperor's own robe, called *hsüan-tuan-fu*, was black with blue borders. The sun and moon were displayed on the shoulders, while the chest had a large circular plaque with a single coiled dragon, and the back a square plaque with two confronted dragons. Many very small dragons writhe_ in the border, one hundred and eighty-nine in all.[11]

The robes of the princes, by the laws of 1528, were known as *pao-ho-fu.* They were plain blue with cloud-figured blue borders, and had square dragon patterns on breast and back.[12] They corresponded to the similarly designed presentation robes of the officials, *chung-ching-fu,* which were also prescribed at this time, but the squares on the latter had animals or birds to indicate the wearers' ranks, instead of dragons.[13]

Meanwhile, although dragon robes were never officially decreed during the Ming, several varieties —especially those with four-clawed *mang* dragons, called *mang-i*—gradually came back into wide use. The first reference to them states that in the reign of Yung-Lo (1403-1425) the eunuchs who stood on either side of the Emperor, as his principal attendants, were required to wear *mang* robes.[14]

[10] The portrait of the last Emperor, Hsi Tsung (in *Chung kuo li-tai ti-hou-hsiang*), shows only two symbols, the axe and the *fu* symbol on the front of his skirt. The others must have been transferred to the rear. It also looks as though what had been under the skirt was now part of the robe proper, so that all twelve dragon medallions were now on the outer robe.

[11] *Ming shih* 66.6b, 7. Illustrated in *MHT* 60.1486-7.

[12] *Ibid.,* 66.13. Illustrated in *MHT* 60.1513-14.

[13] See S. Cammann, "Development of the Mandarin Square," *HJAS*, Vol. 8 (1944), p. 90, text and note 58.

[14] *Ming shih* 67.15.

The description of these speaks of black robes with dragons embroidered at left and right.[15]

Contemporary paintings show the robes of the eunuch attendants with the two dragons arranged like those on the late Yüan portrait and the portrait of Hung Wu, mentioned above, with their heads on the chest and back of the robes respectively, and their bodies looping back over the shoulders. The paintings also show a background of clouds to round out the four lobes of the design, which reach far down on the breast and back, and out onto the sleeves, with a delimiting border.[16] In short, the pattern makes a huge collar, recalling the Tartar cloud collars. In addition, these robes also had an ornamental band of decoration extending across the skirt below the knees, in the old Yüan style.

During this reign the custom arose of presenting dragon robes to the rulers of the more civilized tribute-bearing nations. In the year 1411, for example, when the Prince of Malacca came in person to the Chinese Court, he was given a pair of brocaded and embroidered robes with *lung* dragons,[17] and at the same period two Sultans of Sulu were also presented with fine robes figured with *mang* and *lung* dragons in gold.[18] These were apparently bestowed to encourage trade, but by the middle of the century the Ming Court found another diplomatic use for them, presenting them to Mongol chieftains on the northern borders who were inclined to raid when they were not bribed into submission. The most notorious case was that of Altan Khan of the Tumets, about a hundred years later (mid-sixteenth century), who received several dragon robes but kept on raiding.[19]

[15] *Ibid.*

[16] Several paintings showing Court scenes, with eunuchs in these robes, can be found in the Wu Family History (see Bibliography), no pagination.

[17] *MHT* 111.2368. This must have been Muhammad Iskander Shah, second Prince of Malacca, who ascended the throne in 1414. See B. H. M. Vlekke, *Nusantara* (Cambridge, 1944), pp. 70-71.

[18] *MHT* 111.2367, and *Ming shih* 325.7b.

[19] The *Yeh-huo pien* (appendix 2.10b) says that the Mongol chieftains first received dragon robes in the (Chêng – túng reign), but the *Ming Hui-tien,* which is often incomplete on such matters, does not mention any gifts of dragon robes to the Mongols before the time of the Altan Khan (*MHT* 111.2371).

Not only the foreigners coveted these robes; Chinese nobles and officials desired them as well. Probably the highest nobles automatically received them, but the custom soon sprang up of awarding them to especially high-placed, or unusually worthy, courtiers and officials. After 1432, when a *mang* robe was presented to Wang Chi on his return from a successful military expedition in Southwestern Yünnan, they were regularly given to Commanders-in-chief as a reward for their achievements.[20]

About this time (mid-fifteenth century), the custom also arose of conferring a *mang* robe on the Chief Eunuch, who had already come to hold a baleful influence over the court.[21] As a mark of his power, his robe had a special dragon, called *tso mang,* or seated *mang.*[22] The Ming texts explain that this meant that it was shown fullface, with its entire body on the front of the robe, like the *lung* dragon on the Emperor's robe.[23] By contrast, the form of dragon shown in profile, and extending back over the shoulders, was called a *tan mang* or simple *mang,*[24] and this of course was the usual type.

We read that in addition to the two forms of *mang* differentiated by their position, the presentation robes also had two types distinguished by a variation in the number of claws. These were the usual four-clawed *mang* and a five-clawed variety.[25] A "five-clawed *mang"* was of course technically a *lung* dragon, but the term was a convenient euphemism, since the laws strictly stated that only the

---

The functioning of the Ming diplomatic system of "honors and decorations" (*ming chi*), in which the presentation of dragon robes to non-Chinese princes and border chieftains played an important part, is well described by T. C. Lin in "Manchuria in the Ming Empire," *Nankai Social and Economic Quarterly,* Vol. 8 (Tientsin, 1935), pp. 37-41. (He translates the term *mang-p'ao* incorrectly as "serpent-embroidered robes," instead of "four-clawed dragon robes," evidently misled by the common dictionary meaning of *mang.* See Chapter 8, Section A.)

[20] *Yeh-huo pien,* appendix 2.10b.

[21] *Ibid.,* 2.10.

[22] *Yeh-huo pien* 1.29.

[23] *Ibid.,* and *Ming shih* 67.15. Portraits in the Palace Museum (reproduced in *Chung-kuo li-tai ti-hou-hsiang*) show that some of the Ming Empresses also wore full-faced dragon patterns on the breast of otherwise plain robes. However, in most cases these are partially hidden by the dragon-figured stoles worn over them.

[24] *Ming shih* 67.15.

[25] *Ibid.*

Emperor and his immediate family had the right to wear a *lung*.[26] No doubt the ambitious Chief Eunuch managed to get the five-clawed type.

The simplest form of presentation dragon robe at this time merely had a *mang* in a square pattern, *mang-p'u,* on breast and back,[27] but the more elaborate ones had dragons on the shoulders, and later on the sleeves, as well. Note that on the robe shown in Plate 2, right, the dragons on the sleeves are incorporated into the design on the upper robe extending down from the shoulders, so that the whole upper robe comprises an enormous cloud collar, though this lacks the traditional serrated border. Meanwhile the standard type of dragon robe with the two main dragons on front and back, extending over the shoulders, continued in favor.

The more honorable and most coveted robes also had the narrow band of design, called *hsi-lan,* stretching across the skirt at the knees,[28] with four smaller dragons, a pair in front and a pair behind. A strip of waves was sketched in beneath them, and a mountain was generally shown rising from the waves at the center, between the dragons. The background color of this band provided a still further distinction in robe types. Its color on the finest robes was yellow, while the secondary ones had a red band. Since the robes were of dark material, these must have stood out prominently.

Still further precedents, and other types of robes, were established in the next century. In 1503, when the Hung-chih Emperor held a celebration to mark his return to court after an absence, he gave *mang* robes to all the members of the Grand Council, the chief governing body of the Empire,[29] a custom followed by his descendants. The robes presented on this occasion were described as deep crimson *mang* robes, *ta-hung mang-i,* and the especially full-cut red dragon robes were characteristic features of the later Ming court,

[26] In the following dynasty of Ch'ing, the Court tried to forestall this by always specifying in the laws "five-clawed *lung*" and "four-clawed *mang*."
[27] *Ming shih* 67.15.
[28] *Ibid.*
[29] *Yeh-huo pien,* appendix 2.10, 10b.

red being the dynastic color.[30] (Plate 2, left, shows an example of the type.) Note that it has the two principal dragons arranged in the standard manner, extending over the shoulders, two lesser ones on the sleeves, and pairs of still smaller ones on the skirt. On these robes the skirt band was the same color as the rest of the garment.

In 1518, the Chêng-tê Emperor was even more generous, and gave robes to all his courtiers according to their rank.[31] An account of this says that the first rank received robes figured with *tou-niu,* a type of three-clawed dragon with down-curving horns.[32] The second rank received robes with *fei-yü,* a kind of winged dragon-fish (literally "flying fish"), and the third rank, four-clawed *mang* robes, etc.[33] There seems to be some mistake in this listing, for other references explicitly state that the *fei-yü* and *tou-niu,* in that order, were considered inferior to the *mang.* At any rate, by this time we find several types of dragons, the five-clawed *lung,* the four- (or five-) clawed *mang,* and the three-clawed *tou-niu,* together with the half-dragon "flying fish." [34]

From that time on, the wearing of dragon robes became very fashionable, so great numbers of officials disregarded the law of 1459 which prohibited anyone from having dragon robes made for himself,[35] and ordered them freely on their own authority. Finally, in 1537, the Chia-ching Emperor was greatly angered by a particularly flagrant case [36] and issued a stern decree against officials

[30] *Ming shih* 67.1b mentions the dynastic color.

[31] *Ibid.,* 67.6, 6b.

[32] The *tou-niu* is graphically pictured in the *San-tsai t'u-hui, niao-shou* 5c, and described on 5d. Shên Tê-fu implies that this animal and the "flying fish" were purely Ming inventions, unknown to earlier dynasties (*Yeh-hou pien,* appendix 2.10b). They were not just invented in time for this occasion in 1518, however, because a law of 1459 had already mentioned both, among the types of robe decoration forbidden to officials (*Ming shih* 67.6).

[33] *Ming shih* 67.6b.

[34] *Yeh-huo pien,* Appendix 2.10b.

[35] Law quoted in *Ming shih* 67.6b.

[36] "In the 16th year of Chia-ching, when all the Ministers of State came to a court audience at the Imperial halting place, Chang Tsan, the President of the Board of War, was wearing a *mang* (robe). The Emperor angrily informed his Minister Hsia Yen, saying, '(Chang Tsan) is of the second rank, how can he take it upon

who wore robes with dragons of any type without having been awarded the right to do so.[37]

The decree of 1537 did not curb the officials' desire to wear the resplendent dragon robes, however. It merely caused them to make greater efforts to get these robes conferred on them. By the beginning of the next century, conditions at the Ming Court had become so lax and corrupt that this was a comparatively easy matter. Shên Tê-fu, a late Ming scholar-antiquarian writing in 1606, complains of the many abuses in the conferring of dragon robes.[38]

First, he tell us, members of the Grand Council and others were getting robes with *tso mang,* full-faced dragons like those worn by the Emperor (which probably had the five claws as well). Secondly, certain high officials were being conferred dragon robes three or four times in succession. Lastly, dragon robes were no longer confined to a few especially worthy individuals. They were being conferred on everyone from the Ministers of the Six Boards, Expeditionary Generals and Commanders-in-Chief, down to the officers and eunuchs in the palaces of the princes—men of barely the sixth rank—who obtained them through the good offices of their patrons.[39]

This sounds as though a tremendous number of dragon robes were being made, especially if the wives of the nobles and officials who had been given the right to wear such robes were also permitted to wear them. We have no definite information about this in the Chinese records, but a series of later Ming portraits shows the wives of marquises wearing the same type of dragon robes as their husbands. The only difference was that the main dragons faced in the opposite direction: the front one looping back over the woman's right shoulder, and the rear one looping forward over her left shoulder.[40]

---

himself to wear a *mang?'* (Hsia) Yen answered him, saying, 'But that which (Chang) Tsan is wearing is an Imperially conferred "flying-fish" robe; it is new and resembles a *mang.'* The Emperor responded, 'Why is it furnished with two horns? This is strictly forbidden." (*Ming shih* 67.7b, 8.)

[37] *Ibid.,* 67.8.
[38] *Yeh-huo pien* 1.29-30; appendix 2.10b.
[39] *Ibid.,* appendix 2.10b.
[40] These portraits are found in the Li Family History (no pagination).

If this was a general custom, there must have been a very considerable number of Ming dragon robes in existence by the time the Manchus conquered China in 1644, yet not one has survived to find its way into a Western collection. This is not surprising, however, considering the fact that only two or three Early Ch'ing robes have come down to our own day.

There are several good reasons for their disappearance. In the first place, the right to wear a dragon robe was an honor, even though many individuals could obtain it. Thus, their owners undoubtedly prized them highly—to the extent of wishing to be buried in them. Then, although the Manchus had another costume tradition, using robes of very different cut, we shall see that they were able to use the Ming dragon robes—except for the red ones, since they had a strong aversion to red [41]—by recutting them to make their own style of dragon robes, as well as court robes. As for the red ones, Ch'ing Dynasty portraits show us that some of them must have been passed down in Chinese families, after the fall of the Ming, to be worn by the wives of Chinese officials in the new dynasty as "dragon coats" (see Chapter 10). It seems probable, however, that many, if not most, of the Ming-style "dragon coats" worn in the Ch'ing were merely copies of the older robes, representing the survival of an obsolete type, like the example shown in Plate 17.

[41] Red was the dynastic color of the Ming, and therefore it was considered unlucky by the Manchus of the succeeding dynasty, who strictly avoided wearing red robes. The one great exception was the Ch'ing Emperor's robe for the sacrifice at the Altar of the Sun, when red was required by the traditions of ancient ritual.

3

Manchu Dragon Robes: Early Laws and General History

WE have seen that the first rules for Ming official costumes emphasized their national character by an appeal to the old Chinese traditions of the Han and T'ang, in protest against alien influences introduced by the Yüan Mongols—although within two generations their informal robes were again reflecting Yüan styles in the dragon patterns. Similarly, the first edicts regarding Ch'ing costume stressed their own national character, and invoked the old traditions of the Manchus in order to forestall the possible deteriorating influences of the new (Chinese) culture, with which the Manchus now found themselves surrounded.[1]

The Ch'ing proscription against Ming styles was directed against the cut of the Ming dragon robes, but did not extend to their patterns. This was because dragon robes were already a part of the Manchu tradition before the Conquest in 1644. Their leaders had been obtaining Ming dragon robes since the early sixteenth century and, although they altered them somewhat, dragon robes had become part of their own culture. In fact, as the dragon robes had never been an integral part of the Ming costume tradition— they were not even specifically mentioned in the Ming clothing laws —it remained for the Ch'ing rulers to make these robes a definite feature of Chinese official costume.

---

[1] These sentiments were expressed in two edicts of Abahai, the second great Manchu ruler, when he warned his princes and highest nobles against adopting the Chinese costume and language, lest the Manchus should lose their national identity and their dynasty collapse. These are found in the *Tung-hua lu, Ch'ung-tê* 1.19b ff.; 2.8b ff.; and the *T'ai-tsung Wên-huang-ti shih-lu* 32.8 ff.; 34.26b ff. The second is paraphrased, with numerous omissions, in the *Ch'ing-shih k̆ao* 109.1.

The full-cut Ming robes were repellent to the Manchus, who considered them not only effete but most impractical. The traditional robes of the Manchus before they entered China were of an entirely different style, conforming to their way of life as horsemen, hunters, and warriors. Like the robes of the Yüan Dynasty, they were relatively close-fitting, but had shorter, rather tight sleeves. Moreover, they had some very distinctive features of their own. The sleeves ended in crescent-shaped "horsehoof cuffs" called *ma-ti hsiu,* that protected the backs of the hands; and the skirts (of the men's robes) were split front and rear for convenience in riding. A narrow, Mongol-style belt of cloth or leather, fitted tightly around the waist with knife, flint-and-steel set, purses, kerchiefs, and other utilitarian possessions hanging from rings at each side. The ornamental buckles on their formal belts (*ch'ao-tai*) with the jewels atop their hats, designated the ranks of nobles and officials. For special occasions Manchus of high degree wore over their robes short-sleeved, knee-length jackets or long-sleeved full-length jackets, of cloth for summer and of fur (or fur-trimmed) for winter. (See Plate 8, left.)

In 1632, Ning Wan-wo, a Chinese official serving with the Manchus in Manchuria, suggested that both Chinese and Manchus in the service of the new dynasty should have identical official costumes to prevent any discrimination.[2] This was approved, so when the Manchus conquered China in 1644, they required the Chinese who joined their government to wear Manchu official dress; while all other Chinese had to wear Manchu-style queues and a modification of the Manchu robe. The only concession to native Chinese custom was the adoption, in 1652, of Ming-style badges of rank ("mandarin squares") for their formal jackets, which were now called *p'u-fu.*[3] (See Plate 8, left.)

---

[2] *T'ai-tsung Wên-huang-ti shih-lu* 10.31b ff. This gives the date of the memorial as February 13th, 1632; though *Eminent Chinese of the Ch'ing Period* (p. 592) says that it was presented in 1631.

[3] *KHHT* 48.12b, 13. The use of squares to indicate rank was in the Ming tradition, but their actual form was modified by the Manchus to make a distinctly new type. See "Development of the Mandarin Square," pp. 81-82, 97 ff. (On p. 81 of that article the date given for the first Ch'ing laws for squares is incorrect. It should be May 26th, 1652.)

Early in the Ch'ing Dynasty, the costume for nobles and officials was divided into two classes: ordinary dress, *pien-fu* or *ch'ang-fu,* and court or ceremonial dress, *li-fu* or *ch'ao-fu.* The ordinary robes were simply cut, in the usual Manchu style, and were rather plain. If they had any pattern at all, this was of the same color as the background. The court or ceremonial robes, on the other hand, were very highly ornamented in order to make an impressive showing when they were worn at imperial audiences and at the great annual sacrifices. They consisted of a fairly tight-fitting jacket with a broad, flaring collar, and a rather full, pleated skirt, which had no slits—unlike the other robes worn by the Manchus. (See Chapter 11, and Plate 18, left.)

A third type of robe comprised those for semiformal occasions. These were cut very simply in the usual Manchu style, like the ordinary robes, but were made of more colorful and more costly fabrics than the latter. Collectively, they were called *ts'ai-fu,* colored garments; *hua-fu,* patterned garments; or, later, *chi-fu,* festive garments.[4] At first, these semiformal robes were made of silks or satins, figured in gold or bright colors, with various patterns such as small dragons, clouds, flowers, or mere arabesques. Sometimes these motifs were used singly, but combinations also were popular, such as cloud masses alternating with coiled dragons, or small dragon medallions in the centers of peony flowers. Such robes were often worn beneath more formal ones, as we see in Early Ch'ing portraits.

As time went on, the dragon designs became more and more accessible, until even officials of comparatively low degree could wear them, and robes patterned with these crowded out the other types of figured robes. Finally, they became the only acceptable semiformal robes, and they alone were collectively known as *chi-fu.* However, the Manchus never considered the dragon robes as just a mere subtype of their semiformal dress. They valued them very highly in themselves.

[4] The term *chi-fu* is of great antiquity, as it appears in the *Chou li.* See the *Chou-li chu-su* 21.7. It was also used in the Sung (*Sung shih* 151.4), but it seems to have died out again after this, to be revived in the eighteenth century by the tradition-loving Ch'ien-lung Emperor.

The Manchus' interest in dragon robes began in the century before their conquest of China. In 1522, the Ming Court presented a silken *mang* robe to one of the Manchurian chieftains, an ancestor of Nurhachi, when he requested it. Two years later, they gave another to a second Manchu leader who asked for one. Still a third chieftain sent a memorial to Peking begging for a *mang* robe with a hat and belt. The Chinese, becoming exasperated, sent him the official hat and belt without the robe, but again he wrote to ask for one. This was the last straw. The Ming Court then announced that the "Northern barbarians" could no longer wear the robes with insignia that had originally been bestowed on them, and forbade them to buy any more. If they did so illegally, the sellers would be punished along with the buyers.[5] This decree makes it clear why the Manchus from this time were so eager to get Ming dragon robes. It is easy to see how the prohibition against wearing elaborate robes must have annoyed them, especially when their Mongol cousins were getting dragon robes and rich brocades simply as blackmail.

The records in the Ming Dynastic Statutes concerning Manchu tribute relations end with 1587, but we know from other sources that not long after this the growing power of the Manchus and the increased weakness of Ming control in the North enabled the "Northern barbarians" to do a little blackmail on their own. In the loot from their raids as well as in "tribute gifts," they managed to obtain the coveted dragon robes as well as dragon satins from which to make others.[6] We have no record of the numbers they acquired, but the Manchus obviously got numerous dragon robes before the Conquest. We read, for example, that in 1621 Nurhachi,

[5] The first presentation is recorded in the *Ming shih-lu* (*Shih-tsung chia-ching shih-lu* 12.14b), and the second is in the same, 36.5b; while the third, together with the sequel, is in *MHT* 111.2373. Further information may have been given in the Early Ch'ing sources, but the Ch'ien-lung Emperor suppressed all references to the pre-Conquest Manchus which told that they had been vassals of the Ming, in an effort to "purify" the memory of his ancestors. (See *Eminent Chinese*, p. 598.)

[6] In 1596 Nurhachi requested from the Ming court additional *mang* satin in tribute, indicating that he was already receiving some. See Mêng Sên, *Ch'ing-ch'ao ch'ien-chi* (Shanghai, 1930), p. 122. Then in 1609, Nurhachi's fifth son, Manggultai, is reported as having obtained loot in the form of *mang* satin, oxen, and liquor in a raid on Fu-shun Kuan in Liaoning (*Ibid.*, p. 136). The latter instance was apparently just one among many.

their principal chieftain, bestowed nine *mang* robes and six bolts of *mang*-figured satin apiece on a couple of Mongol princes who came to visit him.[7] This was only one of several such presentations. The first accounts speak only of the Manchus' having *mang* robes, but by 1636 they must have had five-clawed dragon robes as well. For in that year the Court decreed that no one under the rank of first degree prince could wear yellow or five-clawed dragons, thus keeping the latter an Imperial monopoly.[8]

Most of the pre-Conquest robes must have been Ming robes, obtained either made up or still in the bolt, as Manchuria had poor facilities for fine silk weaving, even though some was attempted in the early seventeenth century (see Chapter 9). However, we can be sure that the Manchus retailored the Ming ones to fit their own conceptions of what a robe should be, taking them in at the sides and altering the sleeves.

The matter of sleeve alteration brings up an interesting point. We know that the sleeves on the Ming robes were very long, falling well below the hands when the arms were at the sides, also very wide, and that they had large dragons decorating them below the elbows. By contrast, the Manchu idea of a practical sleeve, as we have seen, was one that was fairly snug—though not so tight as to bind the arms in shooting a bow—and reaching only to the wrist exclusive of the cuff. If, in altering a Ming robe, they had simply cut the sleeves narrower and chopped them off at the wrist to add their characteristic horsehoof cuffs, this would have resulted in cutting away large portions of the sleeve dragons, leaving ugly, incom-

---

[7] *Tung-hua lu, T'ien-ming* 3.26b. Pictures of Nurhachi and his nobles in the *Man-chou shih-lu t'u,* which tells of the Manchu rise to power, show various forms of robes with dragons. However, this book was re-illustrated, as well as rewritten, in 1781, by order of the Ch'ien-lung Emperor, who wished to delete anything that might seem uncivilized from the Chinese point of view. Therefore the pictures express Middle Ch'ing, rather than pre-Ch'ing traditions, and are useless for evidence.

[8] *KHHT* 48.14. Yellow was first used as the color for the Emperor's robes by Wên-ti of the Sui Dynasty (581-605 A. D.), according to Chiu Hsün (quoted in the *T'u-shu chi-ch'êng, li-pu* 330, (first) 7, 12). This did not mean, however, that the Emperors of China could not wear other colors if they chose. The Ming Emperors frequently wore red robes, and the Manchu rulers were fond of blue.

plete patterns on the lower sleeves. To avoid this, they apparently cut off the sleeves at the elbow and added new lower sleeves from the same, or different, material. This would explain the origin of the strange Ch'ing convention of the two-part sleeve, which is otherwise incomprehensible. We can be sure, however, that by the eighteenth century the original reason was long since forgotten, and the two-part sleeve was merely maintained as part of the Manchu national tradition.

The first definite reference to dragon-figured robes in Ch'ing China dates from 1652, the year in which the Manchus adopted the use of mandarin squares. In that year, the Court ordered the Imperial silk factories in the South to send annually to Peking two robes of silk tapestry (*k'o-ssŭ*) with five-clawed dragons, one of bright yellow and one of blue (see Chapter 9). The order also included bolts of satin for robes in bright yellow, *ming-huang,* and tawny yellow, *ch'iu-hsiang-sê,* all having five-clawed or three-clawed dragons.[9] Inasmuch as a law of that year expressly forbade the use of these two colors and these two forms of dragons—unless they were especially conferred by the Emperor [10]—these must obviously have been for Imperial use only.

No actual rules for the dragon robes of the Emperor and his immediate family were made until 1759, as the Early Ch'ing rulers still retained the power to make their own decisions for less formal dress. However, the laws for the ceremonial robes (*li-fu*), issued in the meantime, give us some clues. In 1683 it was announced that the Emperor's ceremonial robes were to be of yellow, tawny yellow, or blue satin—or other fabrics—with five-clawed or three-clawed dragons.[11] A little earlier than this, in January 1676, when the

[9] *KHHT* 136.4b, 5.
[10] *Ibid.,* 48.14b. This is the first mention of a taboo against the color tawny yellow and three-clawed dragons, both of which may have been innovations at this time. Although yellow had been an Imperial prerogative for a thousand years (see Note 8), the Ch'ing was apparently the first dynasty to use off-shades of yellow, several of which were later used for the robes of persons closely related to the Emperor who were not permitted to have pure yellow.
[11] *Ibid.,* 48.1.

K'ang-hsi Emperor decided to appoint his second son to be his successor, it was decreed that the Heir Apparent's ceremonial robes should be tawny yellow with five-clawed or three-clawed dragons.[12] Finally, in 1690, when the first edition of the *Ta-Ch'ing hui-tien* was issued, it proclaimed that the Empress' ceremonial robes should be yellow or tawny yellow satin, with five-clawed dragons or "phoenixes," etc., and that the Imperial consorts should have satin of any colors except these, with five-clawed dragons or "phoenixes," etc.[13]

As for the rest of the Imperial family, and other Manchu nobles, it had been formally announced in 1652 that first-degree princes and their sons, and also second-degree princes, could wear five-clawed dragon satins, while third- and fourth-degree princes, imperial dukes, and the lesser imperial nobles, should wear satins with *mǎng* dragons.[14]

The above laws never mention dragon robes, as such, but we can draw some inferences from them. Since the dragon robes were rather informal (during the first third of the dynasty, at least), the Emperor and his family could no doubt take their choice of colors and patterns, with the following limitations, as suggested by the laws for the more formal robes: no one but the Emperor and Empress could wear yellow;[15] no one but the Emperor and Heir Apparent (between 1676 and 1712) could wear three-clawed dragons; and no one below the rank of second degree prince could wear five-clawed dragons—unless any of these forbidden elements were especially conferred.

In May 1652, the laws announcing the adoption of mandarin squares also decreed that Chinese dukes, marquises, and earls, offi-

[12] *Ibid.,* 48.2. This law only applied for the period 1676-1712, for in the latter year Prince Yin-jêng, the Heir Apparent, was finally deposed in disgrace, and no new one was appointed.

[13] *Ibid.,* 48.1b (the Empress); 48.2 (Imperial consorts).

[14] *Ibid.,* 48.2b, 3 (first and second degree princes); 48.3b, 4 ff. (third and fourth degree princes).

[15] A special exception was made for the robes of High Lamas, which could be yellow, but had to have four-clawed dragons unless five-clawed ones were specially conferred. (See Chapter 14.)

cials down to the fourth rank, officers of the Imperial Guards, and gentlemen of no official rank attending the Emperor, could wear four-clawed dragon satins.[16] These men could also wear five-clawed or three-clawed dragons, or even the forbidden colors, if these were especially conferred on them by the Emperor.[17]

These same laws said that the (principal) wife of a Chinese noble, or of an official (Chinese or Manchu), should dress in conformance with her husband's rank, that his father and mother should also wear clothes following their son's rank; and that his sons who had not yet left home or taken office, and his daughters who had not yet married and left the family, should wear the costume of their father—except his actual insignia: hat jewel, belt ornaments, and squares of rank, none of which could be used by the junior members of the family.[18] Thus whole families could, and did, wear dragon-figured robes.

As we shall see, some of the Chinese women did not wear the Manchu style of dress, but those who did had robes essentially the same as those of their husbands. The only difference was that their skirts were slit at the sides, rather than at front and rear.

Nothing is said in the Chinese sources about the size or distribution of the dragons on these first Ch'ing robes for non-nobles. Possibly the decoration on them consisted merely of small dragon medallions, two or three inches in diameter, scattered over the robe in a regular pattern. Such robes are often shown in Early Ch'ing portraits, visible under the outer jacket. In fact, it would appear that dragon robes as such—that is, robes with large, bold dragon patterns like those of the Ming—may first have been confined to the highest nobles and especially worthy military officials. For we find a law of 1664 specifically permitting civil officials above the fourth rank to

---

[16] *Shih-tsu Chang Huang-ti shih-lu* 64.11, 11b (Chinese nobles and officials); 15b (nonofficials in the Emperor's presence).

[17] *Ibid.*, 64.12. If these special robes were kept or worn without being conferred by the Emperor, the penalty was serious. If anyone (of high degree) used or kept them, he would be punished according to his rank, and common people would be flogged. If a wife or minor disobeyed this rule, the head of the family would be punished. (See also *KHHT* 48.14b.)

[18] *Shih-tsu Chang-huang-ti shih-lu* 64.13, 13b.

wear "dragon robes" (*mang-fu*), as though this were a new privilege.[19]

The first reference to a *mang-p'ao* by this name dates from 1667. In that year it was arranged that government officials worthy of special recognition should have an audience with the boy-emperor, and the military officials who came to the Court were each presented with a *mang-p'ao*.[20] Again, in 1740 the military officers of outstanding merit were once more rewarded with dragon robes. Those of the first two ranks were conferred satin robes with "large *mang* dragons," and those of the third and fourth ranks were given robes with "small *mang* dragons." [21] (This distinction in size of the dragons may represent the difference in pattern between the robes of Type 2 and 3 and those of Type 4, as described in the next Chapter, if we can assume that the former persisted that long.) Although these are the only recorded instances of mass bestowal of dragon robes on worthy officials, individuals were given them from time to time as a mark of imperial favor.

In 1713 the Court announced that dragon robes (*mang-p'ao*) were to be worn, with *p'u-fu* jackets, as court dress for the birthday celebration of the K'ang-hsi Emperor, who was then sixty years of age.[22] This is only the first of many such references, for on frequent occasions throughout the rest of the dynasty, the dragon robes were prescribed for birthday festivals, court ceremonies, and even for some of the great sacrifices.[23] The announcement of 1713 is important, however, because it shows that by that time the dragon robe had finally become an accepted element in Ch'ing costume, for practically all ranks.

[19] *KHHT* 48.15.
[20] *KHHTSL* 317.18b. The Early Ch'ing records (*Tung-hua lu*, etc.) generally used the old Ming term *mang-i* in speaking of dragon robes. Then they were called *mang-fu*. The term *mang-p'ao* is relatively late.
[21] *KHHTSL* 317.18b. This distinction between "large *mang* satin" and "small *mang* satin" is repeatedly made in the accounts of Early Ch'ing tribute gifts. See *ibid.*, ch. 506-7, and Chapter 14, below.
[22] *Ibid.*, 296.2, 2b.
[23] The Ch'ing Emperors wore their dragon robes, with the outer jacket (*kun-fu*), for the first day of the annual sacrifice at the Altar of Heaven (*ibid.*, 415.1).

Dragon robes are not specifically mentioned in the dynastic laws for costume until 1759. This is because the Early Ch'ing lawmakers were exclusively concerned with the actual designations of rank: the jeweled hat spikes and belt ornaments, and (after 1652) the badges on the outer jackets. While the use of fabrics of certain colors and various types of dragons were permitted to some ranks and forbidden to others, before 1759 there was never any mention of the specific form or pattern of the decoration on the robes.

Even after the dragon robes came into wider use in the reign of K'ang-hsi, it seems to have been taken for granted that they should be cut according to the Manchu tradition. Provided a person who was authorized to wear only a four-clawed dragon did not take it upon himself to wear the five-clawed one (unless granted the right to do so), the way the dragons were disposed on his semiformal robes probably made little difference. However, we may assume that fashion, as active in imperial China as anywhere else, played its part in making some patterns more popular than others at a given time. For, as we shall see in the next Chapter, the few examples of actual robes that remain from Early Ch'ing show a considerable range of distinct patterns, following several apparent lines of evolution.

Finally, in 1759, one stereotyped pattern for dragon robes, which had been achieved after an evolution of many decades, was fixed by law.[24] Within this basic pattern there were only slight variations for different ranks, resulting in a comparative uniformity. From this time on, the standardized dragon robes formed the only acceptable garment for semiformal wear, and were required for all but the lowest ranks of officials.

The acting officials were not the only ones who wore dragon robes. Throughout the Ch'ing Dynasty the Government sold ranks in exchange for contributions of grain or silver—ostensibly to pro-

---

[24] Another, variant pattern was prescribed for the lowest officials (seventh to ninth rank), but this was apparently never used, for reasons stated in Chapter 5, below. Chapter 5 also presents in greater detail the laws regarding the dragon robes worn after 1759. These were originally published in the *Huang-ch'ao li-ch'i t'u-shih,* chs. 4-7.

vide funds for relieving famines and other distress—and this included ranks without office.²⁵ The purchasers of these nominal ranks were then permitted to wear the costume appropriate to the rank they had bought, including of course the dragon robes, for the sake of heightened prestige.²⁶ This measure was especially popular with merchants and bankers, who were classed quite low in the social scale as compared with the officials, for by this means they could buy their way into higher social circles.

The sale of ranks and the attendant privilege of wearing dragon robes gradually increased during the eighteenth century, reaching its height in the nineteenth. In the reign of Tao-kuang especially, elaborate price tables were issued.²⁷ Finally, after the Taiping Rebellion, when the Imperial Treasury was depleted by the wholesale destruction of revenue-producing lands in the southern provinces and by the alienation of taxes by the rebels, etc., the Chinese government came to depend on such sales as an important source of revenue and the practice became even more widespread.²⁸ The ensuing mass production of dragon robes, and the necessity of conforming to the fairly rigid basic pattern established in 1759, resulted in a marked deterioration of workmanship, and a comparative monotony of decoration. However, as the outer jacket was required to be worn over the dragon robe on all public occasions, the decoration of the robe itself was probably no longer considered very important.

Meanwhile, the Ch'ing Dynasty apparently had the same trouble that the Ming had had in trying to restrict the five-clawed dragon to the use of the Imperial family. We have seen that in 1636, at the founding of the dynasty in Manchuria, five-clawed dragons had been forbidden to all below the rank of first-degree prince, but that in

²⁵ Yang Ching-jen in *Ch'ou-chi pien* (published in 1883) gives samples of laws for the sale of ranks, beginning in 1653 (10.13 ff.)

²⁶ For example, a law of 1727 said, "Merchants who have purchased real, or nominal, rank should dress in conformance with their degree," (*KHHTSL* 328.23).

²⁷ These were published by the Board of Revenue (*Hu-pu*) in the *Cho-tsêng chang-li* (1827). We are indebted to Edwin Beal, Jr. for this reference.

²⁸ A number of books of the early T'ung-chih period reflect this. See for example the *Che-kiang mi-chuan chang-ch'êng* (1862); and the *Tsêng-hsiu ch'ou-hsiang shih-li t'iao-k'uan* (1866).

1652 they were permitted to be worn by those of lesser rank on whom the privilege had been specially conferred by the Emperor as a reward for merit. Apparently they must have been granted on such a large scale that they soon weakened the Imperial monopoly, for, in 1687, the Court felt compelled to take corrective measures. It decreed that Ministers of State and other officials, who had been bestowed satins with five-clawed *lung* dragons, must take out one claw.[29]

The problem came up once more in the next century, and in 1738, the Court announced that no one below the rank of second-degree prince could wear robes with five-clawed *lung* dragons. If anyone below that rank had had such a robe conferred upon him by the Emperor, he could wear it if he took out one claw. And if princes or other high nobles had rewarded their subordinates with robes having woven *lung* dragons, even though they had been worn, it was also required that one claw be removed.[30]

Though these laws for the removal of an extra claw remained in the statutes until the fall of the dynasty, they were obviously widely disregarded—probably with the excuse that they referred to five-clawed *lung* dragons, and not the "five-clawed *mang*". We have evidence, however, that this law was sometimes enforced. The Dayton Art Institute has an eighteenth-century brocaded dragon robe that originally had five-clawed dragons, but the threads have been pulled out to remove one toe and claw from the foot of every dragon (except on the collar), and the same thing has been done on a dragon jacket at the Textile Museum of Washington, D.C. The law was carried out in an even more literal fashion on a late eighteenth-century dragon robe in the collection of Mrs. Walter Beck, which incidentally demonstrates the continued enforcement of the law long after it was issued for the second time. On this robe only the extra claws have been removed, leaving the toes intact, so that at a slight distance the dragons still appear to be the five-clawed variety. Conversely, Mrs. William Mayer has a portion of a Middle

---

[29] *KHHTSL* 328.15b.
[30] *Ibid.*, 328.22b.

Ch'ing brocaded dragon robe on which a fifth claw has been added to each foot of every dragon by later embroidery. Possibly this was done to replace claws that had previously been removed to conform to this law, after it had ceased to have effect.

As the dynasty progressed, the higher officials were apparently more and more frequently granted the right to wear an additional claw on their *mang* dragons, and by the latter part of the nineteenth century, the fifth claw was apparently freely assumed by lesser nobles and officials, whether or not they had earned the right to wear them by special merit.[31] In all these cases, the dragons were still called five-clawed *mang,* like those of the later Ming, and the robes were called *mang-p'ao,* thus preserving at least a token of conformity. This state of affairs in Late Ch'ing accounts for the enormous number of five-clawed dragon robes, of varying degrees of quality, still obtainable all over China. Obviously, the popular myth that the five-clawed dragon was always restricted to the Ch'ing Emperors is utterly without foundation.

Apart from the extensive spread of five-clawed dragons, two or three other developments not specifically mentioned in the laws should be noted in this general survey, before we move on to consider the evolution of the patterns. In the first place, on the Early Ch'ing dragon robes (before the eighteenth century), although the lower sleeves were made from different pieces of cloth, they were usually of the same material as the body of the robe, or were at least of the same general color. During the Late K'ang-hsi period, however, lower sleeves of darker fabric began to make their appearance, and by the mid-eighteenth century their use had become an established custom.

The reason for this minor change was quite logical. Early

---

[31] For an example of a lesser official wearing the five-clawed dragon, see P. K. Kozlov, *Mongolya i Amdo i Mertvii Gorod Kara-koto* (Moscow and Petrograd, 1923), pl. 35, facing p. 518. This portrait of the Provincial Judge of Kansu, in 1909, shows him as an undistinguished-looking third-rank official, wearing a *k'o-ssŭ* robe with five-clawed dragons on it. (Incidentally, the subtitle of the photograph calls him "Ne-tai, the Governor of Lanchow-fu," an amusing misconception, apparently based on his familiar title of *Nieh-t'ai,* the colloquial equivalent of *An-ch'a-shih* or Provincial Judge.)

Ch'ing portraits show us that, on formal occasions, Ch'ing noblemen and officials wore the long outer jackets which had sleeves that came down to the cuffs of the dragon robe worn beneath it; while their wives wore similar jackets, or "dragon jackets" that also had long sleeves (see Chapter 7). In Middle Ch'ing, however, the short-sleeved *p'u-fu* jacket was worn much more frequently—it is the only one pictured in the illustrations for the laws of 1759—while the later dragon jackets, which these same laws confined to the use of noblewomen, had half-length sleeves also. It must have been generally felt by the Court that brighter colored sleeves projecting beyond the shorter ones of the dark jackets would look undignified if not absurd. In any case, after the middle of the eighteenth century, custom—not laws—required dark lower-sleeves for the dragon robes and court robes, when they were to be worn with the short-sleeved *p'u-fu* jackets.

Thus, only two types of dragon robes would not have required this type of sleeve. These would have been, first, the winter dragon robes which were worn with the long-sleeved winter-style *p'u-fu* or the fur jackets, and, secondly, the dragon robes which the Emperor might wear in the privacy of the Palace's inner apartments, where he would not need to bother with an outer jacket.[32]

Sometime during the second half of the nineteenth century, the fashion arose of wearing an extra collar with the dragon robes and ordinary robes, when wearing the *p'u-fu* or the fur jacket for formal visits and other social occasions. As this was only a social custom, it was not prescribed by law, so we have no precise date for the innovation.[33] This collar, called *ling-t'ou,* was round and stiff, and was faced with black silk, velvet, or fur, depending on the season. It was not fastened directly to the dragon robe, but merely fitted down over the neckband of the outer jacket. As such, it was not an

[32] *CTTHH* 3, pl. 16, shows an informal portrait of the Ch'ien-lung Emperor in his study, wearing a robe with light lower sleeves.

[33] For mention of this collar see Fr. Simon Kiong (Kung Ku-yü), "Politesse Chinoise," *Varietés Sinologiques* 25 (Shanghai, 1906), 34, and pl. 20 (p. 28). The earliest instance known to us of the use of this extra collar is a portrait of "Chinese Gordon," dating from the second half of the nineteenth century. See H. B. Morse, *In the Days of the Taipings* (Salem, 1927), photograph facing p. 299.

integral part of the dragon robe, comparable to the spreading collar on the court robes, but was merely a costume accessory.

As a last development, at the end of the nineteenth century it became customary to wear the cuffs of the dragon robes turned back, and they were made very large to fold back more easily. The over-large cuffs on the men's robes looked grotesque enough, especially when turned down, as may be seen on one of the dragon robes of the Kuang-hsü Emperor now in the National Museum of Washington, D.C. But those on the women's robes were several times larger, and their general effect was ridiculous. (See Plate 12, right.) This distortion of the traditional Manchu cuff was as much a sign of decadence as the overelaboration and disintegration of the pattern itself, which, as we shall see, reached their culmination at about the same period. Thus the final developments of the dragon robe seem to have foreshadowed the fall of the Ch'ing Dynasty.

4

Early Ch'ing Dragon Robes:
Evolution of the Patterns

NOW let us turn from the general development of Early Ch'ing dragon robes to specific examples, either in surviving garments or in the representation of costumes in reliable, datable portraits. Among these we find a number of widely diverging basic patterns in use from the founding of the Manchu Dynasty until 1759, after which there was one standard design. For stylistic analysis, then, we may divide the dynasty into two periods: Early Ch'ing (1644-1759) and Later Ch'ing (1759-1911). At first the many variant patterns from the former period may seem confusing, but investigation has shown that in general they fall into six basic types depending on the number and disposition of the dragons. Most if not all of these types can ultimately be traced back to Ming prototypes. The Ming derivation is particularly obvious in the case of the first group.

TYPE 1. SIX DRAGONS. We have seen that the most familiar decoration on the later Ming dragon robes was a pattern consisting of two large dragons and six smaller ones. One of the large dragons had its head on the breast of the robe and curled back over the left shoulder, while the other had its head on the back of the robe and curled forward. Then the smaller ones were disposed in pairs on a horizontal band across the front and back of the skirt, and on the sleeves. In the Early Ch'ing this Ming pattern was continued almost unchanged on the court robes worn by Manchu nobles, and a modified form of it appeared on the first type of Early Ch'ing dragon robe; in both cases, of course, without dragons on the sleeves.

On the Ch'ing dragon robes of this first type, the principal dragons on chest and back were shown in profile, arching over the shoulders

as the Ming ones did. However, the pairs of smaller dragons on the
front and back of the skirt were no longer confined to a band.
Furthermore, the waves with the world-mountain rising above them,
which had figured on the lower edge of the band on the Ming skirts,
were dropped to the bottom of the robe. With this change in the
lower portion of the robe, the whole pattern now portrayed an
ancient conception of the Universe: the world-mountain standing
in the midst of the sea, with the heavens above. The whole upper
portion of the robe, in which the dragons were soaring, was considered as the cloud-filled sky. This pattern seems to have persisted
throughout the first century of Manchu rule, but it does not appear
on the dragon robes after 1759, and may have gone out of fashion
for the semiformal official robes long before that.[1] The writer has
seen only one early Ch'ing dragon robe of this type in the Occident,[2]
but the basic pattern is found on a Chinese bride's robe of the middle
Ch'ing now in the Seattle Art Museum, shown in Plate 17. (See
also Plate 4.)

TYPE 1a. As a variation on the first type, some robes had the heads
of the principal dragons on chest and back facing, instead of being
shown in profile. One of these is shown in an informal portrait
of the K'ang-hsi Emperor's fourth son, Prince Yin-chên, who succeeded him as the Yung-chêng Emperor.[3] It was painted about the
beginning of the eighteenth century, and is now in the Palace
Museum in Peking. The robe is of dark-colored silk, with the
dragons in gold against a cloud-strewn background. The large
facing dragon on the chest has its body curling back over the shoulder of the robe in the traditional Ming fashion, the two smaller ones

[1] This robe, seen in a private collection, was announced as being Ming because
of its unusual pattern. However, its narrow sleeves, ending in horsehoof cuffs,
identified it as early Ch'ing beyond any doubt.
[2] An apparent survival of this pattern on dragon robes is found in the illustration
for the robes of the lowest officials in the later Ch'ing laws of 1759 (LCTS, 5.96).
But this is no real exception to our statement, for the text of the law thus illustrated
describes the pattern differently, speaking of five dragons instead of six. Furthermore,
these particular robes were apparently never made or worn. See Chapter 5 for a
fuller discussion of this point.
[3] CTTHH 1, pl. 27.

are coiled at the knees, and a simple wave pattern is barely visible at the base of the garment. Incidentally, this portrait also provides the earliest instance of the dark lower sleeves and embroidered cuffs, so characteristic of the Later Ch'ing, but the collar is still severely plain.

TYPE 2. TWO GIANT DRAGONS. The Royal Ontario Museum of Archaeology in Toronto has a magnificently embroidered dragon robe on which the basic pattern consists merely of two giant dragons. Their heads are shown in semiprofile like those on the robes of the first type; but the bodies, instead of looping back over the shoulders, continue down the front and back of the robe, respectively, in several broad curves. As an additional feature, this robe has sixteen very small dragons to ornament the background, not counting those on the cuffs. It probably dates from the K'ang-hsi period. (See Plate 5.) [4]

In a number of Early Ch'ing portraits from the late seventeenth or early eighteenth centuries, the lower half of the dragon robe as revealed through the open slit of the formal jacket discloses a section of an enormous dragon (see Plate 8, left, for example). In such cases, it seems obvious that the whole design on the front of the robe must have consisted of a single huge dragon. But as the jacket always conceals the upper part of the robe in these portraits, it is impossible to tell whether there were additional dragons on the shoulders of the robe; if so, it would fall into the next category.

TYPE 2a. A subtype of this second type of Early Ch'ing robe had two giant dragons extending down the front and back, like those of Type 2. But it also had one more on each shoulder, with their bodies stretching down the sleeves, making four dragons in all. Mrs. D. C. Martin has recently acquired a handsome robe of this

---

[4] This is also pictured in *Chinese Court Costumes*, pl. 1. The back of a similar robe in woven satin, never actually cut out but made into a hanging instead, is in the Nelson Gallery. It is green, suggesting that it was made for a palace eunuch or a woman (men never wore green), and it has the additional peculiarity that the dragon is facing left, as though the finished robe were intended to fasten on the left side instead of the right.

type which had been found in a tomb. (See Plate 6.) All four of its dragons are in profile; those on the shoulders are both looking forward toward the front of the robe, following a convention of that period. The robe is made of soft satin, which unfortunately has become discolored in burial. Details of the pattern are woven in peacock feathers. On both sides of the main dragons are arranged groups of objects from the series popularly known as the Hundred Antiques, showing bronze vessels, vases, and other ornaments. On either side of the central mountain, below, a small *ch'i-lin* is shown prancing on the waves, and near the bottom, where the skirt has been turned under prematurely to shorten the robe, are bell and halberd symbols.

The use of extraneous symbols in general, and the last-mentioned ones in particular, is characteristic of textiles from the Yung-chêng period, although the shapes of the dragons and of some of the cloud forms seem to be earlier. If the latter elements were survivals, this robe might possibly date from the Yung-chêng period. The 1740 reference to "large *mang* robes" as opposed to "small *mang* robes," mentioned in the preceding chapter,[5] suggests that robes of this type may have persisted well into the eighteenth century. Perhaps they did not drop from favor until the standardization of dragon robes in 1759 made such variations in pattern obsolete. We shall see in the last chapter that this type of robe was still being worn in Tibet before the Communists came to Lhasa in 1951.

As to the origin of these giant dragon patterns, it seems likely that they had Ming prototypes, especially if one recalls the Ming reference to the dragon which had "its entire body on the front of the robe, like the *lung* dragon on the Emperor's robe."[6] Incidentally, this Ming quotation was referring to facing dragons, and it is very possible that the Manchu Emperor or his princes had robes with patterns of Type 2 and its subtype (2a) on which the giant dragons were facing. If this were the case, there would also have been two further subtypes (2b and 2c).

---

[5] See Chapter 3, Note 21, for references.
[6] See Chapter 2, Note 23, for reference.

TYPE 3. FOUR GIANT DRAGONS. Another type of early dragon pattern, related to the last mentioned, was characterized by a pair of dragons, instead of a single one, extending down the front and back on each side of the central seam. A subtype (3a) had a smaller dragon on each sleeve. Our evidence for these comes from an old pattern of confronting dragons surviving on Later Ch'ing women's court robes, as well as from two related robes: a woman's dragon jacket and an archaic dragon robe in modern Tibet.[7]

TYPE 4. EIGHT DRAGONS IN TWO SIZES. The fourth basic pattern had large dragons on chest and back and on each shoulder, and pairs of smaller ones on the front and back of the skirt. (See Plate 9, left.) We are probably safe in assuming that this was ultimately derived from a pattern on Ming presentation robes, as was the first type. In this case, the Ming prototype would have been the kind of robe on which four creatures filled the four lobes of design around the collar, with four smaller ones on a band across the skirt, and others on the sleeves (as in Plate 2, right). If this assumption is correct, after first cutting off the sleeves with their animals, the boundary lines of the four-lobed collar device and the skirt band would have been abandoned to leave the dragons free, while the waves from the lower portion of the band would have been dropped to the bottom of the robe.

The evolution of the standard form of Type 4 was very possibly completed by the end of the K'ang-hsi reign in 1721. But all the typical examples preserved in our American museums seem to date from considerably later, apparently from the Yung-chêng or early Ch'ien-lung reigns. They are generally of satin in rather soft colors, with the dragons woven in gold. Their pastel shades have led to their being called women's robes. However, most of them that we have seen have the skirts split at front and rear for horseback-riding males.[8] In other words, their common American designation, "consort robes," is a misnomer.

[7] See pp. 74, 174, and 149.
[8] See *Imperial Robes and Textiles of the Chinese Court,* pl. 1, for an example.

The Early Ch'ing robes of the first three types and the earliest examples of Type 4 generally had merely the surface of the sea depicted on their lower borders. However, some of them also had a suggestion of the turmoil below the waves indicated by cloud-shaped swirls pressing up from below. On the fully developed examples of the fourth type of robe, the tails of these swirls extended downward as wavy stripes, and the rest of the deep sea beneath the waves was also represented by stripes, usually in contrasting colors. At first these lines were short and rather tentative, but in time they became longer and gradually straightened to form strong diagonals. This convention was known to the Chinese as *li shui* or "upright water," as opposed to *p'ing shui,* "flat water," the latter term being used when only the surface of the sea is represented, as on the court robes.[9]

The completely developed form of this fourth type of robe is shown in a portrait of the Yung-chêng Emperor (1722-35) after he had ascended the throne.[10] The upper dragons on his yellow robe are especially large and vigorous, those on the shoulders being as big as the other two and extending down the upper arms. The principal one on his chest is shown firmly clutching the sacred pearl in his right foreclaws. At the bottom is the world-mountain as a triple peak rising from the waters. Four of the waves curl high above the rest, giving special distinction to the lower border. Below these are cloud-shaped swirls terminating in thin, wavy bands of *li shui* in various colors at the base of the robe. The background of the robe as a whole has a few colored clouds, but absolutely no trace of the bats and other lucky symbols that came into favor with the Ch'ien-lung Emperor. And, of course, there is no trace of the Twelve

[9] The terms *li shui* and *p'ing shui* first make their appearance in *Huang-ch'ao li-ch'i t'u-shih* (1759, 4.10, 19, etc.).

[10] *CTTHH* 1, pl. 29. A previous portrait in the same book (pl. 12) shows the K'ang-hsi Emperor in an even more developed type of dragon robe. However, this robe has so many later elements, such as the highly evolved *li shui*—not only at the base of the robe but on the sleeves as well—and late wave forms, that we are convinced this is a posthumous portrait, painted at least thirty years after his death. As such, we discard it for contemporary evidence.

Symbols, which were not introduced until the reign of the latter sovereign.

Another interesting variation of the Yung-chêng Emperor's dragon robe is the development of accessory ornamentation. Most of the earlier dragon robes, including the so-called "consort robes," had a plain collar and lapel, at most edged with a thin strip of brocade as on the Toronto robe. Now, we find an elaborate collar lapel, embroidered with dragons to match the cuffs.[11]

An earlier variant of Type 4, not sufficiently different to be called a subtype, is a robe in the Metropolitan Museum which has been casually attributed to the reign of Shun-chih at the beginning of the dynasty.[12] Essentially this is a simple Type 4 robe, with the four large dragons on the upper robe and the four smaller ones in confronting pairs on the skirt. However the latter four dragons are almost lost among a multitude of even slightly smaller dragons which have been included as background decoration like those on the Toronto robe. (Both this robe and the Toronto one were women's robes, and in view of their very high quality they probably belonged to imperial consorts, and may thus legitimately be called "consort robes."[13]) The Metropolitan robe is also remarkable for the fact that its background is strewn with fanciful representations of the longevity character (*shou*), although the use of these did not become a common feature on Ch'ing robes until the Ch'ien-lung period, some time after this must have been made.[14]

---

[11] As noted above in connection with the earlier portrait of the Yung-chêng Emperor as a prince, the embroidered cuffs seem to have been an earlier development, before the ornamental collar and lapel.

[12] *Costumes from the Forbidden City*, pl. 16.

[13] Since both the Metropolitan and Toronto robes are probably consorts' robes, this may possibly supply the explanation for the many small dragons on both. As stated in Chapter 1, Note 1, the Emperor was often referred to euphemistically as the Dragon, and the word "dragon" was commonly used instead of "imperial" to qualify his possessions. Accordingly, the Imperial princes were known as "the Dragon's offspring," *lung chung*. Therefore, the addition of many small dragons on the robe of an imperial consort might have been a symbolic expression of the wish "May you have many sons by the Emperor."

[14] This Metropolitan Museum robe is the earliest instance known to the writer on which multiple *shou* characters appear.

The dating of this robe presents problems. In the first place, the sleeves have additional sleevebands, a characteristic of Later Ch'ing Manchu noblewomen's robes which we have first observed in a portrait dated 1728; [15] secondly, the ornamental lapel and cuffs are characteristic of the Yung-chêng or Early Ch'ien-lung periods. These features would make it seem likely that the robe had been made sometime between 1725 and 1740. But, since the lapel and collar cover up the top of the principal dragon, these additions were evidently not intended by the original weaver; furthermore, the dragons are a well-developed K'ang-hsi style. It seems probable, therefore, that this was actually woven earlier, but not made up before the Yung-chêng period, after the styles had begun to change.

Type 4a. The front section of an Early Ch'ing robe of this type, with all eight dragons shown in profile, is preserved in the Dayton Art Institute, having been made up into a hanging at some later time. (See Plate 7.) Not only are the dragons on this of a good Early Ch'ing style, characteristic of the K'ang-hsi period, but it also bears three sets of phrases in Manchu seal script—one above each dragon—which indicate that it must have been woven at a time before the Manchus had completed taking over the Chinese culture to the almost total exclusion of their own. [16] Therefore, we assume that it was probably made sometime before 1700. Note especially that the clouds in the background have exactly the same form as the prominent swirls among the waves, showing why we have called the latter "cloud-shaped swirls." From a technical point of view, this robe was a magnificent achievement in weaving.

Type 4b. The dragon jacket shown in Plate 14 suggests that there might have been another variation of Type 4, with large facing dragons on chest and back but having those on the shoulders in profile, like the dragons on the skirts. For the patterns on the

[15] The portrait in question is in the collection of Dr. and Mrs. S. B. Rentsch of Derby, Conn.
[16] At the writer's request, several specialists in the Manchu language have examined these inscriptions. But as yet they have been unable to decipher the highly conventionalized seal forms.

dragon jackets usually followed those on the contemporary dragon robes. Further evidence for this is provided by the (uncut) back of an image robe in the Boston Museum, which had the same arrangement of two dragons facing and six in profile. And, lastly, a portrait in the Royal Ontario Museum of Archaeology shows a Manchu nobleman of the Early Ch'ing wearing shoulder dragons in profile on a court robe which seems to have been made up from a contemporary dragon robe, as was then frequently the custom. These examples would seem to imply the unquestionable use of such a subtype.

The problem is to determine what if anything was meant by the differences in the number of facing and profile dragons. There is nothing in the laws to indicate that they conformed to distinctions in rank, and yet they very likely did. Perhaps some contemporary account not yet known will still turn up to tell us about the unrecorded styles and conventions of those times.

Type 5. Eight Dragons in Medallions. The earliest example known to us of the common type of Early Ch'ing robe on which the dragons are coiled in eight medallions is a portrait of the K'ang-hsi Emperor as a boy, presumably painted sometime in the 1660's.[17] This is a light blue robe with the usual eight medallions apparently rendered in gold. It has no collar design, plain cuffs, and no ornamentation at the bottom of the skirt. The four upper dragons are facing, while those on the skirts are in profile. This is a standard example of the fifth type.

It would seem that these medallion robes, like the first type of dragon robe, had been derived from earlier Ming examples. For the eight-medallion pattern on the robes of the Early Ch'ing emperors was apparently a simplification of that on the robes of the later Ming emperors which had the eight dragon medallions and the Twelve Symbols. If so, they first discarded the Twelve Symbols, which were completely alien to the Manchu tradition. Then, although they kept the four main medallions on the upper robe exactly

[17] *CTTHH*, 1, pl. 7.

as they were—on the shoulders, chest, and back—they altered the position of those on the skirt. They must have found that the pairs of large medallions which the Ming emperors had worn vertically on the front and back of their skirts were impractical, because their Manchu skirts were split up the front and back for riding, and if the medallions were split they would lose their dignified appearance. Accordingly these were placed horizontally, so that one came in the center of each panel of the skirt, two in front and two behind.

Type 5a. A medallion robe of this subtype is illustrated in a second portrait of Prince Yin-chên, the future Yung-chêng Emperor, when he was still only a third-degree prince, painted about 1705.[18] This robe is dark in color, with plain collar and cuffs like those on the robe in his other early portrait, but all eight medallions have the five-clawed dragons in profile. As in the case of the other Early Ch'ing dragon robes, there is nothing in the laws to tell whether the way the dragon faced indicated distinctions in rank, but we might infer from this portrait, and others of the same period, that nobles below the rank of second-degree prince had to have profile dragons in their medallions.

This fifth type of robe, with the dragons confined to medallions, a plain collar, and no background decoration, must have persisted well into the eighteenth century, as the Royal Ontario Museum of Archaeology has a portrait of a Manchu noble wearing such a robe— also having all the dragons in profile—that must have been painted after 1726. (See Plate 8, right.) We can safely use this date because the subject is wearing a spherical hat jewel of the kind prescribed for semi-informal wear with the dragon robes in a law of 1727. (Before that, the formal hat spike was simply removed for informal occasions, and no hat jewel was worn, as shown in Plate 8, left.)

For many years the only change in these plain types of medallion robes was apparently in the substitution of dragon-figured cuffs for the undecorated ones. However, in the meantime, some variation was afforded by differences in technique. Sometimes the dragon

[18] *Ibid.*, 1, pl. 21.

medallions were woven into the solid color background in gold thread, and sometimes they were woven or embroidered in colors. In addition, those of the imperial nobles were sometimes executed in the same color as the background, subtly distinguished from the latter by changes in weave, or voiding—particularly on the summer robes of gauze. We learn about this use of "hidden pattern" dragon medallions on robes and fabrics from laws which forbid their use to lesser nobles and officials, unless they were specifically awarded them. These injunctions were repeated in the same laws that required the removal of the fifth claw on the dragons.[19]

TYPE 5b. About the third or fourth decade of the eighteenth century, elaborations began to appear in the medallion robes. Several of these are illustrated by robes in the Nelson Gallery which are supposed to have come from the tomb of Prince Kuo (Kuo Ch'ing-Wang), who died in 1738.[20] The earliest of these cannot have been made much before his death, and several which were women's robes—supposedly those of his consorts—are obviously later.[21] The first of these robes has the usual eight dragon medal-

[19] *KHHTSL* 328.22b.

[20] Prince Kuo's biography is given in the *Ch'ing-shih kao* 226.15. The facts of his life contrast strangely with the false legend that has recently grown up around his name. He was born in 1697, the seventeenth son of the K'ang-hsi Emperor, and half-brother to the Yung-chêng Emperor. When the latter succeeded to the throne under extremely suspicious circumstances (many believed that he had poisoned his father, and he almost certainly altered the terms of succession), most of his brothers turned against him. They were savagely punished for this, and several died in prison. The future Prince Kuo, who seems to have been a rather weak and unpleasant character, was one of the few who did not criticize his evil brother, and was accordingly rewarded. He was made a prince of the second degree in 1723, shortly after his brother ascended the throne, and five years later was promoted to the first degree, with the title of Kuo Ch'ing-Wang by which he is now generally known. From 1723 to 1732 he held a series of important positions in the government, acting successively as head of the Board of Dependencies, the Board of Works, and the Board of Revenue. In 1734 he escorted the Dalai Lama back to Tibet from Peking, and returned just before his brother's death. His nephew, the Ch'ien-lung Emperor, who succeeded to the throne, may have mistrusted him. At any rate Prince Kuo was not given any office under the new reign. He died without heirs in 1738 after an illness of less than two months. He was then only forty-one.

[21] The robes from the tomb of Prince Kuo have been discussed by various writers. The best descriptions of them are found in Lindsay Hughes, "The Kuo Ch'in Wang Textiles," *Gazette des Beaux Arts,* 6th series, Vol. 24 (1943), pp. 129-48. The original group in Kansas City is very heterogeneous. Some are men's robes, some women's robes, and there are considerable differences in sizes and lengths.

lions (the upper ones facing and the lower ones in profile) on a background of very small dragon medallions,[22] such as were used by themselves to ornament another kind of semiformal robe known as *ts'ai-fu*.[23] Thus combining two types of pattern on a single garment, it indicates the trend away from plain backgrounds, a symptom of the new sophistication which was then creeping in, nearly a hundred years after the Manchu Conquest. This type of robe with large medallions on a background of smaller ones we can call Type 5b.

TYPE 5c. Still another development in the period covering the later Yung-chêng and early Ch'ien-lung reigns was created by adding to the bottom of the eight-medallion robes the device of the world-mountain standing amid the waves, which had long ornamented the lower portion of other types of dragon robes. This pattern is represented among the robes from the tomb of Prince Kuo only on an undergarment or burial dress.[24] Yet we know that it must have occurred on dragon robes proper, as well, for it survives among the types of dragon robes worn by the highest Manchu noblewomen after 1759. The tomb dress just mentioned has facing dragons in all eight medallions, which would constitute another subtype if found on a proper dragon robe. Such a robe may still turn up.

TYPE 5d. Lastly, there was a variation among the medallion robes, which not only had the mountain and waves below, but also

---

One man's dragon robe seems much later than the rest in style, and the group also contained a set of medallions taken from the jacket of a nineteenth-century emperor. One gets the impression that the grave robbers who produced them for sale had looted many tombs. Meanwhile, in the case of the robes ascribed to the Kuo Ch'ing Wang burial in other museums, there is apparently no evidence whatever to support this claim, and the robes are very likely of much later origin. Unfortunately, a situation has arisen where most Ch'ing tomb robes that are not obviously imperial are called "Kuo Ch'in Wang," the way most late jades are called "Ch'ien-lung" with the implication that they were carved during that reign in the eighteenth century.

[22] "The Kuo Ch'in Wang Textiles," fig. 19, p. 141.

[23] While the dragon robes technically speaking might be called a form of *ts'ai-fu*, the type of *ts'ai-fu* that had only the very small dragon medallions for decoration would not conversely have been considered a "dragon robe."

[24] "The Kuo Ch'in Wang Textiles," fig. 17, p. 140, and *Costumes from the Forbidden City*, pl. 27.

had a background filled with conventionalized cloud wisps as on the other types of dragon robes. This is found on a third robe said to come from Prince Kuo's tomb.[25] It is a woman's robe, for in addition to having an ornate collar and cuffs with an early Ch'ien-lung pattern, it has the extra sleevebands which were then coming into favor for the robes of Manchu noblewomen. The pattern shows eight very elaborate dragon medallions against a background of clouds, with a broad band of waves and *li shui* below.

TYPE 6. EIGHT DRAGONS, ALL THE SAME SIZE. This was the ultimate dragon pattern. It may well have been a fear that further experimentation might lead to an even greater variety in types which caused the Ch'ien-lung Emperor to freeze the tradition in 1759. In that year, the Board of Rites decreed that the pattern for all dragon robes down to those of the seventh-rank officials should be standardized in what we shall call Type 6. The only exception was that the Empress and other high Manchu noblewomen were allowed to continue using eight-medallion robes as well.[26] Type 6 had eight dragons of the same relative size, the four upper ones facing, and the four lower ones in profile, against a background of clouds, with the mountains and waves below. (See Plate 9, right.)

This final pattern is almost undoubtedly a later development of Type 4, in which the size of the upper dragons was decreased while the lower ones were slightly enlarged, so that all were practically uniform in size. But the idea of having dragons of a similar size might possibly have been suggested by the medallion type of robe. If this were so, Type 6 would have resulted from a merging of the most highly developed patterns from the two main streams of evolution. At any event, this final type is a late development of the mid-eighteenth century, representing the culmination of Ch'ing experiments in dragon robe design.

[25] "The Kuo Ch'in Wang Textiles," fig. 2, p. 130, and *Costumes from the Forbidden City*, pl. 26. It is interesting to compare the pattern on this robe with the somewhat similar one on a robe of considerably later date (probably early nineteenth century) in the Victoria and Albert Museum. See *Brief Guide to the Chinese Woven Fabrics* (London, 1925), pl. 4.

[26] See Chapter 7 below.

Of course this pattern was not newly invented in 1759. It had probably been in use for at least twenty years before that, and was merely selected as the only one of several patterns considered worthy of perpetuation at the time when the official costume was standardized and all variations were outlawed. Perhaps the earliest example known to us is another robe in the Nelson Gallery, said to have belonged to Prince Kuo, which shows equal-sized dragons of a type popular in the Ch'ien-lung period and well-developed *li shui*.[27] If the attribution to Prince Kuo is correct, it would seem to indicate that the pattern was already evolved by 1738, the year of his death.

Another interesting early example of Type 6 is an imperial robe in the Minneapolis Institute of Arts.[28] All the dragons on this are nearly of the same size and they represent a typical Ch'ien-lung form of dragon, with crushed-in snout and undershot lower jaw. Furthermore, the clouds in the background are a middle Ch'ing type commonly found on robes of the Ch'ien-lung period. The only unusual variation consists in the fact that the four dragons of the upper robe are represented encircling a sun disc that displays the three-legged sunbird, which indicates that the robe must have been made for an emperor. Probably it was ordered by the Ch'ien-lung Emperor, before he adopted the Twelve Symbols, as he seems to have been the first ruler of his dynasty to fancy himself a *roi soleil*. It is true that the mist swirls below the waves appear to hark back to an earlier period, but the upper waves are typical of the early Ch'ien-lung period, as a carryover from the previous reign. The preponderance of Ch'ien-lung elements makes it clear that the robe must date from that period, sometime between 1736 and 1759.

After the sixth basic pattern was fixed by the laws of 1759, we find no more distinctions between facing and profile dragons on the dragon robes. The only changes were slight differences in the proportion of the various elements of the design, which were dictated by fashion as the dynasty progressed. For example, we can trace

27 "The Kuo Ch'in Wang Textiles," fig. 20, p. 142.
28 *Costumes from the Forbidden City*, fig. 18.

a continual decrease in the size of all the dragons and a gradual broadening of the sea portion below, together with minor alterations in the background pattern which were caused by the increasingly excessive use of lucky symbols among the clouds and waves. (See Plate 10.)

5

Later Ch'ing Dragon Robes:
The Laws of 1759

I N 1759, the Board of Rites issued an illustrated book of sumptuary
laws called the *Huang-ch'ao li-ch'i t'u-shih,* which had been compiled by order of the Ch'ien-lung Emperor. This contained elaborate
rules and specifications for the form of sacrificial vessels, other ceremonial accessories, and official dress, including dragon robes.

The Emperor himself wrote the preface to this book, and the
portion of the preface in which he discusses his attitude toward
changes in costume is an important document in the history of
Ch'ing costume in general. It reads as follows:

> Previous dynasties used sacrificial vessels just to make up the required
> numbers, but we have changed them [the vessels themselves] in order to
> conform to the ancient traditions. As for robes and hats, however, each
> dynasty sets forth its own regulations. Anciently, the *shou* [-hats] of
> the Hsia, and the *hsü* [-hats] of the Yin were not passed down [to
> succeeding dynasties]. We, accordingly, have followed the old traditions
> of Our Dynasty, and have not dared to change them, fearing that later
> men would hold Us responsible for this, and criticize Us regarding the
> robes and hats; and thus We would offend Our ancestors. This We
> certainly should not do. Moreover, as for the Northern Wei, the Liao,
> and the Chin [dynasties] as well as the Yüan, all of which changed to
> Chinese robes and hats, they all died out within one generation [after
> abandoning their native dress]. Those of Our sons and grandsons who
> would take Our will as their will shall certainly not be deceived by idle
> talk. In this way, the continuing Mandate of our Dynasty will receive
> the protection of Heaven for ten thousand years. Do not change [our
> Manchu traditions] or reject them. Beware! Take warning! [1]

This is in essence merely a defense of the Ch'ien-lung Emperor's
decision to continue to follow the old tradition of the Manchu, defi-

[1] *LCTS,* Introduction, 5.6.

nitely un-Chinese, way of dress which had been maintained since the "founding of the dynasty" in 1636, when the Manchus had not yet entered China. As his ancestor Abahai had done in enjoining his family and their descendants to continue the wearing of Manchu costume in 1637,[2] the Emperor warns that a change to Chinese styles of dress would result in the fall of the dynasty, and urges his children and grandchildren to maintain the Manchu traditions. He justifies this by citing an ancient precedent to show that changes in costume from one dynasty to another were permissible, but recalls the fate of the previous alien dynasties, after they adopted Chinese costume and lost their national identity, as a warning to his own people to keep up their native traditions of dress.

In any case, he never objects, in any portion of the preface or elsewhere, to changes made within the framework of the Manchu tradition. In fact, it is illuminating to refer to the laws and regulations for costume in the earlier part of his reign, as they appeared in the *Hui-tien tsê-li* of 1748,[3] together with the regulations laid down eleven years later in the *Huang-ch'ao li-ch'i t'u-shih*. On comparing these, it becomes obvious that the changes which were made in the court and official dress of all ranks, to indicate more clearly the distinctions between them, were very sweeping, although none actually broke with the old traditions.

The immediate provocation for the Emperor's statement of policy regarding change in costume appears to have been an increasing insistence (probably on the part of Chinese scholars and officials) that the Manchus should adopt Chinese dress, as a number of previous foreign dynasties had done, in the interest of preserving the ancient Chinese traditions.[4] However, his declaration in the preface was apparently not enough to still the "idle talk" of those who were making the demands. For, some years later, in 1772, he felt com-

---

[2] *T'ai-tsung Wên-huang-ti shih-lu* 34.26b-27. Further references are given in Chapter 3, Note 1.

[3] *Hui-tien tsê-li*, ch. 65.

[4] The first suggestion that the Chinese ceremonial dress should be resumed was made in April, 1651; but it was rejected so forcibly as to discourage any more for a long time. See *Shih-tsu Chang-huang-ti shih-lu* 54.18b.

pelled to issue another statement, again stressing his opposition to breaking the Manchu tradition of their own distinctive costume.[5]

When we turn to the costume section of this book on sumptuary laws, we find descriptions of dragon robes for all ranks of nobles and officials, stating in detail the specifications for each rank, or group of ranks. The variations in these robes were slight, for all were of the same general pattern (Type 6), beginning with that for the Emperor, which was naturally the most elaborate of the series.

The Emperor's dragon robe, *lung-p'ao,* was described as bright yellow (*ming-huang*) in color, having collar, sleeves, and cuffs edged in brocade of blue-black and gold (*shih-ch'ing pien-chin*). The basic pattern consisted of nine golden dragons, the ninth being on the under flap of the robe, so it was symbolically present, though unseen when the robe was worn. Those on the breast, back, and shoulders were facing dragons, *chêng-lung,* while those on the skirts were profile dragons, *hsing-lung.* In addition, it had the Twelve Symbols that the Ming emperors had worn on their dragon robes. The background was figured with auspicious clouds in five colors, and at the bottom of the robe were the Eight Jewels (*pa pao*) and waves with the *li shui* convention below them. As for minor decorations, the front and back of the collar and each cuff had small, facing dragons, while the right and left side of the collar and the lapel all had small dragons in profile. The skirt had four slits, in the traditional Manchu style, at front and rear, and on each side.[6]

The only real innovation in these specifications is the presence of the Twelve Symbols. These are the same which we have seen were used on the semiformal robes of the Ming Emperors. With this earlier precedent the Ch'ien-lung Emperor apparently saw fit to wear them on his dragon robes as well as on his robes of state. It would seem that the regulations of 1759 mark the first time that the Twelve Symbols were all confined exclusively to the use of the Emperor, officially at least. (In previous dynasties they had tradition-

[5] *Kao-tsung Shun huang-ti shih-lu* 919.11-13b.
[6] See *LCTS* 4.19.

ally been worn, in decreasing numbers, on the robes of the chief nobles and officials who assisted the Emperor at the annual sacrifices.) It is also the first time that they were worn at all by a Ch'ing Emperor.[7]

Perhaps it was the plea for the revival of the old Chinese ways in ceremonial dress that induced the Ch'ien-lung Emperor to make the small concession of adding them at all. Or perhaps he thought of them as emblems of Emperorhood, and felt that in using them he was subtly linked with the great rulers of past dynasties. In any case, since they were borrowed from another tradition, he kept them small and unobtrusive so that they would not impose upon the principal scheme of decoration: the dragons and the Universe concept.

The sun and moon disks appeared on the left and right shoulders of the Emperor's dragon robe. The constellation was shown over the main dragon on the chest, and the mountain above the dragon on the back. The (paired) dragon(s) and the "flowery bird" were on either side of the main rear dragon, and the axe and *fŭ* symbol on either side of the main front dragon. The sacrificial cups and water weed were placed on the lower part of the skirt in front, above the waves, while the flames and grains of millet were on corresponding portions of the skirt at the rear. These are all discussed in detail, together with the *pa pao* and other groups of dragon robe symbols, in Chapter 8.

It is important to remember that the fact that bright yellow was prescribed for the Emperor's dragon robes did not mean that he could not use other colors if he so desired. The presence of the Twelve Symbols would amply distinguish his robes from those of everyone else. Moreover, although the Emperor was usually supposed to wear his ceremonial robe (*ch'ao-fu*) when he attended the great annual sacrifices (the robe being of a prescribed color appropriate to the place and occasion), there were periods of fasting at the shrines of the Altar of Heaven, before the actual ceremonies, when

---

[7] The writer has previously pointed out that the Ch'ing Emperors before the Ch'ien-lung period had apparently not worn the Twelve Symbols. See *JAOS*, Vol. 63 (1943), p. 295; *Oriental Art*, Vol. 3 (1950), pp. 7-12; and *The Connoisseur*, Vol. 126 (December, 1950), pp. 206 and 220.

he was obliged by ritual to wear the simpler dragon robe.[8] The latter would then have had to be of blue, the color required there.

The Heir Apparent's robe was also called a *lung-p'ao*. Aside from the fact that it lacked the Twelve Symbols and was an orange-yellow (lit. "apricot yellow," *hsing-huang*) in color, its specifications exactly followed those for the Emperor's robe.[9]

The dragon robes of the other imperial princes, and of all the nobles and officials below them, were called *mang-p'ao,* or "four-clawed dragon robes." In practice, however, five-clawed dragons were used on the robes of the higher princes and of many beneath them who were awarded the privilege. Those of the imperial princes were golden yellow, *chin-huang,*[10] while princes of the first and second degree and all male members of the Imperial Clan wore blue or blue-black robes, unless the right to wear golden yellow was bestowed on them by the Emperor.[11] Like the Emperor's robe, these were also split at front and back and at the sides. The same was true for the robes of all Manchu nobles, but the dragon robes for Chinese nobles and all the officials had only two slits, at front and back.

The robes of third- and fourth-degree princes and other nobles, Manchu or Chinese, down to imperial nobles of the eleventh degree, were blue or blue black (or other colors depending on the occasions for which they were to be worn) with nine four-clawed dragons.[12] These were also worn by civil and military officials of the first three ranks, and first-class Imperial Guardsmen. The men of these groups could also wear five-clawed dragons if awarded the right to do so.[13] In fact, with the breakdown of governmental control in the nineteenth century, most of them appear to have just taken the five-clawed dragons, whether or not they had been granted the privilege of wearing them.

[8] *KHHTSL* 415.1.
[9] *LCTS* 4.40b.
[10] *Ibid.,* 4.51b.
[11] *Ibid.,* 4.60b.
[12] *Ibid.,* 4.77b (lesser princes, Manchu dukes, etc.); 5.12b (Chinese dukes, etc., and first to third rank officials).
[13] *Huang-ch'ao kuan-fu chih,* p. 22.

The robes of civil and military officials of the fourth to sixth ranks, Imperial nobles of the twelfth degree, and second- and third-rank Imperial Guardsmen, were of blue, blue black, or other colors, with eight four-clawed dragons.[14] The absence of one dragon did not change the external appearance of these robes in the least, for the ninth dragon, as we have already remarked, was placed on the inner flap of the robe, where it could not be seen when the robe was worn.

Lastly, civil and military officials of the seventh to ninth ranks and unclassed officials were assigned dragon robes with a variant pattern. This is very briefly described in the laws as having only five four-clawed dragons, without any mention of how they were to be disposed.[15] The accompanying picture illustrating the front of such a robe seems to show the typical old Ming pattern. It has a large profile dragon on the chest, arching over the left shoulder, with a dragon's tail appearing over the right shoulder, and two smaller dragons below.[16] Presumably, the makers of the laws had in mind a single giant dragon on the upper robe, which would begin on the chest of the garment, loop over the left shoulder, and encircle the neck, to end on the right shoulder.

It seems difficult to account for this very unusual pattern, unless it was an attempt to perpetuate the old dragon pattern of the Ming and early Ch'ing (Type 1) after the original models had gone out of use. It is possible that the lawmakers, not having before them an actual robe with the old pattern, may have gotten a false impression from seeing portraits of their forebears. They might have thought that the dragon's tail appearing on the right shoulder of the earlier robes was merely the extension of a single large dragon, without realizing that it had belonged to a second dragon originating on the back of the garment.

No examples can be found of a robe with this five-dragon pattern, and there is no evidence of its actual use in the later Ch'ing portraits.

[14] *LCTS* 5.55b.
[15] *Ibid.*, 5.96b.
[16] *Ibid.*, 5.96.

In fact, it seems that this pattern may never have existed except on paper. There are several reasons that could account for its not having been used. In the first place, the asymmetrical arrangement of a single large dragon on the upper part of the robe was contrary to all the traditions and principles of Chinese costume design. Furthermore, it would have been much more difficult to weave and embroider than the familiar eight-dragon pattern, on which the long panels that made up the front and back had almost identical repeats. Thus the difficulty of making these robes would have made them much more expensive than the eight-dragon ones.

The lowest officials would seldom have found themselves in situations where dragon robes would have been required. Also, their low salaries would generally have made it impossible for them to obtain such luxurious clothing. Moreover, the few officials of these low ranks who did have larger incomes, from other sources, could have used their money or its influence to obtain the right to wear the eight-dragon *mang* robes of the ranks immediately above them. And, after the breakdown of Ch'ing dynastic traditions in the 19th century, when the higher officials were freely using five-clawed dragons, the lowest officials could have helped themselves to the use of the familiar type of *mang* robe with the eight dragons if there had been any occasion to wear one. The fact remains that semiformal portraits of the lowest officials, made from 1759 to the end of the dynasty, always show them wearing plain, solid-colored robes under their *p'u-fu* jackets.

The prescriptions in the laws for all dragon robes, regardless of the wearer's rank, say that they should be "quilted, lined, of gauze, or fur-trimmed, depending on the season." [17] This is further explained by a passage in the Dynastic Statutes which says that in spring the people of the Court were to wear lined robes, beginning in the third (Chinese) month; and in the fall, fur-trimmed robes, beginning in the ninth (Chinese) month. The actual date for the change was decided each year by the Board of Rites, probably depend-

[17] *Ibid.*, 4.19, etc.

ing on the weather conditions of that particular year.[18] In the heat of summer they wore thin silk or gauze robes, and in the winter cold the quilted ones, which had an inner layer of cotton or silk waste.

Even though all the principal elements of the patterns on the dragon robes were now rigidly fixed by law, slight changes continued to be made in the ways of representing them. Thus the stylistic evolution of the dragon robe continued to the end of the dynasty, keeping within the framework of the laws. Most of the chief stages in this development are reflected in the robes of the emperors, which will be discussed in the next chapter. It is sufficient to say here that the *li shui* portion at the base of the robe became increasingly wider throughout the nineteenth century, until it seriously cramped the main field of decoration. Meanwhile, the background became cluttered with symbols of good fortune, scattered among the clouds and waves. As a result of all this extraneous decoration, the dragons were so crowded that they had to shrink back into the relatively small size that they had originally occupied in the medallions. The later robes lost dignity thereby, and in their decadence they mirrored the dynasty in decay.

[18] *KHHTSL* 328.8b. These laws referred specifically to the court robes (*ch'ao-fu*), but they seem to have applied to other robes as well.

6

Later Ch'ing Dragon Robes:
Problems of Dating

THE chief stylistic developments in the final form of the Ch'ing dragon robe are reflected in the later Ch'ing imperial robes which bear the Twelve Symbols. In two notable exhibitions of the last decade,[1] most of the Twelve-Symbol dragon robes in America were sorted into five groups according to their length and differences in their decoration, and were then ascribed to five Ch'ing emperors.[2] It was announced that they had belonged to the Emperors of the K'ang-hsi, Yung-chêng, Ch'ien-lung, Chia-ch'ing, and Tao-kuang periods.[3] Even though it has since been demonstrated that this theory of dating was based on a number of false premises,[4] and we are not yet able to date every Twelve-Symbol robe precisely,[5] we

[1] The first exhibition was held at the Minneapolis Institute of Arts in 1943, and the second at the Metropolitan Museum in 1945.

[2] This theory was devised in 1943 by Alan Priest of the Metropolitan Museum, while helping to catalogue the William E. Colby Collection of Chinese robes and textiles, which had recently been acquired by the Minneapolis Institute of Arts. It was first expressed in a brief, anonymous article in the *Bulletin of the Minneapolis Institute of Arts,* Vol. 32, no. 14 (April 3, 1943), pp. 46-51. It was referred to again in *Imperial Robes and Textiles of the Chinese Court,* and was developed, with embellishments, in "Prepare for Emperors," *Bulletin of the Metropolitan Museum,* new series, Vol. 2 (1943), no. 1. pp. 33-46. Further developed, the theory formed the bulk of the text in *Costumes from the Forbidden City* (pp. 3-13).

[3] "Prepare for Emperors," p. 46. Note that when this theory was first advanced in the *Bulletin of the Minneapolis Institute of Arts* it began the series more conservatively, with the Yung-chêng reign (*ibid.,* p. 47).

[4] See the writer's review of the catalogue for the Minneapolis show in *JAOS,* Vol. 63 (1943), and also his article, "Imperial Dragon Robes of the Later Ch'ing Dynasty," *Oriental Art,* Vol. 3 (1950), pp. 7-16.

[5] S. H. Wang, a curator of the Palace Museum in Peking, who was visiting the United States to inspect our museums, told the writer verbally on December 3, 1948, that several bundles of Ch'ing imperial robes had been preserved in the Imperial Palace, and that the robes had been ascribed to separate sovereigns who were believed to have owned them. He added, however, that the labeling had been done at the end of the dynasty, with no assurance of any scientific accuracy. Thus, even

now have a number of clues to guide us in straightening out the broad groupings.

We have seen that the Twelve Symbols were probably introduced during the Ch'ien-lung period, because of the lack of any evidence that they were used previously in the Ch'ing. But another innovation on a robe of the Ch'ien-lung Emperor provides a more positive clue for ascribing to his reign the earliest of the Twelve-Symbol dragon robes, which have been tentatively placed in the first group. This was merely a decorative element, not a ritualistic one like the Twelve Symbols, so it is not mentioned in the Dynastic Statutes, but we know it from a contemporary portrait.[6]

A painting [7] of the Ch'ien-lung Emperor, made in his old age, shows the dragon on the breast of his court robe coiled around a circular medallion. The latter is figured with the Eight Symbols of the Taoist Immortals and other lucky emblems, which serve to frame an elaborate *shou* character. This particular combination of symbols does not appear on the robes of any previous emperor (except in a falsified portrait of his grandfather [8]), so there is no doubt that the device was invented for, or by, this emperor.

Although the portrait pictures this decoration on a court robe, the Ch'ien-lung Emperor apparently also had it on at least one of his dragon robes, a portion of which has been preserved. This interesting textile fragment, now in the Victoria and Albert Museum in London, still has some of the Twelve Symbols and the central medallion just described, along with a number of other stylistic features

---

if one were able to examine them—which is impossible at present because of disturbed political conditions—they might conceivably be of no help at all in establishing a proper chronology for the Ch'ing imperial robes. In this situation, the search for accurate criteria for dating those we now have in our Western collections must continue in the Occident.

[6] The writer has previously pointed out that in the tradition of Chinese official portraiture the features were considered as less important than the insignia and other designations of rank. See the review of Priest's *Portraits of the Court of China*, in *Far Eastern Quarterly*, Vol. 2 (1943), pp. 310-14; and "Development of the Mandarin Square," pp. 123-25.

[7] *CTTHH* 2, pl. 26.

[8] *Ibid.*, pl. 11. This picture shows the K'ang-hsi Emperor wearing the complete regalia of the later Ch'ing emperors, as developed in the reign of his grandson, and the face is obviously too idealized to have been an actual portrait. The writer has already discussed its falsity in *JAOS*, Vol. 63, p. 296.

which can be used to identify other robes from the same period. (See Plate 15.)⁹ Taking this piece of an authentic Ch'ien-lung dragon robe as a reliable starting point, let us seek its place among the five groups into which the imperial dragon robes in our American museums and collections have been arbitrarily divided.

Unfortunately, the last few inches have been torn off the lower edge of the fragment, so that it is impossible to study the extent of the development of the *li shui,* which, as we have seen, is quite important for analyzing the date of a robe. However, the upper waves still remain, and significantly enough, the most prominent of these are rendered in bold swirls suggesting coiled watchsprings, a characteristic feature of most of the robes in the first group. Furthermore, this fragment has the tall, slender mountains rising from the sea, and the attenuated cloud forms in the background, both of which features are found on the first group of robes, as well as larger and bolder dragons than those on the robes of the later groups.¹⁰ (See Plate 9, right, for a contemporary example.)

In short, there seems full reason to believe that most of the robes of the first group, like the South Kensington fragment, date from the later Ch'ien-lung period (latter half of the 18th century). With this period as our starting point, let us now consider the other groups of later Ch'ing Twelve-Symbol dragon robes.

The second group contains two or three robes which are said to differ from those of the preceding set, though showing a logical progression in style.¹¹ This is what one might expect of the transition from one reign to the next, and if this group does follow the previous one, from the Ch'ien-lung period, these robes must have belonged to the Emperor of the Chia-ch'ing period (1796-1820). It

⁹ This was previously illustrated in the *Brief Guide to Chinese Woven Fabrics,* Victoria and Albert Museum (London, 1925), pl. 5. In the text (*ibid.,* p. 29) this was wrongly described as the back of an imperial robe. Actually, it is part of the front of one.
¹⁰ Compare the description of the robes of the first type in "Prepare for Emperors," pp. 40-42.
¹¹ Two robes were assigned to this group in "Prepare for Emperors" (p. 40), but a third had been added by the time of the Metropolitan Exhibition of 1945. See *Costumes from the Forbidden City,* p. 9.

is said of the latter that he was very conservative, since he was near-ing middle age when he succeeded his father, the Ch'ien-lung Emperor. It is therefore likely that his robes, like his policies in general, would have maintained, with but little change, the tradi-tions of the latter part of his father's reign.

The robes of the third group are the longest of the whole series. If the first group indeed belonged to the Ch'ien-lung Emperor, these of the third group must be the robes of his grandson, the Tao-kuang Emperor, whose portraits depict him as exceptionally tall and thin.[12] In fact, even disregarding the matter of length, there seems to be sufficient evidence of other kinds to suggest that the third group of robes actually does date from the Tao-kuang period (1821-1850).

The greater length of these robes is largely accounted for by a pronounced lengthening of the *li shui* section at the bottom. It has been suggested that perhaps the imperial textile factories, being suddenly faced with a bean-pole emperor, hastily added a few inches of stripes.[13] Whatever the initial reason, this convention of a very long band of *li shui* persisted throughout the rest of the dynasty for dragon robes in general. In fact, on robes for shorter persons the upper portion—originally the most important part of the pattern—was contracted to accommodate it.

Turning to the upper part of the robes in this third group, we find that the decoration has become formalized, almost stereotyped, and that the chief changes which distinguish them from the previous groups seem to be the rather stiff diaper patterns of the background, and a tendency to somewhat crasser and less subtle colors.[14] These characteristics are very noticeable in most of the other textiles of the

[12] A biography of the Chia-ch'ing Emperor says that he was of medium height, stout, and well-proportioned (*Eminent Chinese* 2, p. 967). This is apparently the only reference to the measurements of a Ch'ing Emperor from Chinese sources. However, the official portraits help somewhat: while the Chia-ch'ing Emperor is painted as a rather heavy individual, the Tao-kuang Emperor, his son, is shown as inordinately tall and very gaunt. (*CTTHH* 3, pls. 18, 19 [Chia-ch'ing Emperor]; 4, pl. 1 ff. [Tao-kuang Emperor].)

The portrait of the Tao-kuang Emperor in his dragon robe (*ibid.*, 4, pl. 2) appears to be one of a series of spurious portraits painted at the end of the dynasty. See Chapter 11, Note 12.

[13] "Prepare for Emperors," p. 42.

[14] *Ibid.*, p. 45.

mid-nineteenth century, when the founts of inspiration were beginning to run dry in China. They are particularly apparent in the
mandarin squares of the period.

The robes of the fourth group, in addition to demonstrating an
even greater deterioration in design, are remarkable for the use of a
violent purple dye, which the weavers first experimented with and
then used with abandon. Moreover, they are among the shortest
robes in the series.[15]   The Tao-kuang Emperor, who presumably had
the third group of robes, was succeeded by the Hsien-fêng Emperor
(1850-1861), and we might at first assume that these later robes of
the fourth group had belonged to him. But this attribution is
impossible, in view of the violent purple dye. The writer has had
some threads of this color, from a contemporary Chinese textile,
analyzed by chemical experts. They reported it to be Methyl Violet
2B, an extremely fast aniline dye discovered in Europe in 1861
but not produced on a large scale until 1866.[16]   Thus it was invented too late to have been used on the robes of the Hsien-fêng
Emperor.

All the evidence points to the fact that the robes of the fourth
group must have been worn by the Hsien-fêng Emperor's son, the
T'ung-chih Emperor, after he came of age. During the T'ung-chih
period (1861-75), the Chinese began to take stock of Western culture, and they imported Occidental things on a much larger scale.
Their disastrous defeat at the hands of the Western powers in the
wars of 1857-1860 had impressed them with the fact that the
European nations were more advanced—in technology at least.
Among other foreign goods imported at this time, the Customs
reports list a considerable quantity of European dyestuffs. For
example, in the year 1871, approximately two and a half tons of
aniline dyes (38.46 piculs) were imported from Europe to Shanghai,

[15] *Ibid.*
[16] This dye was identified by the Calco Chemical Division of the American
Cyanamid Company, through the kindness of Dr. E. I. Stearns. It was analyzed by
both absorption spectra and chemical reaction tests. Methyl Violet 2B (Color Index,
No. 680) is a remarkably fast dye, losing its color reluctantly even when treated
with alcohol. Compare the comments on this dye in *Costumes from the Forbidden
City,* p. 12.

by way of Hong Kong.[17] Shanghai, of course, would have been the port of transshipment for materials en route to the imperial silk factories at Kiangning and Hangchow. In the same year, more than five and three-quarters tons of foreign dyes and colors were brought into Tientsin, the port of Peking, where the Imperial Weaving and Dyeing Office was situated (see Chapter 9). However, it would not have been necessary to import the new color as a dye. The Customs reports of this period remark upon a steady import of silk thread from Europe, and some of this, dyed with Methyl Violet 2B, could have been used in making the imperial robes.[18]

As a further clue, several of the robes in this fourth group, for which the new dye had been used, have the marriage symbol, *shuang-hsi*. The Hsien-fêng Emperor had been married before the discovery of aniline dyes, the first of which was found by W. H. Perkin in 1856. However, his son, the T'ung-chih Emperor, was married in 1873, by which time the Customs records attest that some of these aniline dyes had begun to come into China. The eight years that had elapsed since Methyl Violet 2B had been produced commercially would have allowed plenty of time for this particular aniline derivative to reach China, and for the Chinese to discover its possibilities in the way of brilliance and fastness. Moreover, as the T'ung-chih Emperor was only going on seventeen when he married, and probably had not yet attained his full height, this would account for the somewhat shorter length of this fourth group of the Twelve-Symbol dragon robes.

The T'ung-chih Emperor died prematurely in 1875, two years later. This admittedly gives only a short time for the production of the several robes that are said to belong in this group. On the other hand, one point frequently ignored by our Western collectors deserves to be emphasized: *not all of these imperial robes now in our collections were actually worn.* Many of them are unquestionably ex-

[17] See the *Catalogue of the Shanghai Customs Collection* (Vienna, 1873), pp. 46-47, and *Returns of Trade at the Treaty Ports in China for the Year 1871* (Shanghai, 1872), p. 153, for records of the importation of aniline dyes.
[18] *Ibid.*, pp. 222-23, lists the amount of silk thread imported into Tientsin over the period 1865-72.

CHINA'S DRAGON ROBES

amples that were rejected for various reasons. The imperial dragon robes, whether woven or embroidered, were made in several pieces, and each piece would be carefully examined by the official inspectors as it came from the loom or embroidery frame.[19] If these worthies disapproved of the quality of the weaving, or the dyes used, the individual panels might be rejected before the parts of the robe-to-be were cut from the background. These panels were not destroyed, however. Some were presented to the Lama Church as silk offerings,[20] and, after the fall of the Dynasty in 1911, others were undoubtedly made up and sold to foreign buyers. Still other robes might have been actually tailored in the Imperial factories, only to be rejected later by the Imperial Family or their stewards.[21] These rejects would not have been destroyed either, but would have been put away in chests for emergency use. No doubt some of these —obtained during the looting after the Boxer Rebellion in 1900, or in the public sales held in Peking during Fêng Yu-hsiang's regime in the 1920's—help to account for the relatively large number of such robes in American collections.

In short, although the T'ung-chih Emperor occupied the throne of China for only a short time after he came of age, the experimentation required for testing the possibilities of the new color, the fastidiousness of the Inspectors, and the caprice of the Emperor or his mother, the notorious Empress-Dowager, might easily have resulted in the production of a considerable number of Imperial Twelve-Symbol robes at that time, very few of which were ever approved for actual use.

Then, too, since the robes in this fourth group were put there primarily on the basis of their length, some of them might possibly

[19] The dragon robes were woven, or embroidered in three separate, rectangular panels (see Chapter 9). Before being cut out, and previous to being sent up to Peking, they were inspected by the Superintendent of the Imperial Factory. See Chapter 9, Note 17.

[20] While visiting a large Tibetan lamasery near Leh, Ladakh, in 1938, the writer saw a portion of an Imperial dragon robe in yellow silk still forming part of the original bolt, being used as a canopy over one of the principal Buddhas in the main shrine hall.

[21] After being forwarded to the Silk Storehouse (*Tuan-k'u*) in Peking, the robes were again inspected, by the official in charge. See Chapter 9, Note 16.

have belonged to the Kuang-hsü Emperor, who was only seventeen years old at the time of his marriage in 1889, and who also had probably not yet attained his full height when he wore his wedding robes.

The fifth and last group of Twelve-Symbol dragon robes must have belonged to the Kuang-hsü Emperor, who reigned from 1875 to 1908.[22] They comprise the largest number in the series, and his reign was a long one, allowing time for the manufacture of numerous robes. Also, it would seem likely that our Occidental museums and collections would have a considerable number of his garments, in view of the widespread looting of his palaces during the Allied occupation of Peking in 1900, and the frequent sales of Late Ch'ing imperial textiles by destitute Manchu courtiers in the '20's.

This fifth group is characterized by even longer *li shui* stripes on the lower border, so that the waves would reach almost to the knees of the wearer, when standing. Photographs of the period clearly show that this ultimate, excessive widening of the deep-sea portion was a convention of the late nineteenth and early twentieth centuries.[23] This proves that the robes of the fifth group were, as we might logically expect, products of the Kuang-hsü period. (See Plate 10, right, for an example.)

The Kuang-hsü Emperor was succeeded by a small boy, the pathetic P'u-yi, who was deposed by the Revolution of 1911, three years later. But, since all the robes we have been discussing were made for adults, the robes worn by this child do not concern us here.[24]

Thus we have seen that the five groups of Imperial, Twelve-Symbol dragon robes in our American collections probably belonged to the Ch'ien-lung, Chia-ch'ing, Tao-kuang, T'ung-chih, and Kuang-hsü periods.

[22] Compare "Prepare for Emperors," p. 145, where they are wrongly ascribed to the Tao-kuang Emperor.
[23] See, for example, Bland and Backhouse, *China under the Empress Dowager* (Philadelphia & London, 1912), photograph facing p. 90.
[24] A miniature Imperial dragon robe, apparently made for this child, the Hsüan-t'ung Emperor, but never cut out, is in the National Museum, Washington, D.C.

One question still remains: why do we apparently have no robes of the Hsien-fêng Emperor? A possible answer would be that this Emperor probably did not have many dragon robes to begin with, since the Taiping Rebellion had cut off the imperial silk factories in the South by 1853, the third year of his reign; and most of those he did have were probably stolen by the French troops in 1860, during the looting of the Summer Palace.[25] The Emperor had been spending nearly all his time there, going into Peking only when he was required to attend special ceremonies. Thus, practically all his clothing, including his dragon robes, must have been in this palace. And, as he had to escape quickly—he left barely three hours before the foreign troops arrived—he could not have taken much with him. In this case, since the Chinese Imperial robes in our American collections were mostly purchased in Peking during the present century—directly or through dealers—it is not likely that they would include any robes of the Hsien-fêng Emperor.

Thus far we have been assuming, for purposes of discussion, that all the Twelve-Symbol dragon robes assembled in these exhibitions were those of emperors, as has been categorically stated. However, although it is true that in the laws only the Emperor's robes are described as having the Twelve Symbols, existing portraits show that at least two Ch'ing Empresses also wore these symbols.

We shall see in the next chapter that the dragon robes of noblewomen, including the Empress and Empress-Dowagers, were distinguished by extra bands of ornament below the water pattern on the upper sleeves,[26] while women's robes in general were slit only at the sides, and not at front and rear as the men's were.[27] Using these distinctive features as criteria, we perceive that at least one of the

[25] The chaplain of the British forces, describing the French camp near the Summer Palace after the seizure of the latter, is quoted as saying: ". . . while General Montauban assured Sir Hope Grant that 'nothing had been touched' . . . the soldiers' tents and the ground around them were a perfect blaze of silk and embroidery." See *The Times* (London), March 11, 1874, p. 12. General Montauban, himself, testified before a Committee of Investigation that one palace was full of silks, some of which were used instead of ropes to picket the French horses. See *The Times,* March 10, 1874, p. 12.

[26] As prescribed in *LCTS* 6.31-2.

[27] *Ibid.*

"Twelve-Symbol Emperor's robes" displayed at the recent exhibitions of Ch'ing costume must have been an Empress' robe,[28] and
that the cartoon for an Imperial Twelve-Symbol robe in the Nelson
Gallery is obviously a pattern for the robe of an Empress.[29] The
same is true of two "Emperor's" dragon robes in the Chicago Natural
History Museum.

Unfortunately, there is one great obstacle in the way of applying
these criteria for weeding out all the Empress' robes from among
the Twelve-Symbol groups. This is the fact that many of the robes
now in our collections were evidently made up from bolts, or uncut
robes, for sale to foreign buyers. We can tell this by their faulty
cutting, mismatched lapels, and other sloppy features that would
never have been tolerated by autocratic sovereigns who could afford
to have the best.[30] And in this situation, the persons who sewed the
robes together consciously or unconsciously have made faulty
alterations. For example, they might have cut off the second band
of decoration on the sleeves to make an "emperor's robe" out of one
originally destined for an empress, or they might have sewed up the
front and back seams of a robe intended for an emperor, carelessly
neglecting to leave the the required slits.[31] It should be emphasized
that these virtual forgeries should certainly be discarded before trying
to establish a definitive chronology for the dragon robes of the later
Ch'ing Emperors.

As soon as an accurate chronology for the later Ch'ing imperial
dragon robes has been worked out, it should not be too difficult to
set up a tentative scheme for dating the more ordinary later dragon
robes that belonged to lesser nobles and officials.[32] But we must

[28] *Costumes from the Forbidden City,* pl. 22.
[29] *Ibid.,* pl. 43.
[30] For an extreme example of patching see *Costumes from the Forbidden City,*
pl. 1. Plates 34 and 35 of the same catalogue illustrate the mismatched lapels of
robes made up for later sale.
[31] An interesting hybrid in the Metropolitan Collection is a Twelve-Symbol robe
with both the noblewoman's sleevebands and the slits proper to a man's robe. This
is a clear example of a robe made up for the tourist trade, by some one ignorant of
the Manchu traditions.
[32] As for the earlier robes, dating from before 1759, it may take a considerable
time to devise a reliable chronological order. Even if more examples turn up to
work on, the problem will still be complicated by lack of specific regulations, and

remember that it took some time for a new style of decoration or an innovation in symbols to percolate down into the robes of persons of less degree. Furthermore, in the more remote provinces of the Chinese Empire, an old pattern might have been perpetuated for years after it had gone out of style elsewhere.

---

by the great amount of experimentation in pattern then permitted. Such a chronology can only be based on authentic portraits, either bearing dates, or datable by such items as the presence or absence of the round hat jewel, introduced in 1727, or on robes from known tombs that have been opened scientifically.

7

Women's Dragon Robes and Dragon Jackets

A. NOBLEWOMEN'S DRAGON ROBES

AS we have seen, the laws of 1652 decreed that the mother, wife, and daughter of a Ch'ing official were to wear robes conforming to his rank.[1] This did not necessarily mean that they were to be exactly the same; rather, it meant that if he could wear four-clawed dragons they could also. Actually, the robes of officials and their womenfolk—before 1759—were much the same. In the case of their dragon robes, for example, the patterns were exactly the same, and the only real difference was that the women's were slit at the sides, instead of at front and back. (See Plate 11, right.)

The laws of 1759 merely repeated that the dragon robes for women were to be patterned exactly like those of their husbands except for this minor distinction.[2] In practice, however, the wives of Chinese, as distinguished from the Manchu officials—especially those who lived away from Peking, and outside the Manchu garrisons—wore another, unofficial type of dragon garment for most special occasions (see Chapter 10).

Only the dragon robes of the Empress, the Imperial consorts, and the Heir Apparent's wife had any real differences. They not only differed in having extra ornamental bands on the sleeves, but they also came in three types.[3]

The laws of 1759 prescribed three types of dragon robes for the Empress and Empress-Dowager(s). The first was bright yellow, with nine dragons, against a background of five-colored clouds, hav-

---

[1] This convention was apparently first expressed in the laws of 1652 (*KHHT* 48.13), but it may have already been of long standing.
[2] *LCTS* 6.117, 146; 7.15, 33, 43.
[3] *Ibid.*, 6.31-35, 68, 94.

ing symbols of happiness and longevity as the wearer desired, and the Eight Precious Things with *li-shui* below.[4] The laws also say that the sleeves should be like those of the court robes, meaning that they should have an extra band of ornamentation between the upper sleeve and the plainer lower section, or the cuff. This feature and the way the robes were slit—at the sides, like all women's robes— marked the only distinctions between these robes and those of the Emperor, except of course for the presence of the Twelve Symbols on the latter.

However, as we have stated in the last section, even though the laws say nothing about the Twelve Symbols on the robes of Empresses, we know that they sometimes wore them. The Palace Museum has a half-length painting of Hsiao-ho, wife of the Chia-ch'ing Emperor, showing her in a dragon robe of the general style of the Tao-kuang period (she was Empress Dowager from 1820 to 1850).[5] The upper part of the robe has the sun, moon, and stars, and as no dragon robe has come down to us with only four symbols, she was probably wearing all twelve of them. A familiar portrait-photograph of the famous Empress Dowager Hsiao-ch'in (Tzŭ-hsi) shows her wearing a yellow dragon robe with all twelve symbols,[6] and, as we have remarked, the cartoon for a Late Ch'ing Twelve-Symbol dragon robe in the Nelson Gallery, has the sleevebands appropriate for an Empress.[7]

In addition to all this evidence, several of the Empress' dragon robes with the Twelve Symbols have come down to us intact. One, in the possession of Miss Alice Boney, has the very wide sleeves and exaggerated horsehoof cuffs, of which the Empress-Dowager Hsiao-ch'in was very fond, and might possibly be the same robe that she wore for the photograph mentioned above. Another is the magnificent robe richly worked in pearls and coral, that was lent by Lady

---

[4] *Ibid.*, 6.31-2.
[5] *CTTHH* 3, pl. 30.
[6] Princess Der Ling, *Two Years in the Forbidden City* (New York, 1911), photograph facing p. 112; and *Old Buddha* (New York, 1928), frontispiece.
[7] *Costumes from the Forbidden City*, pl. 43.

David to the International Exhibition of Chinese Art in London.[8] In addition to the Twelve Symbols, this has marriage symbols on it, indicating that it was a wedding robe. As the very high *li shui* border, the small dragons, and several other features in its decoration, show without question that it dates from the late nineteenth century, it must have been the wedding dress of the Empress Hsiaoting, who married the Kuang-hsü Emperor on February 26th, 1889. A third, a splendid example in *k'o-ssŭ,* belongs to Herbert Boone of Baltimore. It is obviously earlier than the others. Its sleeves and cuffs are still fairly narrow, and its pattern retains some elements of the Tao-kuang style, though the form of the clouds, with other details, links it to the Kuang-hsü robes. As a transitional robe, we would suggest that it had belonged to one of the Dowager Empresses, either Hsiao-ch'in, or her rival, Hsiao-chên, in the early 1860's.

Two other Twelve-Symbol empress' robes, on exhibition in the Chicago Natural History Museum, provide striking examples of work in *k'o-ssŭ* and embroidered gauze, respectively. Both have the very late, wide cuffs and other late Ch'ing elements characteristic of the reign of the last Dowager Empress, and were probably made for her. It is true that the two robes have in their backgrounds two different types of cloud form, each of which has been ascribed to a different Ch'ing Emperor in grouping the Twelve-Symbol robes (the fourth and fifth groups). However, since the other features of their decoration are similar, we can infer that they must have been made about the same time, and that the designer of one might have gone back to an earlier cloud form for the sake of a little variety. This illustrates once more the pitfalls in attempting to date a robe by only one decorative element, instead of considering all the elements on the robe.

The second type of empress' dragon robe had eight dragon medallions against a background of bright yellow (or other colors), yet it kept the waves with *li shui* and the Eight Precious Things, as

---

[8] *Catalogue of the International Exhibition of Chinese Art 1935-36* (London, 1935), No. 3006, text p. 257, photograph p. 269.

found on the first type.[9] The third type also had eight medallions
on a background of yellow (or other colors), but it had no ornamentation on the skirt, though it retained the ornamental collar, lapel,
and sleevebands of the two previous types.[10] Thus the three recall
three stages in the evolution of the dragon robe, in reverse order.
(Types 1 and 2 are shown in Plate 12.)

Imperial consorts of the first degree could wear the first type as
worn by the empress (without the Twelve Symbols, of course),[11]
while consorts of the second and third degrees could wear dragon
robes of this same pattern but of golden yellow,[12] and those of the
fourth degree could wear this pattern in tawny yellow (literally
"incense color," *hsiang-sê*).[13] The Heir Apparent's wife could also
wear dragon robes of the same pattern, but the color had to be orange
yellow, like that worn by her husband.[14] None of these women
below the rank of empress could wear dragon robes of the second or
third type.

B. Women's Dragon Jackets

Just as the Emperor, with his nobles and officials, was regularly
required to wear a dark formal jacket over his dragon robes, so the
Empresses and Imperial consorts had to wear jackets over theirs
when they appeared in public. Those worn after 1759 were of two
types, corresponding in pattern to the second and third types of
dragon robes, but differing somewhat in appearance. The first was
blue-black with eight gold medallions, and had waves and *li shui* on
the lower border.[15] It had no collar or lapel, and lacked the lower
sleeves, but the short upper sleeve ended in the same ornamental
band that was used on the dragon robes. The second type of dragon
jacket was severely plain, being blue-black with eight dragon medal-

[9] *LCTS* 6.33-4.
[10] *Ibid.*, 6.35-6.
[11] *Ibid.*, 6.32.
[12] *Ibid.*, 6.68.
[13] *Ibid.*, 6.94.
[14] *Ibid.*, 6.117.
[15] *Ibid.*, 6.29.

lions in gold, and no other ornamentation.[16] Like all outer jackets these were buttoned down the front, leaving a slit below, to match those at the sides and back. (Type 1 is shown in Plate 13.)

Though nothing is mentioned about it in the laws, several examples of both types of dragon jacket have come down to us, showing four of the Twelve Symbols—sun, moon, stars, and mountain—on the four upper medallions, respectively.[17] These may have belonged to the last Empress Dowager, who was a law unto herself, but possibly the custom began even earlier. (See Plate 13, right.)

Imperial consorts of the first three degrees, and the Heir Apparent's consort, wore dragon jackets identical with the first type worn by the Empresses. The fourth-degree consorts, however, wore jackets similar to the second type worn by the Empresses, plain except for the eight medallions, but the dragons in the four lower medallions were the highly conventionalized *k'uei-lung* type, without scales.[18]

Wives and daughters of the Manchu princes wore jackets like the *p'u-fu* of their husbands or fathers, while wives of lesser nobles and officials were supposed to wear dark jackets with eight floral medallions enclosing *shou* characters.[19] In practice, the latter generally wore the *p'u-fu* with "mandarin squares" like that of their husbands.

No discussion of women's dragon jackets would be complete without mention of some earlier types which were worn over the *ts'ai-fu* or dragon robes in Early Ch'ing for semiformal wear. Judging by one seventeenth-century portrait, now in Toronto, they were even worn over court robes on occasion.

These are especially interesting for two reasons. In the first place, neither their cut nor their patterns survived into Later Ch'ing. Secondly, their bold patterns probably reflect those on contemporary dragon robes, thus giving us a few more examples of unusual decora-

---

[16] *Ibid.*, 6.30.

[17] The Metropolitan Museum and the National Museum in Washington, D.C., both have examples of this type, and the writer saw another for sale in Shanghai, in 1945.

[18] *LCTS* 6.29 (first three degrees); 6.93 (fourth degree).

[19] *Ibid.*, 6.128, 135, 145, 150 (princesses); 6.154 (lesser noblewomen and officials' wives).

tion on the Early Ch'ing dragon robes, proper. Like the later dragon jackets, they were buttoned down the front, leaving a slit below the knees, and were also slit at both sides and at the rear. Unlike the later ones, however, they had long, straight sleeves, cut fairly full, and ending abruptly with a straight (or slightly oblique) edge. They were worn over robes which had horsehoof cuffs, so that the latter projected slightly, to complete the costume.

Several examples of early eighteenth century dragon jackets are shown in one of the woodcuts illustrating the K'ang-hsi Emperor's Eightieth Birthday Celebration in 1713.[20]   These jackets, being worn by ladies of the Court, have three main types of patterns. The first has eight dragon medallions thé second has four dragons, like the dragon robes of Type 2a; and the third has eight dragons, like the familiar, later dragon robes. A single example shows still another type, with twelve dragons—having two dragons, instead of one, on each skirt panel. Because of the small scale, the patterns in this picture are merely roughly indicated, and although they are valuable for contemporary evidence, it is necessary to turn to portraits or surviving examples of actual jackets to study any details.

A very interesting example of one of these Early Ch'ing dragon jackets is that worn over the court robe in the above-mentioned portrait at Toronto. This has two enormous *mang* dragons in profile, facing each other across the central seam, and extending down the whole length of the robe; while two smaller profile dragons are shown crawling down the sleeves toward the sacred pearls just above the cuffs. The central seam, cuffs, and lower border are all edged in gold brocade.

A slightly later dragon jacket is shown being worn over a *ts'ai-fu* robe with dragon medallions in a more informal portrait from the Late K'ang-hsi or Early Yung-chêng period, now in the Metropolitan Museum.[21] This jacket has a large, facing dragon with both (five-clawed) forefeet upraised, on the breast of the robe; two profile dragons on the shoulders, extending down the arms; and two more

[20] *Wan-shou ch'êng-tien* (Peking, 1714), 41.21b.
[21] Priest, *Portraits of the Court of China* (New York, 1942), pl. 18.

profile dragons soaring upward on the skirt panels. All the dragons are about the same size but are larger and more vigorous than those on later robes. At the base of the robe are slanting stripes of rudimentary *li shui* with *ju-i* heads, but no curling waves. Being a winter robe, it is trimmed with white fur. (See Plate 14.)

The Textile Museum of Washington, D.C. has an actual dragon jacket of a slightly later period, probably contemporary with the robes from the tomb of Prince Kuo. This has the same combination of dragons as on the Yung-chêng dragon robes, the four upper ones being very large, while the four on the skirt are much smaller. A broad band of waves (but no *li shui*) is broken by naturalistic rock masses instead of the more usual, symmetrical tapering peaks. In the waves are bell symbols characteristic of the Middle Ch'ing robes, including at least one of the Kuo Ch'ing-wang series.

An interesting variation, which seems to be a transition between a woman's dragon jacket and a *p'u-fu* is represented by two examples, one in the Yale Gallery and one in the Metropolitan Museum. Both are of red satin with the pattern woven in gold. If they were not split down the front, with relatively narrow sleeves, like the dragon jackets, we would have placed them in the next section, among the dragon robes of Chinese brides, because they were probably intended as wedding garments. Both have dragon medallions on the shoulders, and four more on the skirts (front and rear). Instead of those generally found on breast and back, however, they have the square of the husband's rank (ninth rank, in each case). A strip of waves with the mountain is figured at the base of each robe, and small stags and cranes, emblems of longevity, are shown just above the water on each side of the mountain. It seems probable that these were made at the time when the dragon medallion robes were still in favor and in their most fully developed form; while the squares are in the style of the Ch'ien-lung period. This would date these robes about 1750, shortly before the laws that discouraged further experimentation.

The Metropolitan Museum also has a unique example of Later Ch'ing dragon jacket that belonged to an Empress. Made of yellow silk, it has the familiar pattern of a nineteenth-century Imperial dragon robe, including the Twelve Symbols, but is cut differently. It buttons down the front, and has a small round collar instead of the collar with lapel. It also differs from the Early Ch'ing dragon jackets we have been describing in having short sleeves. (Unfortunately, the sleevebands that terminated them have been removed, spoiling the appearance of the jacket.) No doubt this unusual garment must have been made to order for one of the nineteenth-century Empresses, and as such it has a double interest. Not only does it provide further proof that the Later Ch'ing Empresses could wear the Twelve Symbols, but it also shows that they sometimes wore robes that were outside the main tradition of Later Ch'ing costume—a thing their subjects could never do.

8

The Symbols on the Dragon Robes

A. THE DRAGON AND OTHER BASIC SYMBOLS

W E cannot attempt to review all the details of Chinese dragon lore, and the various cosmic meanings that have been ascribed to the dragon and its pearl.[1] However, as this creature is the primary symbol on the robes we are considering, it is important to study the variations in its representation from period to period. The Chinese had various fashions in dragons, just as they had changing fashions in dress, and some knowledge of these can be of great help in dating.

The dragon, like the *ch'i-lin* and the Chinese "phoenix," with which it is associated in the ancient group of four sacred creatures (*szŭ ling*), is a highly composite animal made up of parts from a number of others. The simplest description of the dragon in Chinese literature says that it is depicted with the head of a horse and the tail of a serpent. This is quoted in a famous Sung encyclopaedia of natural history which goes on to give a much more detailed account. It begins by saying that the dragon has "three sections" and "nine resemblances"—three and nine both being highly auspicious *yang* numbers. The three sections are head to shoulders, shoulders to loins, and loins to (the tip of) the tail. As for the nine resemblances: it has horns like a stag, a (fore-) head like a camel, eyes like a demon, a neck like a snake, a belly like a sea monster (the *shên*), scales like a carp, claws like an eagle, pads like a tiger, and ears like an ox. As an additional feature, it has on its brow a bump like Po Shan, a

[1] For a rather full discussion of Far Eastern dragon lore, see M. W. de Visser, *The Dragon in China and Japan* (Amsterdam, 1913). (This was first published in *Verhandelingen der Koninklijke Akademie van Wetenschappen*, new series, Vol. 13, No. 2.) The highly controversial question of the meaning of the flaming jewel, or pearl, is discussed by him on pp. 103-8.

famous mountain, which is called the *ch'ih-mu*. Without the *ch'ih-mu*, it could not ascend into the heavens.[2] This prominence is often indicated on the facing dragons on the robes by a prominent circle on the forehead. Another Sung account says that the dragon has eighty-one scales, nine times nine, nine being the *yang* number par excellence; as opposed to the carp which has thirty-six, six times six, six being the *yin* number.[3] This latter tradition, however, seems to have been generally overlooked by the makers of the later robes, who apparently did not limit themselves to any definite number of scales.

As we have seen, the earlier Chinese dragons of the T'ang, and apparently the Imperial dragons of the Sung as well, had only three claws, extending the *yang* symbolism still further; and they also had very distinctive, slender horns that curled upward at the tips. Probably it was one of the Tartar dynasties that introduced the idea of Imperial five-clawed dragons. (Was this perhaps to indicate a superiority over those worn by the Emperors of China?) At least, the five-clawed dragon and its dominance over those with fewer claws is first officially mentioned in the Yüan statutes.[4] Note that five is still a *yang* number, though less auspicious than three. At any rate, with the slight exceptions mentioned below, the three-clawed Imperial dragon passed out of Chinese culture after the Sung, though it was retained in Japan, where it still appears.

The Ming robes had both five-clawed and four-clawed dragons, with relatively straight and rather heavy horns. The four-clawed type was called a *mang*, to distinguish it from the Imperial *lung* dragon. Chinese dictionaries define this word as meaning a great snake, the king of snakes, or a boa constrictor. But the fact remains that in Ming and Ch'ing art and costume, the creature called a *mang* was a full-fledged dragon which resembled the *lung* in every respect

---

[2] These descriptions are given in the *Erh-ya i* 28.1b, in which they are ascribed to Wang Fu, a writer of the Later Han period.

[3] Lu Tien, *P'i-ya* 1.1.

[4] See Chapter 1, Note 20, for reference. The three-clawed dragon was apparently never used on robes after the K'ang-hsi period, but was used in Later Ch'ing on rugs made for people of low degree, who were not permitted to use four- or five-clawed dragons. See Gordon B. Leitch, *Chinese Rugs* (new ed.) (New York, 1935), p. 81. The Newark Museum has a pair of such rugs in its Tibetan Collection.

except the number of its claws. And after the dynasty became more corrupt, and persons outside of the Imperial Family were allowed to add a fifth claw, the distinction was one of name only. The Ming also introduced a three-toed dragon known as the *tou-niu,* with stubby claws and large, curving horns that swept up over the ears and down again, in a broad arc.[5] The clumsy horns and feet of these *tou-niu,* however, would prevent them from ever being mistaken for the stately, three-clawed imperial dragons of the past.

The Manchus did not retain the *tou-niu,* but Early Ch'ing references speak of three-clawed dragons, *san-chao lung,* on the robes of the Emperor and the Heir Apparent. The University Museum in Philadelphia has recently been given a fragment of a Ch'ing imperial robe in yellow *k'o-ssŭ* with two dragons that have only three claws on each foot.[6] Why did the Manchus use them at all, and why did they later abandon them? The records fail to tell. Perhaps they originally adopted the idea from Japanese textiles imported by way of Korea before they conquered China, for, as we have seen, the three-clawed dragon had persisted in Japan. In any case, the fully developed claws on these Early Ch'ing three-clawed dragons would serve to distinguish them from the Ming *tou-niu,* while their later style of horns would appear quite different from the slender, more graceful ones of the Sung dragons. The Ch'ing also continued the practice of using the four-clawed *mang* dragon. But by the nineteenth century, if not earlier, this was again a distinction only in name, and the wearing of five-clawed dragons by lesser nobles and officials had become very general.

The Early Ch'ing dragons, as we have seen, were much larger than those on the later robes, and more vigorously depicted. One particular characteristic that sets them apart from those of the Middle and Late Ch'ing is the very long snout or muzzle, ending in a more prominent nose. (See Plates 4, 5, 7, and 18.) This feature

---

[5] The *tou-niu* is first described and pictured as an animal in the *San-tsai t'u-hui* (*niao-shou* 5c and d). Previous uses of this term in Chinese literature obviously refer to a group of stars, or the region of the heavens in which they are seen.

[6] The gift of William E. Colby of San Francisco.

is commonly found on the older dragons shown on Ming porcelains, etc., and thus was no doubt a stylistic carryover from the previous dynasty, as was the spiky, flamelike appendage at the end of the tail, an element which is not found on the earlier dragons.

The dragons of the Yung-chêng and early Ch'ien-lung periods were still quite large—especially those on the upper part of the robes—but they were somewhat tamer looking, with shorter heads which no longer carried on the classical camel-horse tradition. During the middle of the Ch'ien-lung reign, all the dragons began to shrink in size, and they never regained their old stature or their former liveliness. Lesser distinctions can also be noted, such as the fact that on the Twelve-Symbol robes of the Middle Ch'ien-lung period, the upper, facing dragons generally have both forepaws upraised (see Plate 9, right). This convention reappears on one of the robes of the Chia-ch'ing Emperor as shown in a portrait of him, but it then seems to have passed out of fashion, with only an occasional revival for the sake of variety.[7] Examination of the Later Ch'ing robes in our American collections often shows an inconsistency in that the facing dragons on the lapels may have both forepaws up, while the larger ones below them have one turned down, or vice versa. This was probably because the tailors had economically used extra lapels left over from an earlier time.

In addition to the official distinction between dragons, depending on the number of claws they had, we have seen that there were also differences in position that were considered very significant. In the

---

[7] It has been suggested that this dragon with both forepaws upraised might be a characteristic of the Emperor's robes from K'ang-hsi through most of the Ch'ien-lung period (*Chinese Court Costumes,* p. 19). However, the portrait of the Yung-chêng Emperor in his dragon robe shows the main dragon with the left foreleg extending downward (*CTTHH* 1, pl. 26); that of the Ch'ien-lung Emperor shows both forepaws upraised (*CTTHH* 3, pl. 1); while one of the portraits of the Chia-ch'ing Emperor also shows the main dragon with both forepaws up (*CTTHH* 3, pl. 18). Lastly, a late nineteenth-century dragon robe in Minneapolis has this type of dragon (*Costumes from the Forbidden City,* pl. 35).

Two very doubtful portraits of the Tao-kung and T'ung-chih Emperors in dragon robes show both forefeet bent down, like those on the Minneapolis sun-symbol robe (*CTTHH* 4, pls. 2 and 25). However, in addition to the questionable authenticity of the portraits, no such robes from that period have as yet been discovered, so we cannot present this as a definite phenomenon.

Ming, for example, a *tso mang,* shown fullfaced, was considered more worthy than the *tan mang* or "simple mang," shown in profile.[8]

Similarly, on the Ch'ing dragon robes, both the *lung* and the *mang* dragons were qualified by the words *chêng,* or *chêng-mien,* meaning facing, and *hsing* (literally, "walking"), meaning in profile. In Early Ch'ing these seem to have served to distinguish between the robes of the highest nobles and the lesser ones; this was certainly true on the medallion robes at least. But in the Middle and Later Ch'ing, both types of dragon appeared on the same robe. It is important to note that the four dragons shown fullface on the upper part of the Later Ch'ing dragon robes are not all absolutely identical. Three have their bodies curving to the left, with their tails extending out to the right, in the usual convention for depicting facing dragons. But the fourth, the one on the right shoulder, has its body curving to the right, with its tail extending out to the left toward the front of the robe, so as to be exactly opposite to the one on the left shoulder. Thus the two shoulder dragons exactly balance each other, like the profile dragons on the shoulders of the Early Ch'ing robes, which had both been shown facing the front of the robe to create an effect of perfect symmetry.

Still another type of dragon by position appeared in the Ch'ing on women's robes, such as the "dragon jackets." This was the *li lung* (or *mang*), meaning "vertical dragon."[9] It was an ascending dragon shown in profile, facing upward. Note, however, that if the head of an ascending dragon is horizontal, it would still be called a profile dragon, or *hsing-lung.*

We have already mentioned the cosmic symbolism in the basic pattern on the dragon robe, with its Earth symbolized by the mountains, its Sea (waves and *li shui*), and its cloud-filled Sky. We have pointed out the value of the changes in the sea elements at the bottom of the robe—especially the evolution of the *li shui*—for determining the date of a given robe. The mountains and clouds are also valuable for dating, as they, too, underwent an evolution that is

[8] *Yeh-huo pien* 1.29, and *Ming shih* 67.15.
[9] *LCTS* 6.11-12.

particularly apparent in the sequence of the Twelve-Symbol robes. The early, towering peaks gradually shortened and became more squat; while the bold cloud scrolls became slender and attenuated, then bunched together in overly conventionalized, very unnatural-looking forms.[10] However, some caution must be used in applying these criteria, because in the late nineteenth century, several types of clouds seem to have been used on separate robes at the same time, as illustrated by the set of late empress' robes in the Chicago Natural History Museum. This was probably due to a desire for novelty, when the artisans could no longer think up new ways of rendering the old details and turned back to earlier robes for inspiration.

Of these three groups of elements, only the mountain had an especial symbolic importance in its own right. This mountain, which is generally repeated four times around the base of the robe, has often been described by Western scholars as being the Mount Meru of the Buddhists (which is usually rendered in Chinese as the *Miao-kao Shan*). It is undoubtedly the equivalent of Mount Meru, as the axis of the Universe, but the people of China apparently thought of it as representing not Meru, but *K'un-lun Shan,* the traditional center of the Universe in their own cosmology.[11] Unlike Mount Meru, *K'un-lun Shan* is traditionally described as consisting of five parts—four lesser ranges grouped around the central mass. A few Earlier Ch'ing robes have it depicted as five separate peaks, a tall central one with two others on each side, like descending steps.[12] All the later dragon robes, however, represent the world-mountain as seen in profile from each of the four cardinal points, with only three peaks.

Two exceptions to the usual mountain form must be noted. A number of the Early Ch'ing robes showed a highly eroded, weather-

[10] For a representative sequence of Ch'ing robes to show changes in details, take *Costumes from the Forbidden City,* and examine plates 18, 17, 23, 32, 36, in this order—disregarding the dates given in the captions.

[11] This concept is quite ancient. The *Shên-i ching,* which is ascribed to Tung-fang Shuo of the second century B.C., although probably actually written some six centuries later, already spoke of K'un-lun Shan as the center of the Earth (*Han-wei ts'ung-shu* ed., p. 13). For a translation of this passage see S. Cammann, "Cosmic Symbolism on the Dragon Robes of the Ch'ing Dynasty," in *Art and Thought,* the Coomaraswamy Memorial volume (London, 1948), p. 127.

[12] *Costumes from the Forbidden City,* pls. 18, 28.

beaten crag jutting from the jewel-strewn sea. This motif, very common on the contemporary mandarin squares, was known as "the Mountain of Longevity and the Sea of Happiness," *shou-shan fu-hai*. This comes from the ever-popular auspicious phrases, *Shou pi Nan-shan, fu ju Tung-hai*, meaning, "May you be as long-lived as the Southern mountain(s), and enjoy happiness as vast as the Eastern sea." A fine example of this is shown on a dragon jacket in the Textile Museum of Washington, D.C.

The other exception is sometimes found on dragon robes made for the burial of prominent persons, where the world-mountain is supplanted by representations of rocky islands. These were intended to portray P'êng-lai Shan and its neighbors, the islands of Fang-chang and Ying-chou, which collectively formed the Isles of the Immortals in ancient Chinese folklore. There the Dead were believed to enjoy everlasting bliss among the eternal pines, while white cranes flew overhead.[13]

A beautiful example of this is the "Wave and Pine Tree, or Hundred Cranes robe" from the tomb of Prince Kuo, which is briefly described above as an example of Type 5d. The Minneapolis Institute of Arts has another burial robe, of a later period (though ascribed to the same tomb), called the "Crane and Gate robe," which even portrays some buildings from the traditional palace of gold and silver, *Chih-ch'êng-kung,* that is said to be found on the Immortal Isles.[14] In terms of Oriental sympathetic magic, the body of the deceased clad in such a robe was already in the realm of P'êng-lai, in the abode of the Immortals, where it would enjoy eternal life.

In addition to these palace buildings that have been miscalled "gates," another architectural feature occurs quite frequently on later Ch'ing dragon robes. This is a small three-dimensional pavilion, supported on a mist or vapor emanating from the jaws of a dragon-like sea monster which is shown emerging from the waves

[13] *Shih chi* (*Szŭ-pu ts'ung-k'an* ed.) 28.11b; *Shan-hai ching* (same ed.) 2.57b.
[14] This Minneapolis robe is pictured in *Costumes from the Forbidden City*, pl. 29, and *Imperial Robes, etc.*, pl. 3. The gold and silver palace is mentioned in a biography in the *Shih chi* (edition cited) 118.11.

above the *li-shui*.[15] This represents a mirage created by the mythical monster *shên* (or *ch'ên*), over the Eastern Sea.[16] The Chinese name for this motif is *shên shih*, "the City of the Shên," and in North China, where the final *g* is not pronounced, this forms a pun on *shêng shih*, meaning "successful affairs."[17] A variation of this sea monster motif has a golden jewel called a *shêng*, which is also a pun on "success," in the vapors rising from the creature's mouth, as though to emphasize or restate the pun.[18] Perhaps this convention was adopted in regions where the monster's name was not pronounced exactly like the word *shêng*, due to differences in dialect, and the persons who designed the robes wanted to make it very clear that this was still a symbol of success. In Chinese tradition the *shên* monster was capable of changing its form at will into any form of water animal, so sometimes the vapors with a pavilion or a jewel are shown rising from the mouth of a great frog, or from a giant conch shell. Examples of this motif with a frog form are shown on the robe in Plate 17.

To return to the subject of the Universe pattern, we must consider a special feature of the clouds on the imperial robes. The laws of 1759 say that the background of the robes for the Emperor and Empress, Heir Apparent, and Imperial consorts, should have "clouds of five colors." The expression "clouds of five colors" is a very ancient one in Chinese folklore. Reports of their occurrence in nature appear again and again among the auspicious events listed in the

[15] These pavilions in the sea monster's breath have also been called "gates" by Western art critics, probably on the assumption that they represented the "Dragon Gate" (*lung mén*). However, the latter is traditionally always represented by a flat, *p'ai-lou* type of "arch," while these structures are obviously three-dimensional pavilions. Furthermore, on the robes of princes and nobles, the Dragon Gate motif, with its implication of success in the civil examinations, would have had absolutely no meaning because these men of rank were automatically appointed to high positions without having to consider examinations.

[16] The earliest occurrence of this explanation for the phenomenon of the mirage is found in the *Shih chi* (ed. cited) 27.33b.

[17] Dr. Lessing, taking another name for this motif, *hai-shih shên-lou*, has attempted, without success, to give a punning explanation for it, in *Sinica* Vol. 9 (1934), p. 251. It is also described by the name *shên-ch'i lou-t'ai*, "buildings of the monster's breath."

[18] See *Costumes from the Forbidden City*, pl. 15, lower right detail, and *Chinese Court Costumes*, pl. 14.

dynastic histories or local annals.[19] The reason for the frequent use of the expression, as stated in the *Sung shu,* is that "Clouds having five colors are omens of great peace, and are called 'auspicious clouds,' *ch'ing-yün."* [20] The descriptions suggest a mist or vapor in which the sunlight created rainbow-like effects, but in the Middle Ch'ing, when these laws were issued, the term "clouds of five colors" was apparently very literally interpreted. Thus the robes show cloud scrolls bordered with individual colors—red or pink, violet, blue, green and yellow—ornamenting the background. However, in spite of this new way of rendering them, the five-colored clouds were apparently still considered as omens of happy augury, and as such, they took their place among all the other happiness symbols that appeared on the robes in the Ch'ien-lung reign.

B. THE TWELVE SYMBOLS

The first use of the Twelve Symbols in China is traditionally ascribed to the mythical emperor Huang Ti, and even the legendary ruler Shun is supposed to have referred to them as an institution of the Ancients.[21] However this is merely an example of the common Chinese trait of giving an institution greater prestige by ascribing it to remote antiquity. There is even some doubt as to whether the Twelve Symbols were actually worn by the rulers of the Chou Dynasty. But we can be sure that they appeared on the Imperial sacrificial robes in the Han Dynasty, and they were used by all the native Chinese dynasties thereafter.[22] Even the foreign invaders gen-

[19] For some examples, see the *Sung shu* 27.24, 31. The Five Colors in Chinese literature are generally considered as being the five basic "colors"—black, blue, red, yellow, and white. But there were other variant combinations, more appropriate for clouds, such as light green, pale blue, pink, violet, and dark yellow. See the *T'u-shu chi-ch'êng, li-fa tien* 133.3.

[20] *Sung shu* 29.11.

[21] For the Huang Ti tradition, see Ts'ai Shên, *Shu-ching chi-ch'uan* (a Sung work) 1.38b, notes. For Shun, see *Shu-ching chi-ch'uan* 1.38b, text; and Legge, *Chinese Classics,* Vol. 3, 1 (*Shoo King*), p. 80.

[22] There is some debate in the commentaries on the *Chou li* as to whether the Chou Emperors wore all Twelve Symbols on their robes, or only nine of them (omitting the sun, moon, and stars), but the consensus seems to be that they wore all twelve. (See the *Chou-li chu-su* 21, 7.9b.) By the Han Dynasty, there is no

erally took over the custom in time. The Khitan rulers of the Liao adopted the Twelve Symbols in 946, the Ju-chên Tartars of the Chin in 1140, and the Mongols of the Yüan in 1274.[23] In fact, the Twelve Symbols were even used in other countries that came under Chinese cultural influence. The Japanese Emperor adopted them in 820.[24] The Korean kings used nine of the Twelve Symbols since 1065, when the Liao Emperor gave the King of Korea a nine-symbol robe,[25] and in 1896, when the ruler of Korea proclaimed himself "Emperor," he took all twelve of them.[26] Lastly, the Kings of Annam adopted the Twelve Symbols when they took over Chinese dress in 1744, and their descendants wore them for official sacrifices down to the last decade.[27] The last time they were worn in China was in 1914, when Yuan Shih-k'ai, first President of the Chinese Republic, wore them in a ceremony at the Altar of Heaven.[28]

We have seen that the Ming Emperors were apparently the first Chinese rulers to wear the Twelve Symbols on their less formal robes as well as on their sacrificial ones, and that this custom was

---

question that all twelve were being used (see the *Hou-Han shu*, 40.1, 1b). The earliest representation of the use of the Twelve Symbols that has come down to us is on the seventh-century "Scroll of the Emperors," by Yen Li-pên, now in the Boston Museum. Here several of the Emperors of the Six Dynasties period are pictured in ceremonial robes. These portraits have been reproduced by the Commercial Press in the *T'ang Yen Li-pên ti-wang-t'u chên-chi* (Shanghai, 1917), in such a way as to show more details than are revealed in the reproductions contained in Dr. Tomita's *Portfolio of Chinese Paintings in the [Boston] Museum* (Boston, 1933). However, all photographs must necessarily be rather poor, owing to the deterioration of the original painting.

[23] For these dates, see the *Liao shih* 56.1b, the *Chin shih* 43.7, and the *Yüan shih* 78.3.

[24] *Nihon Kiryaku (Kokushi taikei* ed., Vol. 5) 14.434. See also Josiah Conder, "History of Japanese Costume—Court Dress," *TASJ*, Vol. 8 (1880), pp. 553-55, and the *Wakan sansai zue* (1713) 28. 1-2, both of which have pictures of the Japanese Twelve-Symbol robes that were derived from the Chinese.

[25] *TPMHPK* 79.3.

[26] *Ibid.*, 79.17.

[27] In 1458, the Annamese Envoy begged the Ming Emperor for (Nine-Symbol) sacrificial robes like those that had been given to the King of Korea, but the request was refused (*Ming Hui-yao* 78.3b). Full details of the Annamese Twelve-Symbol robes adopted in 1744 are given in the Annamese records (see Chapter 14, Note 28, for reference). Pictures of the Twelve-Symbol sacrificial robes worn by the "Emperor" of Annam, and a brief description of them, will be found in Orband and Cadière, "Le Sacrifice du Nam Giao," *BAVH*, Vol. 23 (1936), pp. 83-84; pls. 39, 40.

[28] For details of the robes worn by Yüan Shih-k'ai and his officials, see the writer's review in *JAOS* Vol. 63 (1943), p. 297.

maintained by the Ch'ing Emperors when they eventually took over the Twelve Symbols in the eighteenth century.

It is interesting to speculate why the Manchus did not use them until the reign of Ch'ien-lung. The probable reason is that they were considered as being too Chinese, and hence alien to the Manchu "national" tradition, until the influence of China's long heritage once again became strong at the Court in Peking. We know, for example, that the Shun-chih Emperor, the first of the line to rule over China, reacted violently when, in 1651, a Chinese official suggested that he should assume the traditional Chinese ceremonial hat and the robes with the Twelve Symbols when he officiated at the great annual sacrifices.[29] The memory of this "insulting" suggestion no doubt rankled for many years.

At any rate, the first mention of the Twelve Symbols in the Ch'ing was in 1759, when they were prescribed for use on the Emperor's court robes, as well as on his dragon robes. We have seen, from existing evidence, that the later Ch'ing Empresses also wore the Twelve Symbols, and we shall soon take up the question of smaller combinations from this group, also found on dragon robes. First, however, let us examine the symbols individually and in detail.

1. The sun disc was red, and contained the three-legged bird associated with the sun in Chinese folklore since early times.[30] In the original tradition this was thought of as a kind of crow, but by the time of the Ch'ing dynasty it was usually represented as a gaily-colored rooster.

2. The moon disc was greenish white (*yüeh-pai*), with the legendary hare of the moon pounding on her mortar under the cassia tree.[31]

---

[29] See the *Shih-tsu Chang-huang-ti shih lu* (54.18b) for the memorial by the Censor, K'uang Lan-chao, in April 1651, and the Emperor's reply.

[30] The three legs are explained by the fact that this bird was considered as the embodiment of the *Yang* principle, and the odd numbers are associated with *Yang*. See the Liang Emperor Chien Wên's preface to the *Ta-fa Sung*, in the *Ch'üan shang-ku San-tai Ch'in Han San-kuo Liu-ch'ao wên* (Canton, 1893), *Ch'üan Liang wên*, 13.1.

[31] The early Chinese thought of the moon-animal as a toad, and it appears as such in representations of the moon on Han mirrors. See P. C. Yetts, *Catalogue of the Eumorfopoulos Collection of Chinese Bronzes* (London, 1930), B.14, Vol. 2, pl. 9.

3. The constellation (*hsing-ch'ên*) traditionally consisted of the seven stars of the Great Dipper, and appeared thus on the dragon robes of the Later Ming Emperors. In the Ch'ing, however, only three stars were used on the Emperor's robes—represented as red or gold dots, connected by thin lines of the same color. The Five-Symbol robes had all seven, but they were divided into two groups for greater symmetry.

4. The mountain—usually shown as a rock mass in Ch'ing, but sometimes having distinct peaks—was a simpler representation of the same world-mountain figured at the base of the dragon robes.[32]

5. The dragon, king of animals, was represented in the Ch'ing by a pair of tiny, five-clawed dragons.

6. The "flowery bird" (*hua-ch'ung*) was shown as a pheasant (the prototype of the "phoenix," as king of birds) according to the ancient tradition.[33]

7. The paired *fú* symbol, or "Symbol of Discrimination," [34] suggests capital E's placed back to back. According to tradition it was originally represented in two colors—one half blue, the other black —as it represented the dualistic forces of Good and Evil, etc., being the alleged prototype of the *yin-yang* symbol.[35] In the Ming and Ch'ing, however, both parts were shown in the same colors.

8. The axe, called *fù,* in a different tone, was traditionally shown as a sacrificial weapon, with the blade emerging from the stylized

---

By the Liang Dynasty, people began to speak of the "hare in the moon," the hare being the embodiment of the *Yin* principle (see reference in previous note), and the T'ang mirrors show the moon as having both hare and toad, on either side of the legendary cassia tree (see Cammann, "A Rare T'ang Mirror," fig. 5, top). By Ch'ing times, the hare was shown alone.

For further details on the hare in the moon, and its possible origins, see Mayers' *Chinese Reader's Manual,* No. 724, p. 235.

[32] A Chinese scholar, Yün Ching, has pointed out that the mountain symbolized Earth, just as the stars symbolized Heaven. See his *Ta-yün-shan-fang shih-erh-chang t'u-shuo* (*Chih-chin-chai ts'ung-shu* ed.) 1.2.

[33] The pheasant was originally the bird of the Empress, like the later "phoenix" (*Ibid.,* 1.3).

[34] This *fú* symbol is popularly, and rather ambiguously, called "the Symbol of Distinction." To most minds, the word "distinction" inevitably conveys the idea of "eminence" or "honor" rather than the distinction between Right and Wrong, which is what this actually symbolized. Thus the term "Symbol of Judgment" or "Symbol of Discrimination" seems much more suitable.

[35] *Shih-erh chang t'u-shuo* 2.1b.

head of a monster. The Ming axe symbol, as shown in the Emperors' portraits, usually omitted the monster but displayed part of the handle. In the Ch'ing, however, it was represented as a simple blade, without embellishment.

9. The two sacrificial cups (*tsung-i*) originally had a tiger and a monkey, respectively, figured on them, and this tradition was preserved by the Ming. However, with the cultural degeneration in Late Ch'ing, the cups were sometimes shown as covered jars, and the animals on each were the same—nondescript, composite creatures, resembling striped monkeys.[36]

10. The water weed (*tsao*) was shown as a number of green leaves branching from a main stem, usually disposed in a square, or circular pattern.

11. The fire symbol was shown in Ch'ing as a cluster of thin, licking flames, also disposed in a square, or circle.

12. The grain, or millet, (*fên-mi*) had been depicted on Ming robes by sixty small grains arranged in vertical lines to form a circular pattern. In the Ch'ing, the symbol was represented by an indefinite number of yellow grains scattered on a white circle.

The Twelve Symbols are often found in Western books on Chinese Art, listed with the more common symbols as though they could be seen anywhere. Moreover, these books generally explain them in terms of the sententious interpretations given them by a seventh-century scholar, Yang Ch'iung of the T'ang.[37] The latter's comparatively late rationalizations cannot be ignored if one is trying to understand what the Twelve Symbols meant to some Chinese, in recent centuries. But they are very misleading if accepted as the sole

[36] See *Costumes from the Forbidden City*, pl. 35, for an example of the covered jars. Even though the two animals on these robes have stripes, they are not intended to represent tigers, as they have the forked tail of the legendary monkey called *wei*, who was believed to plug his nostrils with the two ends of his tail when it rained. See Giles, *Chinese-English Dictionary* (2d ed. 1912), no. 12,597.

[37] The original statements are found in a memorial preserved in the *Chiu T'ang-shu* 45.17, and have been copied in the *T'u-shu chi-ch'êng, li-i tien* 330. (2d) 4. They are translated in *Chinese Textiles* (pp. 55-56), *Costumes from the Forbidden City* (p. 7), and *Chinese Court Costumes* (p. 44), so we shall not bother to repeat them here. We can consider these explanations of the Twelve Symbols as late rationalizations because by the seventh century A.D. these symbols had already been worn for well over a thousand years.

The Twelve Symbols.

explanation, in that they obscure the deeper, original significance of the symbols.

A typical example of late rationalization is the following quotation from the Sung period, which represents the symbols in terms of the qualities desired in a model Sovereign:

> The sun, moon and stars represent Enlightenment; the mountain represents Protection; the dragon, Adaptability; the pheasant, Literary Refinement; the sacrificial cups, Filial Piety; the water weed, Purity; the grain, Ability to Feed [his people]; the fire, Brilliance; the axe the Power to Behead [or Punish]; and the *fú* symbol, Discrimination [between Right and Wrong].[38]

[38] Ts'ai Shên, in *Shu-ching chi ch'uan,* 1.38b, 39. This was written in the thirteenth century, but even later than this the tradition of what was probably the original meaning of the Twelve Symbols was still preserved (see Note 42, below, for reference).

Much earlier, the stars were considered as representing Heaven, and the mountain, the Earth.[39] Thus, the sun disc, moon disc, stars, and mountain stood for the Sun and Moon, Heaven and Earth, to which four of the principal annual sacrifices were offered. The dragon and pheasant were symbols of animals and birds in general, or in a broader sense represented animate nature. The *fú* symbol was an emblem of Imperial (or Divine) power in judgment; and the axe an emblem of Imperial (or Divine) power to punish. The bronze libation cups, the water weed, the flames, and the grain are all symbols of elements in Nature—metal, water, fire, and plant life (by extension, wood), while earth, the fifth of the traditional Five Elements, was already represented by the mountain. Tradition said that these should all be embroidered or painted (or woven) in the Five Colors, which corresponded to the Five Elements, the Seasons, and the Five Directions, thus adding even more cosmic significance.[40]

We see, then, that not only were all of the Twelve Symbols closely associated with the sacrificial ceremonies, but also that collectively they comprised a sort of *maṇḍala,* or symbolic representation of the greater Universe and its component elements, signifying Universal Dominion in an even more comprehensive way than did the basic pattern of the dragon robe.[41] In short, the sovereign wearing the Twelve Symbols was, figuratively at least, the Ruler of the Universe.

[39] *Shih-erh chang t'u-shuo* 1.2.
[40] *Shu-ching chi-ch'uan* 1.38b, text; 39, notes. Y. Harada, discussing the "original" form and use of the Twelve Symbols, has expressed the theory that the first three (sun, moon, and stars) represented heaven, and the next three (mountain, bird[s], and animals) the earth and its creatures, while the last six were merely names given to stylized forms of ornamentation: lines and dots, meanders, etc. See Yoshito Harada, *Kan-Rickuchō no fukushoku* (Tokyo, 1937), pp. 3-56. His explanation for the first six is perfectly valid, but it seems absurd to dismiss the last six as meaningless decorations, at a period in Chinese civilization when symbolism of Nature and natural forces was so important in religion.
[41] Robert Eisler (in *Weltenmantel und Himmelszelt* [Munich, 1910], Vol. 1, p. 21) speaks of the sacrificial robes of the Emperors of China as cosmic robes, because of the cosmic significance of the Twelve Symbols figured on them. However, he apparently did not recognize the fact that in the Ch'ing at least, the dragon robe—even without the Twelve Symbols—was in itself a picture of the Universe, as the Chinese saw it.

That this was evidently the original meaning of the Twelve Symbols is obvious from a passage in the Book of Rites, which was compiled during the Han, from Chou sources. This says, "On the day of sacrifice, the Emperor wears the robe with the symbols in order to represent Heaven (or God)."⁴² For the Emperor was considered as the vice-regent of Heaven, on earth. In fact, this idea must have persisted for centuries, because the History of the Sung Dynasty, written in the Yüan, quotes the above statement in its section on Sung costume.⁴³

The same passage from the Book of Rites goes on to tell, somewhat indirectly, why there are twelve of these symbols, rather than some other number. In explaining why the Emperor had twelve strings of jewels on his ceremonial crown (*mien*), it says, "Twelve is the number of Heaven."⁴⁴

While all twelve of the symbols were worn by the Later Ch'ing Emperors, we find smaller combinations of them on occasional robes from this period. The Metropolitan Museum, for example, has a yellow robe with the sun and moon on the shoulders, but no other symbols from the set. This no doubt belonged to an Emperor, and we suggest the Ch'ien-lung sovereign. He was much interested in past history, especially that of the former non-Chinese dynasties, and it is very possible that he had read that the Liao, Chin, and Yüan rulers, with whom he felt a close affinity, had all used the sun and moon as Imperial symbols, and decided to emulate them. In fact, it is quite possible that he wore only these two symbols before deciding to use all twelve of them as a regular practice.

Next, the Walters Gallery in Baltimore has a finely embroidered maroon robe, with all of the Twelve Symbols except these two. In place of the sun and moon on the shoulders, circular *shou* medal-

⁴² *Li chi, chiao-t'ê-sheng* (2), *Shih-san ching* (Commercial Press ed.) I, p. 924. Legge completely missed the point in his translation of this passage, due to his misunderstanding of the word *kun* (see Chapter 1, Note 4), saying, "On the day of Sacrifice, the king assumed the robe with the ascending dragons on it as an emblem of the heavens" (*Li Ki*, I, p. 429). However, he admits in a footnote that his rendering might be inadequate.

⁴³ *Sung shih* 151.4. This quotation has an extra character, *chiao* (Giles, no. 1312), but the meaning is unchanged.

⁴⁴ *Li chi, loc. cit.* Legge (*Li Ki* I, pp. 429-30) again missed the point.

lions are embroidered in gold. This is a man's robe, in the style of the early nineteenth century, and inasmuch as it lacks only the two highest symbols, it could have been made for an Heir Apparent—specifically, Prince Min-ning—who was proclaimed Heir Apparent in September 1820, and was enthroned as Tao-kuang Emperor a month later.[45]

Lastly, we find in our museums a small series of dragon robes—made for both men and women—that have only five symbols: the sun, moon and constellation (split into two groups of stars), with the axe and *fǔ* symbol. (One of these robes, made for a woman, is shown in Plate 12, right.)

This seems a very significant combination. The first three are the highest of the Twelve Symbols, the ones that former dynasties had considered the prerogative of the Emperor alone, and which they believed represented his spiritual power; while the last two were symbols of Judgment and Punishment, the Emperor's temporal powers. At the same time all the symbols that refer more specifically to Sacrifice are omitted. This suggests that the Five Symbols were probably worn by regents who held the Emperor's powers of rule, without having his privilege—and obligation—to be chief officiant at the great annual sacrifices.

It is possible that the oldest of these were worn by the Ch'ien-lung Emperor (and perhaps his Empress, as well) after he gave up the throne, but not the power, in 1796, following his sixty years of direct rule. However, the style of most of the Five-Symbol robes we have seen suggests a much later date, and they may well have been worn by the regents for the T'ung-chih Emperor, in the second half of the nineteenth century (1861-73).

We have seen that the Twelve Symbols, which are usually said to have been confined to the robes of the Ch'ing Emperors, in some cases actually were not. However, there is one symbol or combination of symbols that does appear to have been used on the Emperor's

[45] This robe appears to have been retailored for someone of stouter build. This would tend to support our attribution, since the Tao-kuang Emperor provided in his will that most of his robes should be distributed among his courtiers. See *Eminent Chinese*, p. 575.

robes alone. This was the circular medallion enclosing a round *shou* symbol, at the center of the breast, and back. Around the *shou* were figured the eight symbols of thě Taoist immortals, lucky peaches, bats, and a jade musical stone, all of which will be explained individually below. We have mentioned (in Chapter 6) that this is found on part of a dragon robe once worn by the Ch'ien-lung Emperor, now in the Victoria and Albert Museum. (See Plate 15.) Apparently this medallion was never used again on dragon robes, for in the later Ch'ien-lung reign it may figuratively be said to have burst like a bomb, scattering the Taoist Symbols, the peaches, and the bats all over the background of the dragon robe, and they were never recombined to form a single motif.

C. The "Eight Precious Things" and Other Common Symbols

The only symbols besides dragons which the laws of 1759 specifically prescribed for the dragon robes worn by those below the Emperor were the "Eight Precious Things," *pa pao*. This phrase permitted considerable latitude, for by the mid-eighteenth century it had come to be used for several sets of symbols.

The primary set, and that to which the name most fittingly applies, was an old group of wealth symbols. It seems very likely that this set was the one that those who wrote the laws had in mind, because various combinations of them were the first extraneous symbols to be used on the dragon robes. On the Early Ch'ing robes of the first four types, for example, four or more of these symbols were generally shown in the waves. Their association with water seems to have been derived from the old Lamaist belief that the sea was the source of wealth.

This first group of the Eight Precious Things seems originally to have consisted of pearls, gold circular ornaments, called *shêng* or *yüan shêng*, gold rectangular ornaments, *fang shêng,* a "wish-granting jewel," *ju-i,* rhinoceros horns, ivory tusks, sticks of coral, and rolls of tribute silk. Sometimes an ingot or "shoe" of precious metal replaced one of the others.

By the time they appeared on the Ch'ing dragon robes, however, their number and variety had greatly increased, giving more than sixteen alternatives which could be interchanged to make up various combinations of the Eight Precious Things.[46] The pearls were now shown singly as "flaming jewels," or were piled in groups. The circular and square *shêng* jewels were shown singly with elaborate decoration, or more simply in interlocked pairs. One form of the circular *shêng,* probably through a misunderstanding of the original symbol, was usually transformed into a pierced coin. One form of square *shêng* was often ornamented with a swastika, or the latter was frequently used alone in the later groups as a golden "swastika jewel." The *ju-i* jewel was now usually supplied with a handle, making a *ju-i* scepter, and the long rolls of silk had evolved into scroll paintings, or long, narrow books (Buddhist sutras) although, strictly speaking, neither books nor paintings were emblems of material wealth like the rest of the group. Apparently through another misunderstanding, probably derived from clumsy renderings of the over-conventionalized rhinoceros horn, an artemisia leaf had joined the group on porcelains and folk textiles, but the writer has never seen this used on a dragon robe.[47]

---

[46] These wealth symbols, often called "the Eight Jewels" by Occidental writers, are usually described as consisting of a specific group of eight, the individual symbols varying with the writer (see *Chinese Textiles,* p. 72 and fig. 28). They are often "explained" by fantastic rationalizations. Among the worst we have seen are those of Charles A. Nott in *Chinese Jades* (Palm Beach, 1942), p. 36. He tried to make them out as Taoist symbols and, of course, was unsuccessful. In so far as they were religious symbols at all, they were always associated with Buddhism.

[47] The names given by Western writers to individual symbols from this group are as fantastic as they are varied. The *shêng* jewels seem to have been given the weirdest appellations, but this is not unexpected since their original function and meaning seem to have been forgotten even in China (see Cammann, "A Rare T'ang Mirror," p. 106). Even familiar ones like the rhinoceros horn are often given ludicrously inaccurate explanations based on Occidental concepts, which would seem strange to a Chinese. See, for example, B. Vuilleumier, *Symbolism of Chinese Imperial Ritual Robes* (London, 1939), p. 19, where he describes the traditional rhinoceros horns as "unicorn horns," and indulges in pure fantasy regarding them. Like Nott, he tries to read his own meanings into the Chinese symbols.

On some Ch'ing robes, we even find articles from one of the
other symbol groups, such as a golden wheel or a vase from the
Eight Buddhist Symbols (discussed below), included among these
wealth symbols. In fact, the uncertainty about the composition of
this group of the Eight Precious Things, and the many divergent
ways of representing a single symbol in it, such as the circular
shêng, suggest that this was either a very old tradition or an alien
one which was never properly assimilated; but we shall not discuss
these questions here.

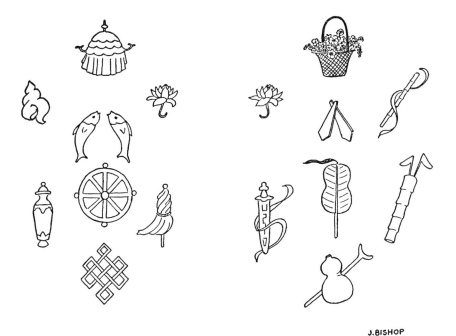

J.BISHOP

The Eight Buddhist Symbols and the Symbols of the Taoist Immortals.

By Middle Ch'ing the term *pa pao* had been loosely, and rather
inaccurately, extended to apply to two other groups: the Eight
Buddhist Symbols, and the eight symbols of the Taoist Immortals.
The former group consisted of the wheel of the Law, royal canopy,
state umbrella, lotus, vase, endless knot, twin fish, and conch shell.
The latter group consisted of a magic fan, a bamboo rattle, a lotus,

castanets, a sword, a gourd and crutch, a flute, and a flower basket. We have already noted these last as occurring in a circular arrangement on one of the Ch'ien-lung Emperor's dragon robes. The Buddhist symbols originally had a sacred meaning—they still figure in Lama ritual—and the Taoist set had originally been closely associated with the semidivine persons whose attributes they were. However, for most people by the Middle Ch'ing they had become completely dissociated from any religous connotations and were merely sets of lucky symbols.[48]

In addition to these three groups, the later robes often displayed a considerable number of common auspicious symbols, which, like the pavilions of the sea monster's mirage, were never even alluded to in the sumptuary laws.[49] Being merely incidental decorations, with no ritual importance, there was no reason why they should be mentioned in the laws. Such trifles were left up to the designers of the robes or the artisans who made them.

Typical of these extraneous symbols were the Flowers of the Four Seasons, which, like the Eight Precious Things, were chosen from a large number of alternates. Winter was generally represented by the plum blossom or the bamboo (the latter, strictly speaking, not a flower); spring, by the grass orchid (on the robes, this resembles a miniature iris) or the magnolia flower; summer, by the peony or the lotus; and autumn by the tree peony or the chrysanthemum.[50] These were either shown scattered individually among the clouds in the background or were used in combination with the Buddhist and Taoist symbols to make the latter more decorative. Frequently the peony, often conventionalized almost beyond recognition, was used alone, because, as "the flower of riches and honor," *fu-kuei-hua*,

---

[48] For a slightly more detailed account of these Buddhist and Taoist symbols, see "Development of the Mandarin Square," pp. 113-114.

[49] Since Ming times, the Buddhist set had simply been called the "Eight Lucky Things," *pa chi-hsiang*, without any trace of religious associations.

[50] Other combinations are sometimes given. The writer has previously pointed out, elsewhere, that in the symbolic group of the Four Flowers, just as with the Eight Precious Things and the "Five Poisons," the idea of the symbolic number of things is more important than the specific objects themselves. See S. Cammann, "Symbolism in Far Eastern Art," *Encyclopaedia of the Arts* (New York, 1946), p. 982.

it conveyed hopes for greater advancement.[51] Like the peony, the marigold has an auspicious name in China. As the "flower of ten thousand years," *wan-shou-chü,* it was often used in the background of robes—especially during the Ch'ien-lung period—as a symbol of longevity. Lastly, the rose, as "the flower of lasting springtime" (i.e., "enduring youth"), *ch'ang-ch'un-hua,* was quite popular on nineteenth-century robes.

Also common were the Three Lucky Fruits: the peach of long life, the pomegranate of fertility or abundance, and the Buddha's-hand citron, signifying happiness. These, too, were often scattered over the background, or were arranged with various auspicious flowers in a basket prominently displayed as a central motif below the main dragon on the front and back of the robe, the basket itself being one of the symbols of the Eight Immortals. Like the peony, the peach is often shown alone as a symbol of long life, or in combination with other happiness symbols such as the bat (see Section D, below).

The pine as an emblem of longevity is found frequently on Later Ch'ing mandarin squares, but on the dragon robes it is almost entirely restricted to those that portray the Isles of the Immortals, which give them a place to take root. The same is true of growing fungus, *ling-chih,* also a symbol of eternal life. However, detached fungus plants are sometimes found along with cranes as emblems of longevity in the background of Later Ch'ing robes. These also are sometimes held in the mouths of bats or cranes.

The cranes of longevity are often shown in the background of the dragon robes, either flying or curled into decorative medallions, to convey hopes for the long life of the wearer. Writers on Oriental symbolism, both Chinese and foreign, often interpret their use as symbols of longevity "because cranes live to a great age." However, their life span is not exceptional among birds. It seems more likely that this association has developed because of their color. Since

[51] The peony was apparently first given this title and this association by the Sung scholar Chou Tun-i in his famous essay on the lotus, *Ai-lien shuo,* which is quoted at length in the *Kuang-ch'ün fang-p'u* 29.13.

antiquity, legend has described them as figuring among the "white birds and white creatures" which dwelt on P'êng-lai Shan, the home of the Immortals.[52]

"Phoenixes" often appear on the dragon coats of Chinese brides, because in old Chinese tradition a bride was symbolically an empress for a day, and the "phoenix" was a symbol of the Empress. Otherwise, I have only seen them on one Later Ch'ing Empress' robe.

An interesting combination of bird symbols is shown on a Late Ch'ing dragon robe in the Murray Galleries, Georgetown, D.C. This has the nine types of birds found on the mandarin squares of the civil officials arranged in pairs in the background.[53] This combination is not unusual on the stoles worn by wives of Chinese officials (see Chapter 10), but it is rarely found on dragon robes.

Animals, except for the Happiness bats, were even more rarely used. However, we have seen the *ch'i-lin* on Mrs. Martin's Early Ch'ing robe, and it occurs on occasional later ones. This expressed a wish for offspring, because of the old saying, "The *ch'i-lin* will send children" (*ch'i-lin sung tzŭ*).[54] As we have previously mentioned, the term "unicorn" is very inappropriate for the *ch'i-lin* of later Chinese art, because this blue, scaly dragon-horse is always shown with two horns.[55]

The deer is also sometimes shown on the dragon robes, but since its use, like that of the bat, depends on a pun, we shall discuss it

[52] For the comparative longevity of cranes in relation to other birds, see P. Chalmers Mitchell, "On Longevity and Relative Viability in Mammals and Birds," *Proc. Zool. Soc.* (London), 1911, pp. 536-37. The white birds and animals on P'êng-lai Shan are mentioned in the *Shan-hai ching,* Ch. 7 (*Szŭ-pu ts'ung-k'an* ed.), 2.57b.

[53] Cranes, Manchurian pheasants, peacocks, and geese are shown on either side down the front of this robe. The silver pheasants are on the shoulders, while the egrets, mandarin ducks, quail, and paradise flycatchers are shown on either side down the back. For descriptions of each type, as shown here, and on the badges of rank, see "Development of the Mandarin Square," pp. 104-6.

[54] The *ch'i-lin* as an omen of successful sons occurs early in Chinese literature. See Legge, *Chinese Classics* 4, 1 (*She King*), p. 19, for an example from the *Book of Poetry.*

[55] Even in referring to the ancient representations, when the *ch'i-lin* had only one horn, the term "unicorn" is an unfortunate expression, as it connotes to the European mind a pure white, smooth-coated horselike animal with a spiral horn protruding from its brow—a very different picture from the Chinese *ch'i-lin.*

with the other punning symbols. The fish is also used as a pun, as well as because of its position among the Eight Buddhist Symbols. We have already mentioned that according to old tradition the sea monster called *shên* was able to change its shape at will, and thus we sometimes see its characteristic image-bearing vapors rising out of giant conch shells.[56]

Auspicious Chinese characters were often used as well, especially to express wishes for longevity. Very common on the robes of the Imperial Family, and sometimes appearing on other robes as well, was the character for long life, *shou*, drawn in countless fanciful ways. It often appears in various archaic forms on the Twelve-Symbol robes.

Sometimes the *shou* character was worked into elaborate medallions with the swastika. For the latter, as an alternative character for the word *wan*, meaning "ten thousand," added the element of endlessness to the long life desired for the wearer: "May (I) live ten thousand years." The allover swastika pattern used as a background for some of the imperial dragon robes had the same general meaning. Similarly, the character for "good luck," *chi*, was sometimes worked into the center of a *shou* medallion.[57] Dragon robes for weddings also had, scattered over the background, the symbol for happy marriages, *shuang-hsi*, formed of two linked characters for "joy." [58]

D. LATER CH'ING PUNNING SYMBOLS OR REBUSES

The same literary tastes that led to the use of unusual variations of Chinese characters on the robes also resulted in the introduction

---

[56] An Imperial robe now in Minneapolis has these vapor-giving sea shells in the lower waves. See *Costumes from the Forbidden City*, pl. 22. Incidentally, this Twelve-Symbol robe probably once belonged to an Empress, judging by its ornamental sleeves.

[57] See detail of the dragon robe in *Chinese Textiles*, fig. 12 (p. 36), where both swastikas and *chi* character are combined to form a *shou* symbol.

[58] As a rule, only very wealthy persons such as members of the Imperial Family could afford to have special robes made for a marriage ceremony. However, a non-imperial dragon robe for a wedding, with the *shuang-hsi* symbols, is shown in Yamanaka's catalogue, *Exhibition of Chinese Textiles, Imperial Robes, etc.* (New York, May, 1940), No. 60.

of punning symbols or rebuses. These are very important because they often occur on the later robes, and other textiles. Yet they have been so neglected that most of them are unknown to present-day students of Oriental art, and meanwhile their meanings have largely been forgotten in China as well. Some of them were brought to the attention of Western students by Professor Chavannes, in his pioneer work on Chinese folk symbols, and others were explained by Mr. Nozaki in his Japanese study of Chinese popular symbolism, but both have missed some of the rebuses that are often found on dragon robes.[59] And Chavannes, in particular, has failed to convey the methods by which the meanings of new rebuses may be worked out through knowing the vocabulary of the more common ones. It is quite easy, however, since simple pictures are used to replace familiar words, and the same ones frequently recur even though the combinations may differ. It is much like learning the vocabulary of a new but simple language.

The commonest of these rebus symbols is, of course, the bat, because its name *fu* is a pun on the word for happiness, which is pronounced the same way but written with a different character. This symbol first appeared on the dragon robes themselves in the Ch'ien-lung period, though bats may have been used in the previous reign on less formal, festive robes.[60]

In the Ch'ien-lung period, the bats in the sky portion of the robe were often shown in red, not only because red is a happy and

[59] See E. Chavannes, "L'Expression des voeux dans l'art populaire chinoise," *Journal Asiatique,* 9th ser., Vol. 18, September-October, 1901 (reprinted as an individual pamphlet, with an additional final note, Paris, 1922). This is an invaluable article, but Chavannes made one big mistake in assuming that the vast number of punning symbols that he observed around him in Peking were a characteristic of Chinese civilization itself, rather than a product of that particular age. See also Seikin Nozaki, *Kisshō zuan kaidai* (Tientsin, 1928).

[60] *Costumes from the Forbidden City,* pl. 1, shows an Imperial dragon robe of the Ch'ien-lung period (mislabeled "K'ang Hsi") with the bats. Plate 28 of the same catalogue shows a woman's informal robe in the style of the previous reign (Yung-chêng), which has bats not only in the background, but also linked in groups of five to frame *shou* characters, making elaborate ornamental medallions. In compositions of this type, called in Chinese *wu fu p'êng shou,* the five bats are intended to recall the five forms of Happiness, which were first mentioned in the *Shu ching.* (See Legge, *Chinese Classics III,* Part 2, p. 324.) We cannot recall having seen bats in groups of five on the dragon robes proper.

auspicious color in China, but also because the descriptive phrase, "Red bats attaining the sky" (*hung fu chih t'ien*), by substituting two characters of the same sound for the first two words, becomes "Vast happiness reaching Heaven." Frequently, the dragon robes have one or more bats, each with a jade musical stone, *ch'ing*, dangling from its mouth, because the phrase "bat and musical stone," *fu ch'ing*, by substitution of characters, becomes "Happiness and Good Fortune." Sometimes this is prominently displayed as a central motif below the main dragons on chest and back, either alone or combined with other rebus figures.[61]

Butterflies are a common punning symbol on the dragon robes, particularly those from South China. Their primary meaning is a wish for long life, because their name *tieh* has the same sound as the word for "seventy or eighty years of age." In addition, in South China—particularly Hunan—the other word for butterfly, *hu,* is pronounced exactly like the word *fu* meaning happiness. So robes made there often had the butterfly instead of the bat, in which case it meant both happiness and longevity.

The deer is also occasionally shown on the dragon robes, and occurred on the Middle Ch'ing dragon jackets described at the end of Chapter 7. This is a symbol of riches, because its name, *lu,* is a pun on the word for wealth and emoluments. Similarly, the fish, *yü,* is used as a pun on the word for abundance to mean "abundant fortune."

Two punning symbols for success are so well known as to require little comment. The first of these involved the addition of a brush to the *ju-i* scepter and an ingot of silver, which were among the Eight Precious Things in the upper waves. The descriptive phrase, "brush, ingot, and scepter," *pi ting ju i,* by substituting homophones for the first two characters, becomes "May everything certainly be as (I) desire." The other symbol used a brush to pierce the center of the Wheel of the Law, among the Eight Buddhist Symbols. For the phrase "brush in the center," *pi chung,* by substituting another character for the first one, and changing the tone of the second

[61] See *Costumes from the Forbidden City,* pl. 29.

from the first tone to the fourth, becomes "(I) shall certainly succeed." [62]

As often happens with symbols in general, a given rebus may have had more than one explanation, either at different periods or when used in other contexts. An example of this, from Late Ch'ing, is the picture of a pair of three-legged bronze cups, *chüeh,* standing on a tray. As we have heard this explained in China, a simple description of this picture would be *tieh shàng liang chüeh,* but the word *chüeh* also means "a rank of nobility." So, by substituting another character of the same sound for the first one, and altering the tone of the second (from the fourth to the third) a new phrase is produced, meaning "May (I) successively ascend two ranks in the nobility." It is possible that this reconstruction is not completely accurate, but such expressions of ambition were typical of the closing years of the decaying Ch'ing Dynasty when ascent in noble rank, formerly awarded only for acts of exceptional merit, was comparatively easy, especially if one had enough money to purchase a title.

A second pun was made from the same motif by having the cups colored green, and supporting them on clouds high above the waves at the base of the robe. Here the descriptive phrase "cups green and very high," *chüeh lu ch'ung kao,* by changing the meaning of the first character and by substituting a homophone for the second, makes the more general wish, "May (my) honors and riches be very lofty." [63]

Another Late Ch'ing pun symbol, often found on the same robes as the last, consisted of a temple bell, *chung,* and a scepter, *kuei.* This is said to be a (rather bad) pun on the name of Chung K'uei, the mythical demon slayer. His mere name, like his picture, was believed able to avert evil influences and maintain happiness. Thus this was a somewhat negative lucky symbol. As the bell and scepter

---

[62] *Ibid.,* pl. 44, shows this pierced wheel symbol in use, on an ordinary official robe (mislabeled "Imperial Robe").

[63] This latter phrase was quite common in the Later Ch'ing. The writer has found it, for example, along with other lucky expressions, on a village bell of that period in the valley of Kunming, in Southwest China.

combination occurs quite frequently on Imperial robes of the Kuang-hsü period, but is not found on earlier ones, it has some value in dating.[64]

The same type of large temple bell is also pictured in the waves on the Earlier Ch'ing dragon robes. It is shown with a halberd on Mrs. Martin's (Type 2a) dragon robe, and with a *ju-i* scepter on the Textile Museum's dragon jacket, while one of the robes from the tomb of Prince Kuo has the bell together with a jade musical stone and a halberd.[65] The presence of the *ju-i* and the halberd, both of which were commonly used in Later Ch'ing punning symbols, suggests that these combinations probably formed the first Ch'ing rebuses. Unfortunately, no one seems to have left any record of what the bell once meant here.

The jade musical stone and the halberd, which we have just seen used with the bell to form one of the first of the punning symbols on the Ch'ing dragon robes, together make up the simplest of a series of halberd symbols that were very popular in Later Ch'ing. In this combination, the halberd or poleaxe, *chi*, is a pun on the word for "good luck," [66] while the musical stone, *ch'ing*, was a pun on "good fortune," just as it was when used with the bat.

On the dragon robes the jade stone, in its function as one of the Eight Precious Things, usually stood in the waves, and the halberd was simply set up behind it. On many of the robes, however, the *ju-i* scepter was added to this combination, extending the meaning to express "May (I, the wearer) have as much good luck and good

---

[64] Ryōzō Nagao, *Shina minzoku-shi* (Tokyo, 1940-41), pp. 305-21, describes the evolution of the cult of Chung K'uei (who, under the name of Shōki, is also popular in Japan), incidentally mentioning the connection with the *kuei* scepter. Although this motif is usually found on the same robes as the preceding one (cups on tray), it is sometimes used alone. See *Costumes from the Forbidden City*, pl. 37; detail, pl. 14, lower right.

[65] See "The Kuo Ch'in Wang Textiles," fig. 9, p. 135, detail. Some Western writers persist in listing the bell among the Eight Buddhist Symbols or the Eight Precious Things. The first is traditionally impossible and we cannot recall ever having seen an instance of the second. Perhaps some case such as this, in which the bell is shown in proximity to objects from one of these groups, gave rise to this popular misconception.

[66] The halberd alone was considered as an exorcising charm. See de Groot, *Religious System of the Chinese*, p. 1074.

fortune as (I) desire," *chi ch'ing ju-i.* Sometimes the scepter merely juts from the waves nearby, but more often it appears in actual conjunction with the other two; crossed with the halberd behind the jade stone, for example.

A second group of halberd symbols depends on another pun for *chi,* meaning "rank." In its basic form, this consists of a vase with three halberds standing upright in it. This picture is described in Chinese as *p'ing shêng san chi,* "three halberds rising from a vase." [67] But by replacing the first, second, and fourth characters with homophones, this gives an expression of ambition, "May (I) rise without opposition three degrees in official rank." [68] Sometimes, to make this rebus more easily understood, a musical instrument called a *shêng* is pictured beside the vase to convey more explicitly the second word of the phrase.[69]

A more complicated form of rebus, conveying two complete auspicious meanings, is a variation on the three halberds and the vase, in which the jade musical stone is superimposed against the shafts of the weapons. This is quite common on the latest of the Ch'ing dragon robes. On considering one of these double-pun pictures it is necessary to disregard one or more of the elements shown, to find the first meaning; then one must take up the object or objects first neglected, and ignore one or more of the other elements, to find the second meaning.

In the case just mentioned, for example, we can first disregard the musical stone, and get the usual hope for an ascent of three

---

[67] A variant form of this rebus symbol uses an ingot of silver (*ting*) to form a slightly different pun. See page 129 for a description of this alternative usage.

[68] The pattern sketches for the Empress' dragon robe (Type 1, in the *Li-ch'i t'u-shih* [6.31])—which, incidentally, depict a Pêng-lai Shan robe—have this vase and halberd symbol among the waves. Even though this pattern was not intended to be followed exactly, the fact that this symbol appears here at all shows that it probably had another meaning besides that of official aspiration, which would have been most unsuitable on the robe of an Empress. In fact, the rebus explanation was probably a Late Ch'ing rationalization for what had originally been a symbol to avert evil. The writer hopes to discuss the origin of this symbol, and its earlier forms, more fully in a later article.

[69] Although this rebus with the addition of the *shêng* musical instrument is fairly rare on robes, a fine example is shown on a nineteenth-century official's summer robe of dark blue gauze in the Chicago Art Institute.

ranks, *p'ing shêng san chi.* Then, considering the musical stone, but neglecting the specific number of the halberds, we get the descriptive phrase "halberd(s) and musical stone, together with a vase," *chi ch'ing ho p'ing.* After replacing the first, second, and fourth characters by homophones, and taking another meaning for the third, we get the hope, "(May I have) good luck, good fortune, and tranquillity."

Another, less familiar series of pun pictures on the Later Ch'ing dragon robes depended on a fish. This was not the handsome gold-fish or carp so frequently used to make a rebus for prosperity or abundance, but an ugly, spotted catfish (*Parasilurus asotus L.*), otherwise known as the sheat-fish, or wels. This was used in the rebuses because its Chinese name *nien* was a pun on the word for year. Thus we find on a Twelve-Symbol Imperial robe in Minneapolis a pair of these catfish on a swastika-figured background with a number of bats, to make the phrase, "May [I] year by year have ten thousand happinesses," *nien nien wan fu.*[70]

Two more catfish rebuses turned up on a portion of a nineteenth-century dragon robe owned by Mr. S. Kriger of Washington, D.C. The principal one, in the center of the robe below the main dragon, consists of a bat shown upside down with a pendant chain from its mouth, from which hangs a lotus, *lien,* and a *ju-i* jewel (like the head of a *ju-i* scepter). From these, in turn, hang two catfish, each with a swastika. Taking one *nien* fish with its swastika and the lotus and bat, we get the pun phrase, "For ten thousand years may (I) have continuous happiness," *wan nien lien fu.* Then, since this is a compound rebus, if we omit the bat and lotus, but take the other catfish and swastika along with the *ju-i* jewel, we have the wish, "For ten thousand years may everything be as (I) desire," *wan nien ju i.* The second rebus on this textile is much simpler in design but even more exaggerated in meaning. It has a single catfish lying on two swastikas with red bats hovering around it, to make the

---

[70] See *Imperial Robes and Textiles,* pl. 4; and detail, pl. 6, top. Rebus symbols with this catfish were used as early as the Ming. See the *Ming kung shih* 3.5b. They do not reappear in the Ch'ing until the nineteenth century.

phrase, "For ten thousand times ten thousand years may (I) have vast happiness," *wan wan nien hung fu.*

After the Fall of the Ch'ing Empire, when unsettled conditions made it possible to seize power by force, without having to pass civil service examinations or win promotion by merit (or wealth), the symbols of aspiration became meaningless. The Chinese people, plagued by famines and civil wars as the result of the breakdown of central control, became cynical and lost faith in auspicious symbols in general. This explains why few modern Chinese can interpret the symbols on the dragon robes. The meanings of even the common ones are now almost completely forgotten in the land of their origin.

9

The Making of Dragon Robes:
Techniques and Dyes

FOR centuries, the process of making the decorated robes, including dragon robes, has been essentially the same in China. However, the materials used to make them have differed from period to period, as some fabrics have been more popular than others at a given time.

From the time of the Yüan Dynasty, and probably earlier, the robe proper was always made in three oblong panels. The first panel contained the whole left side (front and back) of the robe-to-be. The second panel contained the back and the inner front flap of the right side, while the third panel, usually smaller, contained only the overlapping, right front portion. In the Middle and Later Ch'ing the ornamental collar and curving lapel, together with the horsehoof cuffs, were made separately on a fourth, much smaller panel, usually of very dark cloth, and the lower sleeves were also made of separate material.

When the robes were woven, they would come off the loom in these large rectangles. Then, if the quality was approved by the inspectors, they would be cut out and made up. In making embroidered robes like the one shown in the frontispiece, large silk panels of the same size as those for the woven robes were affixed to wooden frames, and embroidered with threads of fine silk or even gold. The workers would carefully join together the two vertical panels for the front and back of the robe before embroidering the main dragons and their pearls and some of the other central designs, all of which were sewn to span the middle seam. When the needlework was completed and had been inspected and approved, the embroidered robes were tailored just like the woven ones.

As exceptions to this basic method, the Ch'ing dragon jackets that buttoned down the front were woven or embroidered in only two panels, right side, front and back; and left side, front and back. For the Ch'ing court robes, on the other hand, the upper portion was usually made in three panels like the dragon robes, but the skirt required two more; not to mention the large collars, ornamental waist bands, and other applied decorations, which had to be separately made.

When we turn to a study of the actual materials used, a basic problem is the vagueness with which Chinese writers habitually described colors and fabrics. We could wish for a little more scientific precision. For example, the dragon-figured robe of the Sung Emperor referred to on page 5 is described as being of a color called *chiang,* which in modern dictionaries is defined as being of various shades of red or purple. However, in this case, since mediaeval works on plants speak of madder as "the plant that dyes *chiang* (-color)," and since madder produces a deep red dye, it seems safe to infer that the robe was a crimson one. We shall have more to say about dyes below.

We cannot begin to discuss all the techniques of embroidery and weaving available to the Sung rulers, as it would take us too far off the main subject. Suffice it to say that the pearl-studded dragon robe presented by the first Sung Emperor to Tung Ch'iu-hui (see Chapter 1), does not seem to have been particularly exceptional at that period, for we read of Sung presentation robes of gold brocade and kingfisher feathers, and robes for officials' wives sewn with gold-plated ornaments and pearls, as well as a variety of different fabrics the exact definitions of which could only be determined by long research.[1]

The Mongols of the Yüan Dynasty seem to have been very fond of heavy gold brocades and embroideries in gold. This is exactly what one would expect of "barbarians" from beyond the Great Wall, who for the first time had all the riches of China and Persia and the ability of the Chinese weavers as their exclusive monopoly.

[1] *Sung shih* 153.10b ff.

Even though woven in China, the brocades were given foreign names such as *nakhut,* and *nachidut,* which is called *na-ch'i-shih* in the Chinese records.[2] No doubt their dragon robes were woven in such materials.

When we come down to the Ming, the texts still give very few technical details about the dragon robes. One exception is the *T'ien-kung k'ai-wu,* a Ming work on basic industries. Its writer, in discussing weaving, gives a passage on the making of Imperial dragon robes, but he does not say too much about the actual process. He begins by telling that the Imperial weaving factories for this purpose were in Hangchow and Soochow. (The Ming had another weaving factory in Nanking, their southern capital, but apparently this turned out other things, such as the tribute silks.) The draw looms used to weave the dragon robes must have been much larger than those used to make the usual brocades and dragon satins, for the Ming writer describes the dragon robe looms as having super-structures, which he calls "pattern towers," *hua-lou,* fifteen feet high. He says that they required two trained men, acting as "draw boys," to sit up there and raise the successive sets of loom harness to make the pattern. Going on to stress the need for exactness, he says that if the draw boys made a mistake of a few inches they could throw off the shape of the dragons. The dyers who prepared the threads beforehand had to be equally careful, since it was very difficult to distinguish the proper shade of Imperial yellow (*chê-huang*) from the common yellow ochre until the threads were

[2] E. V. Bretschneider, in *Mediaeval Researches from Eastern Asiatic Sources* (London, 1910), p. 124, defines *nakhut* as "a kind of gold brocade," and *nachidut* as "a silk stuff interwoven with gold." On page 125 he says that *nakhut* and *nachidut* represent the Mongol plural forms of *nakh* and *nachid,* and that the latter apparently represents the stuffs that Pegolotti called *"nacchi"* and *"nacchetti"* in his descriptions of the trade of Cathay and of Constantinople, in the early fourteenth century. See Yule, *Cathay and the Way Thither* (2d ed.), Vol. 3 (Hakluyt Society, 2d series, No. 37, London, 1914), p. 155, especially note 4. Both these terms were borrowed from Persian, the original words being *nakhkh* and *nasij.*

Na-ch'i-shih is defined by the *Yüan shih* (78.7) as gold brocade, *chin chin.* In the later editions it is called *na-shih-shih.* Some varieties of this fabric were sewn with pearls. The *Yüan shih* (78.10) speaks of *ta-na-tu na-ch'i-shih,* consisting of large pearls sewn on brocade, and *su-pu-tu na-ch'i-shih,* consisting of brocade decorated with small pearls.

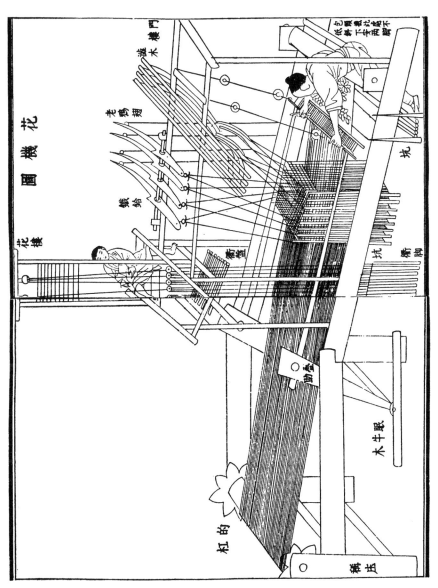

Ming Draw Loom for Weaving Brocades, from the *T'ien-kung k'ai-wu*.

woven. In conclusion, he says that the weaving was so fine on these Ming Imperial dragon robes that one could not even find the knots.[3]

Not all the Ming dragon robes were woven, for the dynastic records state that those for the Imperial eunuchs had their *mang* patterns embroidered.[4] In the case of the dragon robes for the lesser nobles, on which the decoration was confined to squares on chest and back, the squares were probably woven in silk tapestry (*k'o-ssǔ*)[5] or brocaded, and then sewn onto robes of another fabric. Two favored materials for Ming robes were a satin damask figured with wavy diagonals of cloud motif, and a twilled silk fabric called *lo,* which is usually translated as "serge." The dragon squares were probably generally sewn to robes made of either of these.

Whether they were embroidered or woven, the Ming dragon robes must have been exceedingly colorful, for the textile workers of that period had developed dyeing as a fine art. Probably the use of dyes for coloring silk had deteriorated during the Yüan, when the chief emphasis at the Mongol Court seems to have been on gold and silver brocades rather than patterns in colors, but the surviving Ming mandarin squares reveal an extensive range of bright, fast colors, with subtle tints for shading.

The *T'ien-kung k'ai-wu,* in addition to its brief mention of the problems of dyeing the threads in making the Imperial dragon robes, has a section describing how many of the contemporary dyes were made, while the *Pên-ts'ao kang-mu,* a Ming work on useful plants and animals, also provides valuable supplementary information on the materials used for dyes. The former refuses to divulge how the particular reddish yellow for the Ming Imperial dragon robes was made—doubtless in order to prevent unauthorized persons from making and using it. However, the *Pên-ts'ao kang-mu* explains that

[3] Sung Ying-hsing, *T'ien-kung k'ai-wu* (1637) 2.12.
[4] *Ming shih* 67.15.
[5] The Chinese have had several alternative combinations of characters for the term *k'o-ssǔ,* since it was apparently an expression taken from another language. See S. Cammann, "Notes on the Origin of Chinese K'o-ssǔ Tapestry," *Artibus Asiae,* Vol. 11 (1948), pp. 90-110.

it was made from the wood of a thorny tree, related to the mulberry, called *chê* (*Cudrania triloba*).[6] The same book also says that a very bright yellow dye was obtained from the buds of the *huai,* which we call the "Japan Pagoda tree" (*Sophora japonica*).[7] This dye may well have produced the *ming-huang* color of the Ch'ing Emperors' robes.

The making of "golden yellow," *chin-huang,* which was later used for the robes of Ch'ing Imperial princes, is described in the *T'ien-kung k'ai-wu.* They boiled the wood of a kind of sumac tree, *huang-lu,* or *lu-mu,* (*Rhus cotinus*), dyed the silk with this decoction, using potash made from hemp straw as a mordant to set the dye, and finally bleached it with lye.[8] This gives some idea of the advanced technical ability of the sixteenth-century Chinese dyers. Still other yellow dyes for embroidering the patterns, etc., were obtained from the fruits of the common gardenia, *huang-chih* (*Gardenia florida*), and from the inner bark of the Amur cork tree, *huang-po* (*Phellodendron Amurense*).[9]

The principal red dyes for the Ming robes were obtained from safflowers, *hung-hua,* the flowers of a type of thistle (*Carthamus tinctorius*), and from the roots of the madder plant, *ch'ien-ts'ao* (*Rubia cordifolia*), both of which were extensively cultivated for the purpose; as well as from sapan wood, *su-mu* (*Caesalpinia sappan*), imported from countries to the south. The *T'ien-kung k'ai-wu* explains that the deep crimson, *ta hung,* used for the dragon robes of Ming

---

[6] *Pên-ts'ao kang-mu* 36.9. The *T'ien-kung k'ai-wu* in its section on dyes (1, 3. 1b) merely says, under the name of this Imperial yellow (*chê-huang*), "Manufacture not explained."

[7] *Pên-ts'ao kang-mu* 35 (Pt. 1) .32. The *Sophora japonica* was introduced to the United States many years ago as a shade tree, and is frequently known here by an alternative name, "the Chinese Scholar's tree." Ironically enough, in spite of its numerous practical uses in the Orient, our Western dictionaries and botanical books usually speak of it as "a Japanese or Chinese ornamental tree."

[8] *T'ien-kung k'ai-wu* 1,3.1b.

[9] For the gardenia, see *Pên-ts'ao kang-mu* 36.21. For the use of the Amur cork tree see *T'ien-kung k'ai-wu* 1,3.1b. Fine examples of the latter can be found growing behind the main building of the Library of Congress in Washington, D.C. We have the names of many other plants and trees that also produced yellow dyes, but, having mentioned the chief ones used for the dragon robes, I shall save the rest for a longer, detailed study of Chinese dyes in general.

officials, was made by boiling [chips of] sapan wood, and then adding alum and gall nuts—for their tannic acid—to serve as mordants.[10]

The basis for the blue dyes came from various kinds of "indigo,"
lan-tien, including what the Europeans knew as "woad." One of the
chief indigo-producing plants, *liao-lan* (*Polygonum tinctorium*),
comes from northernmost China and Manchuria, and was undoubtedly widely used by the Manchus before the Conquest. This may
explain why blue was such a popular color for Ch'ing official robes.
The *T'ien-kung k'ai-wu* explains, however, that sapan wood was
added to the indigo to make the darker shades of blue,[11] and this no
doubt accounts for the Ch'ing *shih-ch'ing,* or blue-black, which is
actually a very deep purple.

Black dyes were made from the previously mentioned gall nuts,
wu-pei-tzŭ, which were growths caused by insects on the leaves of
a tree from which lacquer was made (*Rhus semi-alata*), and from the
acorn cups of the chestnut oak (*Quercus serrata*), called *hsiang-wän-
tzŭ.* However, the particular black color used for Ming ceremonial
robes, known as *hsüan,* was more complicated. It was made with
indigo, the bark of the wax myrtle, *yang-mei p'i,* and sumac wood
(*Rhus cotinus*), with copperas, or ferrous sulphate, and gall nuts for
mordant.[12]

The preceding colors, yellow, red, blue and black, together with
white (the artificially bleached silk), made up the traditional five.
Other tints could be made by varying the strength of the dye solu-
tions, or by blending. For example, even though they knew that
certain varieties of *Rhamnus* could produce green dyes, the Chinese
textile workers more frequently colored the silk green by first using
a yellow dye—usually from the buds of the *Sophora japonica*—then
re-dyeing with indigo. As the yellow color was less fast, this explains

[10] *T'ien-kung k'ai-wu* 1,3.1b. Sapan wood as a source of red dye is mentioned
in *Pên-ts-ao kang-mu* 35 (Pt. 2) .36; safflower, *ibid.,* 15.40; and madder, *ibid.,* 18
(Pt. 2) .19b ff. Many other plants were also used for red dyes, but these are the
important ones used on the dragon robes; and the rest I hope to discuss in the
later study.

[11] *T'ien-kung k'ai-wu* 1,3.1b. The various kinds of "indigo" are listed, and the
process of preparing the dyes from them is explained, in *Pên-ts'ao kang-mu* 16.70b ff.

[12] *T'ien-kung k'ai-wu* 1,3.1b. *Pên-ts'ao kang-mu* 39.19b mentions gall nuts as
a source of dye.

why the portions of old Chinese textiles that were originally green so often have assumed a pronounced bluish tinge with the passing of time. Purple dyes could either be made by blending blues and reds or, more directly, by using the roots of an herb called gromwell, *tzŭ-ts'ao* (*Lithospermum officinale*). Brown was made from the bark of the wax myrtle, *yang-mei,* with ferrous sulphate as a mordant.[13]

Thus we can see that the Chinese had made dyeing a fine art. Unfortunately, it was never permitted to become a science, because the chief dyers always kept the proportions in their heads, and concealed the equally important information concerning the length of time the threads should be steeped in each solution to produce the required shade. They passed these secrets on to their successors without ever recording them. This enabled certain families to preserve their monopolies, but it also resulted in the loss of much valuable knowledge. When such calamities as the Manchu invasion and the Taiping Rebellion ravaged the silk districts, all too often those who had the secrets were killed before they could pass them on.

. . . . . .

For a long time before the Conquest, the Manchus were entirely dependent on gifts or loot from Ming China for their dragon robes and dragon satins. Then, in 1616, the year in which their leader Nurhachi proclaimed a new dynasty, the Manchus flaunted the Chinese monopoly on silk raising, as one symbol of their break with China. They began to rear their own silkworms and reel the silk, in order to make their own silk and satin fabrics.[14] Seven more years passed, however, before they attempted to weave their own dragon satins.

In 1623 Nurhachi selected seventy-three men to weave *mang* satins and insignia in his first capital at Liaoyang.[15] It is probable that these weavers continued to follow Ming patterns, not having had enough experience to devise their own, and that their work was in-

[13] *T'ien-kung k'ai-wu* 1,3.1b. Gromwell is mentioned as a dyestuff in *Pên-ts'ao kang-mu* 12 (Pt. 2) .36b.
[14] *Man-chou mi-tang,* p. 22.
[15] *Ibid.,* p. 75.

finitely crude compared to that of the highly trained artisans of South China who made the Ming dragon robes. Thus it is likely that the ruling family continued to wear robes made in China, using the Manchurian products for gifts to friendly Mongol princes and favored chieftains.

It was not until 1652, nine years after they came to China, that the Manchus set up their elaborate system to provide fine textiles for the Ch'ing Court. This system was in large measure an inheritance from the Ming, but apparently the devastating effect of the Conquest sieges on the southern industrial cities had so disrupted them that it took at least nine years to restore textile production to normal working order.

The capital at Peking had its Imperial Weaving and Dyeing Office, *Nei chih-jan-chü*,[16] but the actual weaving was done in factories at Hangchow, Soochow, and Kiangning (modern Nanking).[17] In general, all satins for Imperial use were produced by the Office in Peking and the Kiangning factory. The former seems to have furnished the patterns as well as the dyes, while the weaving was done at the latter. Meanwhile the weavers at Soochow annually provided the satins for presentation. (The Ch'ing Court, at least in the first part of the dynasty, usually conferred materials for making robes rather than the robes themselves. See Chapter 14.)

Strict regulations were issued from Peking in 1652, when this system was set up, to instruct the factories how to proceed. The Court commanded that the bolts of satin for Imperial use—those having either four or eight dragon medallions, or of yellow or tawny yellow (*ch'iu-hsiang-sê*)—should all be woven with three-clawed or five-clawed dragons. Aside from these, all the satins produced should be

[16] The Imperial Weaving and Dyeing Office was a department of the Imperial Household, along with the Silk Storehouse, *Tuan-k'u*, and the Imperial Wardrobe, *I-k'u*. It was supervised by a Manchu prince, or Minister of the Household, who held the title of *Kuan chih-jan-chü ta-ch'ên*. See Mayers' *Chinese Government*, No. 76, p. 7; and Brunnert, *Present Day Political Organization of China*, No. 96, p. 24.

[17] The three Southern factories were managed by superintendents especially appointed from the Manchu members of the Imperial Household. These officials had the title of *Shang-i*, or *Ssŭ-fu*. See Mayers, No. 325, p. 43; and Brunnert, No. 845, p. 425. Of course, the work at Kiangning and the other Southern factories was completely disrupted by the Taiping Rebellion. See Chapter 13.

divided into three portions, of which one third should be woven with five-clawed or three-clawed dragons for the use of the Imperial Family, while the other two thirds should be woven with four-clawed dragons for presentation to nobles and high officials.[18] The bolts of satin and gauze for the Imperial dragon robes, and for all other kinds of robes woven with four or eight five-clawed dragon medallions, were commanded to be made two (Chinese) feet broad, and either twenty or forty feet in length. Every other type of fabric, including the satin and gauze with four-clawed dragon patterns, was to be made two feet broad and forty-two feet long.[19]

In addition, the Imperial factories in the South were ordered to send annually to Peking two robes of silk tapestry (*k'o-ssŭ*) with five-clawed dragons: one of yellow with blue collar and cuffs, and one of blue with dark blue collar and cuffs. These were to be sent alternately in the Spring and Fall of each year to the Palace Storehouse in Peking. At the same time, other weaving in *k'o-ssŭ* was forbidden.[20]

Note that, except for the two annual robes of tapestry weave, the chief fabric mentioned is satin. It was only natural that "barbarian" conquerors should think satin very wonderful and *k'o-ssŭ* little short of miraculous. Therefore it does not seem surprising that the Ch'ing Court kept the latter an imperial monopoly and made satin, called *tuan,* the prescribed material for court and official robes.

The Early Ch'ing sumptuary laws of 1652 mention several kinds of satin to be used for robes. The lists include three forms of dragon satins: three-clawed *lung tuan,* five-clawed *lung tuan,* and *mang tuan;* [21] "decorated satin," *chuang tuan,* either embroidered or having ornaments of gold and seed pearls sewn to it; [22] "Japanese satin," *Wo tuan,* which apparently did not actually come from Japan because in 1651 six hundred bolts of it were ordered from the Kiangning factories; [23] gold-brocaded satin, *chin-hua tuan,* having flowers or other

[18] *KHHT* 136.4b-5.
[19] *Ibid.,* 136.4.
[20] *Ibid.,* 136.5.
[21] *Ibid.,* 48.1b, *san-chao* and *wu-chao lung tuan;* 48.3b, *mang tuan.*
[22] *Ibid.,* 48.33 ff., *chuang tuan;* 49.15 same embroidered; 49.10 ff., same embroidered with pearls.
[23] *Ibid.,* 136.4.

patterns rendered in gold; and satin damask, *hua su tuan,* self-figured, with clouds and other patterns.[24]

There would seem to be an overlapping of categories here, as the dragon satins were named for their chief motif, and the others for their technique. Thus the material of an Early Ch'ing dragon robe might have been classified as *mang tuan* because it had four-clawed dragons on it, or as *chin-hua tuan* because these animals were rendered in gold. Again, one occasionally finds an Early or Middle Ch'ing satin dragon robe on which the pattern is rendered in the same color as the background, produced merely by a change in weave. When the pattern is a bold one this may represent the *hua su tuan,* but in the case of some of the medallion robes (Type 5) on which the coiled dragons and their attendant symbols were worked in the same general technique but so finely woven that they were indistinctly seen, this was probably that "hidden pattern" satin, *an-hua chih tuan,* which we have seen mentioned in the laws as a restricted medium.

A magnificent example of the "decorated satin," *chuang tuan,* is the Early Ch'ing robe of Type 2 in the Royal Ontario Museum of Archaeology, which is apparently the only embroidered robe from that period in an Occidental collection. (See Plate 5.) The dragons on it and the background are couched in two shades of heavy gold thread on a plain cloth base, while the clouds, waves, and details of the dragon—horns, whiskers, claws, etc.—are done in satin stitch.[25] This technique of couching with heavy metal threads must have been very popular at the time when this robe was made, to judge from the numerous contemporary mandarin squares in our museums which have backgrounds embroidered in this way. In fact, embroidery in heavy gold thread may well have been fairly common for the dragon robes of Early Ch'ing dignitaries, the robes later being destroyed for their gold thread after the patterns went out of fashion. Some of the

---

[24] *Ibid.,* 48.5b ff., gold brocaded satin, and satin damask.

[25] Couching consists of anchoring heavy threads of metal (or thick silk) by more delicate filaments of silk. This is done primarily so that valuable metals will all appear on the surface, and none will be wasted. The anchoring threads are usually white or neutral, but in the Later Ch'ing they were often colored so that they imparted soft tints of other colors to the gold or silver.

mandarin squares of that period have come down to us with the gold threads of the background ripped away, but on a robe like this, if one took off the gold there would be nothing left worth saving.

In spite of the considerable number of Imperial robes in *k'o-ssŭ* that must have been woven—at the rate of at least two a year—only one has come down to us from before the Ch'ien-lung period, and that is the Metropolitan's Early Ch'ing consort robe.[26] Though the workmanship is excellent, it seems slightly coarse in weave when compared with the *k'o-ssŭ* robes of the Ch'ien-lung period. Possibly this is because more robes in this technique seem to have been made in the mid-eighteenth century, and the later weavers no doubt got more experience.

The *k'o-ssŭ* robes of the Ch'ien-lung period have never since been equalled. A favorite combination of this Emperor was light gold dragons on a blue ground, but one of his robes in the Metropolitan has a background entirely made of writhing cloud-scrolls in the five auspicious colors, showing the Chinese tapestry weaver at the peak of his art.[27]

Not only in tapestry weaving, but in other techniques as well, the textile craft seems to have reached its height in the Ch'ien-lung period. The brocaded dragon robes of this reign are notable for the use of heavy gold and silver threads, made by winding fine metal foil around thin silk thread, instead of the flat gold foil on a strip of leather membrane generally used earlier. The embroiderers of this period also used metal threads of this type, as may be seen on a particularly fine Ch'ien-lung Twelve-Symbol robe in the Walters Gallery, Baltimore, which has the pattern entirely couched in gold and silver thread against deep blue silk.[28] (Frontispiece.)

Some of the more delicately embroidered robes of this period are marvels of technical skill. The Ch'ing craftsmen had already developed to a high degree the execution of fine details, as may be seen on

[26] *Costumes from the Forbidden City,* pl. 16, and *Chinese Textiles,* fig. 6, p. 23: detail in the latter, fig. 5, p. 22.

[27] *Costumes from the Forbidden City,* pl. 21.

[28] For a detailed description of this robe, see S. Cammann, "A Robe of the Ch'ien-lung Emperor," *Journal of the Walters Gallery,* Vol. 10 (Baltimore, 1947), pp. 9-19.

some of the robes from the tomb of Prince Kuo, notably the one with the many cranes,[29] but the embroidery on some of the Ch'ien-lung robes seems even better. The satin stitch was frequently used to make long floats of untwisted floss silk on a satin background, producing soft patterns of a velvet-like finish. Mrs. Martin has a pair of such robes in Imperial yellow, only one of which has the Twelve Symbols. Possibly they belonged to the Ch'ien-lung Emperor and his second Empress—the first died before 1759, when the Twelve Symbols were re-adopted for Imperial use.

During this reign, complicated over-all diaper patterns became popular. A fine example of this is shown on the dragon robe in Minneapolis, mistakenly ascribed to the tomb of Prince Kuo.[30] A few robes of the period had backgrounds of couched peacock feathers. The Cleveland Museum of Art has a particularly fine example which must have produced a handsome, shimmering effect when worn.[31] The "Peking knot" was sometimes used for details and small sections of design, such as lucky symbols, but it was so difficult and time-consuming that we cannot expect to find whole robes in this technique.

It must have been during the latter part of the eighteenth century that wide-meshed gauze came into favor for summer robes. This gave opportunities for embroidery with several forms of counted canvas stitches, some of which do not seem to be characteristically Chinese and may have been introduced from the West. They include both tent stitch (petit point) and the Florentine stitch, familiar in Western embroidery. The latter is darned on the background in short stitches, rising and falling to make a zigzag effect.[32] The Metropolitan has at least one dragon robe on which the whole background is of tent

[29] *Costumes from the Forbidden City*, pl. 26.

[30] *Ibid.*, pl. 29.

[31] The biography of Crown Prince Wên-hui of the Southern Ch'i Dynasty (latter part of the fifth century A.D.) speaks of a robe woven from peacock feathers, "sparkling and resplendent with a golden iridescence" (*Nan-Ch'i shu* 21.5b). This is the earliest record of the use of woven peacock feathers in Chinese textiles, as far as we know. Woven peacock feathers reappear in Late Ming mandarin squares, and are very common on the finer Early Ch'ing textiles.

[32] *Chinese Textiles*, p. 26. The distinction between petit point and Florentine stitch given in this reference is rather poor, being very ambiguous.

stitch, with the bodies of the dragons couched in heavy gold thread,[33] and another having a background of surface darning stitch in very small squares, giving the appearance of a woven fabric,[34] while the Minneapolis Institute of Arts owns a dragon robe entirely worked in Florentine stitch (with the Twelve Symbols falsely added).

After the Chia-ch'ing reign, during which the traditions of the Ch'ien-lung period seem to have been maintained with no further progress, the technical skill of the embroiderers and weavers rapidly deteriorated. In part, this was probably due to the fact that the widespread corruption of officials had extended to the inspectors and others in charge of producing textiles for the Court, causing them to be less strict about the quality of the robes that passed through their hands. Formerly the responsible officials had been strictly punished for any carelessness or inefficiency,[35] but from the early years of the nineteenth century they could act virtually as they pleased.

Another reason for the nineteenth-century decline was probably the fact that the general breakdown of economic conditions within the Empire increased the cost of materials, while lowering the wages. This produced a sense of apathy and despair among the workers, so that they lost interest in doing their jobs well. Lastly, after 1850, the loss of the Southern factories during the Taiping Rebellion (described in Chapter 13) must have severely overtaxed the Peking Weaving and Dyeing Office, which was then forced to handle the total production of Imperial robes for a number of years.

The Imperial robes, however, show less of this general deterioration than the robes for officials, because they were still made by chosen workers, and had to be finally approved by the autocrats for whom they had been commissioned. Yet even the power of the famous Empress-Dowager could not command, or obtain, robes of the quality worn by the Emperors and Empresses of the Middle Ch'ing. The last truly magnificent Imperial dragon robe seems to have been the

[33] *Ibid.*, Fig. 12, p. 36, shows the details.
[34] *Ibid.*, Fig. 15, p. 41; detail, Fig. 14, p. 40.
[35] In 1676, a memorial was sent to the K'ang-hsi Emperor, calling his attention to the fact that the satin sent to Court was not of the finest quality; whereupon the official in charge was demoted one rank and transferred (*KHHT* 136.5).

one embroidered with pearls and coral for the marriage of the last Empress in the 1880's. But this, too, had elements of decay in its design.

One of the principal reasons for the decline of workmanship in the lesser dragon robes must have been the ever-growing demand for these by persons who had purchased the right to wear them. With the greater number of orders, the makers of these robes could not afford to spend as much time and care over them.

The faultiness of the later workmanship is especially apparent in the tapestry dragon robes of the nineteenth century. By this time, the Imperial monopoly on *k'o-ssŭ* had either broken down or was generally disregarded, and robes in that technique became accessible to anyone who could afford them. These robes are a sorry contrast to the *k'o-ssŭ* examples made at an earlier period for the Court. The overworked weavers turned them out rapidly, with coarse backgrounds and crudely drawn patterns, often painting in the details with a brush.

Occasionally, for a wealthier patron, the later tapestry weavers attempted to create richer effects, as shown by a robe in the Beck Collection that has peacock feathers woven into the background, and by a more common type that had rather coarse gold-wrapped thread for the background. These last tend to be rather pitiful, however, because the dragons, waves, and lucky symbols were still badly drawn and poorly executed, making a general impression of tawdriness rather than wealth.

The brocaded dragon robes of the late nineteenth and early twentieth centuries also have a rather cheap appearance, owing to the use of a poor quality, imitation gold foil on a paper base that was inclined to tarnish and to crack and break off in small pieces. Many of the latest ones were not really brocaded, as the metal threads run the full width of the fabric. Quite a number of them had white or unbleached silk for the patterns, intended to give the effect of gold and silver brocade at a distance. Some of the late robes are rather well woven, though the dragons and other details tend to be flat and mechanical-looking.[36] Perhaps they were done on power looms.

[36] *Costumes from the Forbidden City*, pl. 44, shows a typical example.

In spite of the glitter produced by using a single metallic color for the design, these late, brocaded dragon robes seem restrained in comparison with the embroidered ones of the period. Late Ch'ing embroidery was not very good to begin with, showing the prevailing carelessness in design and execution. And, especially after the introduction of aniline dyes in the second half of the nineteenth century, the color combinations were often excessively bright. Some of the details worked in the new dyes seem especially harsh to our Western eyes. No doubt this is because of their contrast with the background colors of rich yellow and deep blue that were still being produced with the older dyes, which, being less fast, have mellowed with the years.

A favorite combination of colors in the later embroidery was the vivid, reddish purple which we discussed in Chapter 6, together with a very bright green. This green we have also had analyzed by the latest scientific methods, and we are told that it was achieved by a mixture of two foreign dyes, Malachite Green with picric acid, which was added to make it brighter. The yellow of the latter, like that of the vegetable dyes, tends to fade on exposure, while the other is very fast, so the result is a strengthening or deepening of the green color on the outer surface of the robe.

Someone has said that it is very doubtful that aniline dyes were ever used by the notably conservative Imperial factories.[37] This remark is obviously based on a misconception, since our museums have Twelve-Symbol Imperial robes with patterns in aniline colors. It is true that, after 1759, the Court textile workers had little latitude as regards patterns, but there were no similar prescriptions to say what dyes and techniques must be used.

The Chinese textile workers, whether employed by the Court or otherwise, had no objection to foreign dyestuffs just because they were foreign, as long as they were effective. They sought strong or vivid shades of red first in the sapan wood imported from Siam and Malaya, then, briefly, in cochineal brought from South America or Mexico, and finally they discovered the superior qualities of the Methyl Violet from Europe. The last was not only very vivid, but was also

[37] *Ibid.*, text, p. 12.

much faster than any other red or purple known to them. As one symptom of their high opinion of the new aniline dyes, the Chinese originally called them "first rank colors," *i-p'in sê*.[38]

While it is true that the original cost of the imported aniline dyes was not low, in the end they were cheaper for the Chinese silk workers. In the first place, the foreign officials who controlled the Chinese Maritime Customs had set a low duty on foreign products, including dyes, to encourage their importation, and by agreement there was no further tax. Meanwhile, native dyestuffs from the Interior had to contend with high transit levies, complicated by Provincial likin taxes. The latter had originally been established to help pay the expenses of the Taiping Rebellion, but had rapidly become a highly organized racket.

This foreign commercial penetration into the native dye industry was only a small example of the evil combination of Western imperialism and internal corruption which was wrecking China's economy. The whole Chinese silk industry underwent a rapid decline in the last quarter of the nineteenth century. The Customs lists of that period show that the Chinese were importing bolts of dyed silk as well as silk thread, and real and imitation gold and silver thread,[39] as well as great quantities of dyestuffs including artificial indigo. In view of this, some of the latest dragon robes must have been made almost wholly of foreign materials.

In short, the Later Ch'ing dragon robes are interesting chiefly as examples of decline in technique, reflecting political and economic decay. For specimens of textile skill and real beauty, it is necessary to go back to the satin dragon robes of Early Ch'ing, or the fine *k'o-ssŭ* robes and the richly embroidered ones of the Ch'ien-lung period.

[38] This term appears in the *Catalogue of the Shanghai Customs Collection* (1873), p. 46. Later, as these dyes became more familiar, more descriptive or phonetic names were used for them.

[39] See S. W. Williams, *Chinese Commercial Guide* (5th ed., Hong Kong, 1863), p. 93. He said, "The quantity [of gold thread] imported is large; but being of great value in little bulk, much of it is not reported in the trade returns." In other words, considerable amounts of it were being smuggled into China.

PLATE 1. Persian Robes with Elements Introduced by the Mongol Conquest. Early fifteenth century miniature painting.

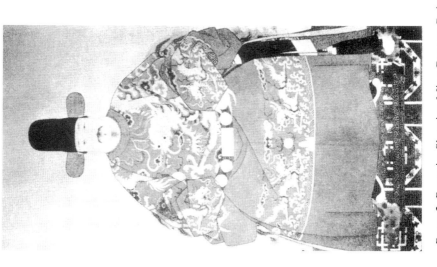

PLATE 2. Portraits Showing Ming Dragon Robes in Use. Left: The usual type of Ming dragon robe. From the Li Family History. Right: Ming presentation robe. From the Wu Family History

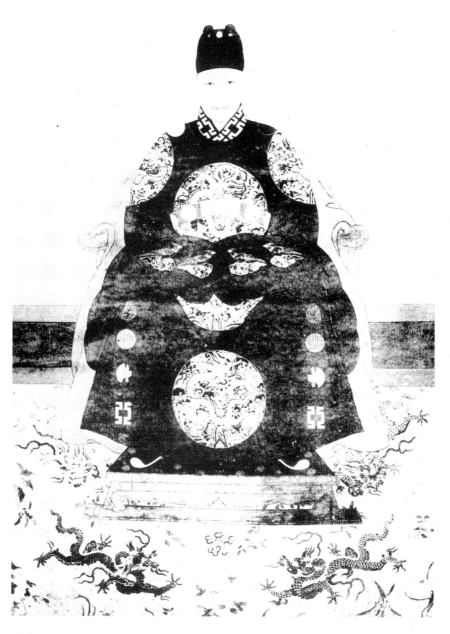

PLATE 3. Portrait of the Ming Emperor Kuang-tsung in Informal Dragon-Figured
Robe. From the *Chung-kuo li-tai ti-hou-hsiang*.

PLATE 4. Upper Part of Early Ch'ing Robe, Showing Part of Type 1 Pattern.
(Courtesy of the Philadelphia Museum of Art.)

PLATE 5. Early Ch'ing Dragon Robe with Type 2 Pattern.
(Courtesy of the Royal Ontario Museum of Archaeology.)

PLATE 6. Early Ch'ing Dragon Robe with Type 2a Pattern.
(Collection of Mrs. D. C. Martin.)

PLATE 7. Portion of Early Ch'ing Dragon Robe with Pattern of Type 4a.
(Courtesy of the Dayton Art Institute.)

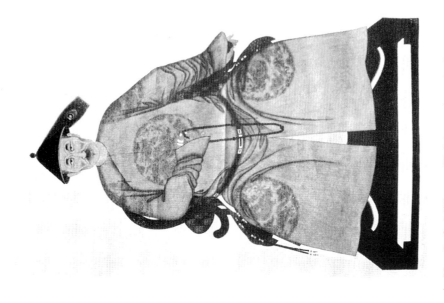

PLATE 8. Early Ch'ing Portraits Showing Dragon Robes in Use. Left; Military official wearing *p'u-fu* jacket over dragon robe. Right: Manchu nobleman wearing medallion dragon robe (Type 5a).

PLATE 9. Development of the Pattern on Ch'ing Imperial Dragon Robes I. Left: Middle eighteenth century. Yung-chêng or early Ch'ien-lung period. Right: Later eighteenth century, late Ch'ien-lung period.

(Courtesy of the Metropolitan museum and the Dayton Art Institute.)

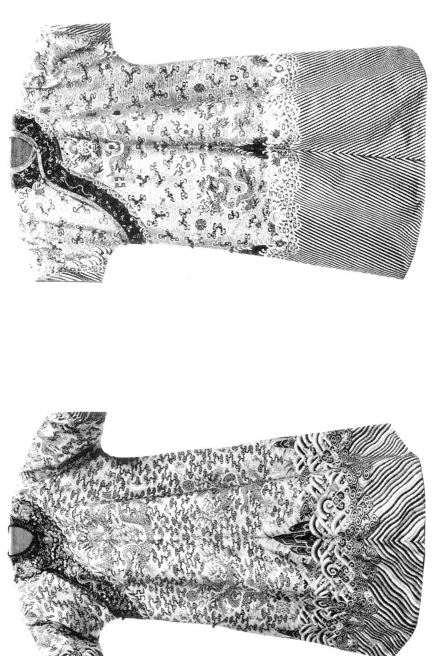

PLATE 10. Development of the Pattern on Ch'ing Imperial Dragon Robes II. Left: Middle nineteenth century, Tao-Kuang period. Right: Late nineteenth century, Kuang-hsü period. [Lower sleeves not shown.] (Courtesy of the Metropolitan Museum.)

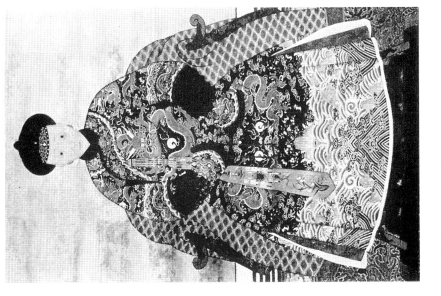

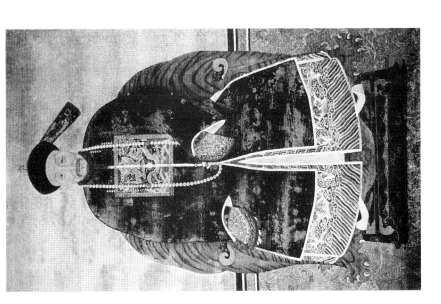

PLATE 11. Early Nineteenth Century Manchu Duke and Noblewoman in Dragon Robes.
(Courtesy of the Nelson Gallery and the Royal Ontario Museum of Archaeology.)

PLATE 12. Manchu Noblewomen's Dragon Robes, Nineteenth Century. Left: Type 2, old from, showing survival of medallion pattern. Right: Type 1, a late Five-Symbol robe, showing degenerated sleeves.

(Courtesy of the Metropolitan Museum.)

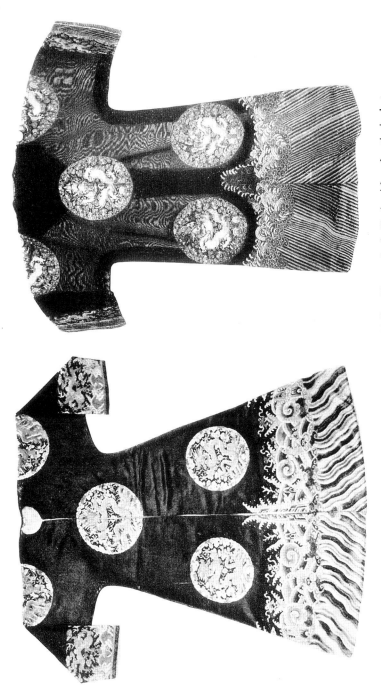

PLATE 13. Manchu Noblewomen's Dragon Jackets, Late Ch'ing Types. Left: Embroidered satin jacket, Ch'ien-lung period. Right: Gauze summer jacket with Four Symbols, Kuang-hsü period. (Courtesy of the Metropolitan Museum.)

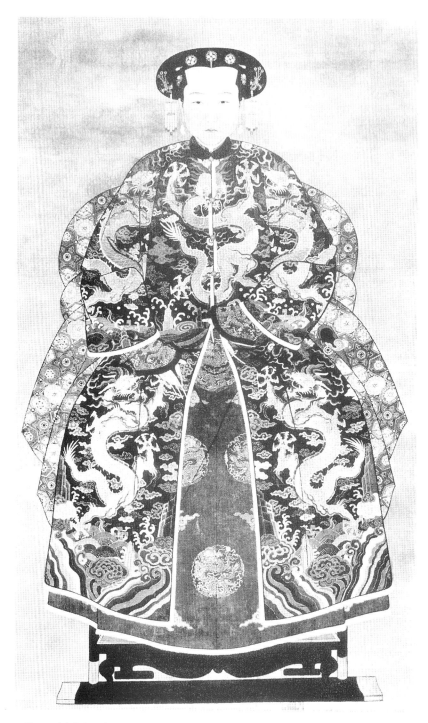

PLATE 14. Manchu Noblewoman Wearing an Early Ch'ing Dragon Jacket.
(Courtesy of the Metropolitan Museum.)

PLATE 15. Portion of the Ch'ien-lung Emperor's Dragon Robe, Showing
Symbol Details.
(Courtesy of the Victoria and Albert Museum.)

PLATE 16. Chinese Official's Wife Wearing Dragon Coat, Eighteenth Century.
(Courtesy of the Royal Ontario Museum of Archaeology.)

PLATE 17. Chinese Bride's Robe with Survival of Early Ch'ing Pattern (Type 1). (Courtesy of Seattle Art Museum.)

PLATE 18. Portraits Showing Early Ch'ing Court Dress. Left: Manchu noble in summer court robe.
Right: Manchu noblewoman in winter court robes and court vest.
(Courtesy of the Royal Ontario Museum of Archaeology and the Nelson Gallery.)

PLATE 19. Late Ch'ing Emperor's Court Robes. Left: Winter robe (Type 1). Right: Summer robe. From a sketch book brought back by the Macartney Mission, 1793.

(Courtesy of the Victoria and Albert Museum.)

PLATE 20. Late Ch'ing Court Dress for Nobles and Officials. Top: Court robe for lesser princes and dukes. Center: Court robe for officials form fifth to seventh rank. Bottom: Court robe collar. (Courtesy of the Metropolitan Museum.)

PART II
RELATED ROBES

10

Unofficial Dragon-Figured Robes

A. Chinese Women's Dragon Coats

THE "dragon coats," *mang-ao,* worn during the Ch'ing Dynasty by wives of Chinese—as opposed to Manchu—officials, and by wives of other prominent Chinese citizens, had almost nothing in common with the official Ch'ing dragon robes beyond occasional correspondences in pattern. These dragon coats and the costume to which they belonged were completely unofficial. The wearing of them was as much a matter of personal preference as was the choice of patterns, and they are never mentioned in the dynastic clothing laws. The elaborate court dress and the complete semiformal outfit including the dragon robe, which were prescribed by law for the wives and daughters of nobles and officials, were only intended for the Manchus, or for Chinese women whose husbands or fathers were serving in the capital. In general, the only Chinese women permitted at Court were those from the renegade Chinese Banner-families which had gone over to the Manchus in the seventeenth century. Otherwise, Chinese women of the middle and upper classes wore this other, unofficial costume for their bridal dress and for special occasions throughout the rest of their life, often being buried in them.

In the absence of laws regarding this form of dress, we are completely dependent on portraits for tracing its development. These show that the full costume consisted of the dragon coat, cut with excessively full sleeves in the Ming fashion and worn over an elaborate pleated skirt, usually ornamented with dragons (and "phoenixes") and hence called *mang-ch'ün.* With these were worn an ornate "phoenix bonnet," *fêng-kuan,* copied from the hats of Ming women of rank, the wide Ming hoop-belts, *chüeh-tai,* and usually a long, figured stole, *hsia-p'ei,* which eventually evolved into a kind of sleeveless vest.[1] However, after the Manchus took over China, the old traditions immediately broke down, so that these Ming-style hats, belts, and stoles no longer showed the proper designations of the wearers' ranks as they had during the previous dynasty.[2] (The complete costume is shown in Plate 16.)

The earliest portraits show these robes as plain red, the favored Ming color, with the "mandarin square" of the husband's rank sewn directly on them, and worn with or without the stoles. Since they lacked any dragon pattern, they were not "dragon coats," so they need not concern us. It is impossible to say when the fully developed dragon coats came into favor, but they are first shown in portraits from the eighteenth century. The patterns of the earlier ones strongly resemble those on the Ming dragon robes (see Plates 16 and 17). They had two large dragons with their heads on the breast and back of the coat and their bodies looping over each shoulder, while a pair of smaller dragons appeared on the very full sleeves, and, two pairs occupied a horizontal band at front and back of the skirt. This band was not necessarily confined by bordering lines as it had been in the Ming, and sometimes the dragons were entirely free, though they usually maintained their horizontal position. These garments generally had the four-clawed dragon, but a portrait in the Metropolitan shows a wealthy woman, apparently of no official rank as she has no insignia, wearing hoofed dragons on her dragon coat.[3] This is probably because true clawed dragons were not permitted to persons without official status.

We do not know how long this style of dragon coat, with the Type 1 dragon pattern, continued in favor. The Seattle Art Museum has just acquired an example from Peking, which, judging by stylistic elements at the bottom of the robe, must date from the early Ch'ien-

---

[1] See J. J. M. de Groot, *The Religious System of China,* Vol. 1 (Leyden, 1892), pl. 3, facing p. 53, shows the skirt; pl. 4, facing p. 54, shows the dragon coat with the hat and belt; and pl. 5 shows the stole-vest with cloud collar attached.

[2] The Ming stoles for ladies of rank had carefully prescribed patterns. See Appendix G.

[3] *Portraits of the Court of China,* cover and pl. 1.

lung period. And in the more remote provinces it is possible that this pattern with the two huge, arching dragons may have lasted on into the nineteenth century. The coat now in Seattle, illustrated in Plate 17, has the usual background of Ming red. The upper half is largely occupied by the giant dragons and their jewels, while "phoenixes" and peonies, and many-seeded pomegranates decorate the broad sleeves.

Although the rest of the pattern, below the waist of the coat, closely resembles the conventional decoration of the Ch'ien-lung dragon robes, it is distinguished by being particularly rich in unusual rebus combinations. The first consists of a boat (*ch'uan*) bearing an official belt (*tai*) and a pomegranate (*liu*), while an official hat (*kuan*) rises from the fruit on a wisp of cloud. Together these form a pun on *kuan tai ch'uan liu*, conveying the hope that the family of officials might continue on for generations.[4] Above this group, the three halberds, rising from an ingot of silver (*ting*), instead of the vase, have cassia flowers attached to their staffs, giving an unfamiliar twist to an old rebus. With these variations, the halberd symbol says, *i ting shêng san kuei-chi*, "May you certainly rise three grades in the (non-Manchu) nobility." Lastly, on the rocks at each side, a monkey is shown embracing a huge peach, making another rebus, to wish that the wearer's descendants might cherish long life.[5] The writer has seen only one other example of the boat device, and that was on another Chinese woman's dragon coat, also from Peking but dating from a much later period. The variation on the halberd pun is entirely new, and although the monkey grasping the peach is a familiar folk symbol, frequently shown on carvings in wood and jade, it has not previously been seen on a robe.

The later dragon coats for the wives of higher Chinese officials during the later eighteenth and early nineteenth centuries had the usual eight dragons like those on the official dragon robes of that period, shown in the same places, with two more on the sleeves. Those

---

[4] See Arthur H. Smith, *Proverbs and Common Sayings from the Chinese* (Shanghai, 1914), p. 152.

[5] The word for monkey, *hou,* has the same sound as the word for descendant(s).

for women of lesser rank had only four dragons (on breast, back, and shoulders), or sometimes merely two. These robes with fewer dragons made up for the lack of more by having several pairs of "phoenixes" and mandarin ducks as symbols of marriage and domestic felicity, as well as a profusion of peonies, happiness bats, and other symbols of good fortune.[6] They were usually embroidered by the bride-to-be, as part of her premarital education, and as a result the workmanship varies greatly from one to another, depending on the artistic ability of the individual woman and her degree of sophistication.

The dragon coats of the later nineteenth and twentieth centuries were cut fairly short and were much narrower in the body. By this time, the bridal costume as a whole tended to emphasize the highly decorated stole-vest, worn over the coat, and also gave considerable prominence to the under skirts which projected below the coat and extended out through slits in its sides. The shortness of the coat left little room for *li shui,* and frequently it was omitted altogether. The decadence of the age expressed itself in ever-increasing ornamentation on the dragon coat, vest, and skirts. And some Chinese women of the later Ch'ing made up for the simplicity of the coat's plain neck by wearing elaborately embroidered detachable cloud collars, which detracted attention from everything else.

B. Theatrical Dragon Robes

Like the women's dragon coats, theatrical dragon robes have no real place in a discussion of official Chinese costume, except for the fact that they occupy a prominent place in Chinese culture and many examples have found their way into American collections. Before 1950 in China, one's Chinese friends invariably said, "If you are interested in Chinese costume, you must go often to the Chinese theater." Such advice is worse than useless. As China has no tradition of theatrical research, both actors and their managers lack any true conception of what the costumes and furniture and weapons were like

[6] De Groot, *op. cit.,* 1, pl. 4, facing p. 54.

at earlier periods. Anachronisms are countless and often very ridiculous, even in plays about the last dynasty.

In historical plays, T'ang and even Han statesmen will stride out upon the boards in voluminous dragon robes of modified Ming cut, but of blue instead of the traditional red or purple, bearing Ch'ing dragon patterns, and usually *li shui,* which, as we have seen, was a development of Middle Ch'ing, unknown to previous dynasties.[7]

Rarely, actual Ch'ing dragon robes will be worn, especially in plays that portray Manchu rulers, but more often they are archaistic ones made up for the individual actors at their own expense. In addition to having anachronisms in color and design, these theatrical dragon robes are usually unmistakable because of the portrayal of the dragons themselves. They are usually drawn very boldly so that they can be seen at some distance, and are embroidered in heavy gold or in very bright silk, to impress the spectator with their splendor. Very often, too, the more prominent features of the dragons are grotesquely exaggerated, such as protruding eyes, very red and bulbous nose, and wandering whiskers. This provides a note of humor in otherwise serious plays. Lastly, the *li shui* is often greatly emphasized, so that its broad stripes of gold or bright colors will shimmer nicely when the actor takes those long ducklike steps, conventionally used on the Chinese stage, which cause his skirts to swirl about him.

Structurally, the theatrical robes differ from the dragon robes proper in that they are fastened with cloth straps instead of buttons. It has been said that this device is used to facilitate quick changes of costume between scenes. However, as it is also sometimes found on the brides' dragon coats, it may merely represent a conservative survival from an earlier period before the use of buttons.

In short, the theatrical dragon robes are admirable for their purpose, which is to create the illusion of dazzling opulence or ancient splendor, but they are utterly useless for studying the development of the form and patterns of the official robes.

[7] Cecilia S. L. Zung, *Secrets of the Chinese Drama* (Shanghai, 1937) on pp. 92, 224, has photographs of a play about the Ch'in Dynasty (third century B.C.) in which two of the actors are wearing robes with excessively wide *li-shui,* as developed some twelve hundred years later.

C. ROBES FOR RELIGIOUS IMAGES

The images in the temples of the Chinese national cult (neither specifically Buddhist nor Taoist) often show the statues of the gods of the locality, together with those of deified heroes such as Kuan Ti, clothed in silken robes, usually figured with dragons. These robes are often recognizable when off the image by their overlarge size. They are usually far too big for even an exceptionally heavy man to wear, although it is also possible to find very small ones, since the images were made in all sizes. One constant feature of the image robes, however, is that they have very wide sleeves. Sometimes the bottom seam of each sleeve is left unsewn but fastened with strings, so that they can be fitted on an image, even when its hands are clasped together around a mace or scepter, or otherwise engaged.

The image robes, like those made for the actors, often show the main dragon with a grotesquely large face and a bulbous red nose, in this case to make a dramatic rather than humorous effect on the beholder. Their color differs according to the image for which they are intended, since most of them are ex-votos, made in the home or commissioned, to deck the figure of a specific deity. Huang Ti and other legendary emperors of Chinese folklore traditionally were given yellow or crimson robes, deified officials commonly had dark red ones, while Kuan Ti generally had his traditional green. The dragons on the robes for images practically always had only four claws, until the end of the Ch'ing dynasty, when distinctions in the numbers of claws no longer had any real meaning.

The Boston Museum of Fine Arts has a fragment of a giant image robe in yellow, with the principal dragons and other details hand-somely worked in woven peacock feathers. It appears to have been designed and woven in the first half of the eighteenth century, judging by the form of the dragons, clouds, and other elements in the decoration, but it was apparently never cut out and made up for actual use. An interesting feature of this robe is the fact that the dragons on the shoulders were in profile, as we have already mentioned in discussing Type 4b of the early Ch'ing dragon robe patterns. The Nelson Gallery has a complete image robe in dark green, with early nineteenth-century dragon and wave forms, which may have been made for a huge image of Kuan Ti.

The Victoria and Albert Museum in South Kensington has a pair of very unusual, large image robes, which, on stylistic grounds as well as the evidence of a cyclical date woven into the fabric of one, can be ascribed to the year 1731.[8] These are extremely interesting, and perhaps unique, for several reasons. The basic design represents a strange hybrid, combining patterns from robes of several types. The upper section has a large facing dragon arching over the shoulders, enclosed in a four-lobed reserve like those on the contemporary Ch'ing court robes, while the pair of dragons on the lower portion are also shown full face. Although all their dragons are the non-imperial four-clawed variety, both robes bear the Twelve Symbols: the sun and the moon on the shoulders, and the rest symmetrically arranged in a broad band across the stomach. Several gods of the Chinese pantheon had been awarded the honorary titles proper to an Emperor, *huang* or *ti,* and hence, they could have rated Imperial emblems such as the Twelve Symbols at a time when these were not the sole prerogative of a living Emperor as they were before 1644 and after 1759. Since one of these robes is red, it might have been made for the Ch'êng Huang, or "City Emperor," of some great metropolis like Peking. The other is green, a color considered improper for males in China, except for Kuan Ti who as god of War had his virility unquestioned. Thus the latter must have been made either for an image of Kuan Ti himself, or for the wife of the Ch'êng Huang, who was often presented with robes which matched those of her consort, but of a different color. Another peculiarity of this pair of robes is that the pattern is not continued on the right side or at the back, where it would not have been seen on a seated image which had its right arm raised. The writer has not found this measure of economy prac-

[8] See the writer's reasons for this dating in *The Connoisseur,* Vol. 126 (December, 1950), pp. 206 and 220.

ticed on any other image robe. But it might once have been quite common, especially on robes such as these which had the main design richly worked in costly gold thread.

The workmanship on the image robes varies extremely, depending on whether a given example was especially commissioned by the Emperor or one of his courtiers as a gift to a prominent temple in order to obtain merit, or whether it was simply made in a farmhouse as a thank offering. However, beginning with the nineteenth century the quality of the weaving or embroidery is almost invariably rather poor, and by the end of that century the raw foreign dyes were generally used in profusion.

11

Ch'ing Court Robes for Men

SINCE the Ch'ing court robes, or *ch'ao-fu,* also had dragon patterns, it seems appropriate to mention them briefly here, especially in order to compare them with the dragon robes proper.

The men's dress consisted of a rather short jacket with a spreading collar, and a flaring skirt pleated at the top. The collar, which extended beyond the shoulders, was called a *p'i-chien* or *p'i-ling.* The latter was the chief distinguishing element of the court and ceremonial robes of the Ch'ing, without which they could not be worn. According to Ch'ing tradition, the wearing of this type of collar was an old Tartar usage, dating back to the Liao Dynasty, at which time it had been called a *ku-ha.*[1]

Another characteristic element found only on these ceremonial robes was a small square flap, called *jên,* which extended below the bottom of the jacket on the right side. Originally it seems to have covered the skirt fastening, but on the Later Ch'ing court robes, which did not have detachable skirts, it was apparently only a vestigial survival with no real function.

The best sources for studying the patterns on these robes would seem to be reliable portraits of the Emperors, because we know their approximate dates, and because changes would be apt to come first on Imperial robes, later filtering down to the robes of nobles and officials. Unfortunately, these are no help before the K'ang-hsi reign. The Palace Museum has ancestral portraits of the first three Manchu

---

[1] *Ko-chih ching-yuan* (1718), 18.22. The contemporary description quoted in this leads us to suspect that the Liao Dynasty *ku-ha* was a form of cloud collar, but the Ch'ing writers apparently assumed that it was like their own *p'i-ling* collar. The first references to the *p'i-ling* date from 1625 (See the *Tung-hua lu,* T'ien-ming 4.8 and 10). As they are mentioned separately from the robes, they may have been detachable at that time.

rulers—the chieftains Nurhachi and Abahai, and the Shun-chih Emperor—showing them all wearing court robes, but these were obviously all painted at the same time, long after their deaths, so they are useless as evidence.[2] The ornamentation is probably quite different from what they actually wore, so we shall not bother to describe it. Only the color seems right, since the robes are yellow, and this was specified for the Emperor's robes in 1636, at the beginning of Abahai's reign.

In view of the doubtful authenticity of the preceding paintings, a portrait of the K'ang-hsi Emperor as a boy is probably the first reliable picture of an Imperial court robe.[3] In design, at least, it is the forerunner of all the later ceremonial robes, and its pattern has all the essentials of the later ones, though it lacks some of the superficial ornamentation that was later added.

The pattern on the upper jacket consisted of four facing dragons, on breast and back, and on each shoulder. These, with their background of clouds, and waves below, formed four lobes of design extending down the chest and back, and down each arm to the elbow. In addition, a strip at the bottom of the jacket had two horizontal, profile dragons confronting a jewel. The skirt had a horizontal band of design running across it, showing a small facing dragon flanked by two more in profile. Except for the strip of ornamentation on the lower border of the jacket, this pattern was essentially like those on the Yüan and Early Ming robes, with the upper decoration in four lobes, recalling a "cloud collar," and the horizontal band across the skirt.

Even more interesting from the point of view of surviving traditions, are the court robes of the Early Ch'ing nobles, shown in portraits of this period. These robes have two large principal dragons on the upper jacket. One dragon has its head on the chest of the

[2] *CTTHH* 1, pls. 1, 2, 4. The patterns shown, consisting of large and small dragon medallions, conform exactly to that prescribed by the Yung-chêng Emperor in 1723 (*Hui-tien tsê-li* 65.1b), which was used for only a short time and then abandoned. It is quite possible that he had had these anachronistic portraits painted at that time to give him an apparent precedent. In any case, in cut and pattern the robes depicted do not represent actual Early Ch'ing types.

[3] *CTTHH* 1, pl. 9.

robe and its body looping back over the left shoulder, while the other on the back loops forward over the right shoulder. (See Plate 18, left.) This is the old Ming pattern which was continued on the first type of Early Ch'ing dragon robe, but the horizontal strip of decoration across the skirt, containing two dragons flanking a small mountain, carries us more directly back to the dragon robes bestowed on Ming officials. (See Plate 2.) In addition, these court robes for Ch'ing nobles and high officials had a narrow ornamental strip at the bottom of the jacket, which is shown in portraits to have been made from extra pieces of satin, usually without any complete pattern. And of course they also had the flaring collar.

We have been discussing the commonest type of Early Ch'ing court robe, as shown in ancestral portraits. This type was made of light silk for summer use, and of heavier material, with interlining and fur trimming, for early spring and autumn. The winter robes are also occasionally shown in portraits, and these were slightly different in form and decoration.

The winter court dress consisted of a jacket of heavy brocade, showing the two principal dragons on chest and back looping over the shoulders—or four dragons for those of highest rank—while the bottom of the jacket had an extra strip of brocade added to make it longer. This much was like the style used in the other seasons, but in addition, the jacket was edged with sable, and the collar and cuffs were of sable. The upper part of the skirt had the horizontal band with the confronting dragons, as did the other type; however, the lower part was faced in sables.

A very early Ch'ing portrait in the Metropolitan shows a variation of the winter court robe, in which the horizontal band usually shown on the skirt was added to the bottom of the jacket, and the whole skirt was made of sable skins.[4] This might have been the earliest winter type; if so, it is reasonable to suppose that it went out of use because it required more sable skins and was therefore too costly.

The sable-decked court costume was eminently practical for creating the maximum effect of awe in a very cold climate. But robes of

[4] See *Portraits of the Court of China*, pl. 17.

this type for all nobles and courtiers, and higher officials in the capital, required an enormous amount of sable skins. In fact, it was chiefly the conflict over the sable tribute from the Northern Manchurian tribesmen, which the Manchus needed for making their winter court robes and formal jackets, that first brought the Ch'ing Dynasty into conflict with the Russians. After the Cossacks reached the Amur in the mid-seventeenth century, their greed for sable skins led to an intense rivalry that finally culminated in open battles. The warfare ended with the Treaty of Nerchinsk (1689), which compelled the Russians to withdraw beyond the Amur watershed. However, since the Manchus did not colonize the region north of the river, the Russians gradually moved in, so the Ch'ing Court, especially after the mid-eighteenth century, became more and more dependent on Russian traders for their sables.[5] It seems probable that the custom of using fewer skins for the court robes, as indicated by the portraits, began at the time of the frontier war of 1680-89, when hostilities interrupted the flow of sable tribute to Peking.

Now that we have discussed the form and general pattern of the Early Ch'ing court robes, let us see what these elements tell us about the origin of the garment. The fact that the lower part of the jacket had to be made out of another strip of cloth, instead of being an extension of the upper fabric; that pleats needed to be taken in the upper skirt in order to make it fit tightly at the waist without disturbing the sweeping pattern of the horizontal band below; and the fact that the sleeves were pieced together, as on the dragon robes—all are evidences of a makeshift origin.

[5] The Russian drive across Northern Asia had been activated largely by an unbridled greed for sable skins. See J. F. Baddeley, *Russia, Mongolia, China* (London, 1919), Vol. 1, pp. 76, 88; Vol. 2, p. 21. The latter part of Vol. 2 has considerable information on the Russian-Chinese rivalry in the disputed territory of the Amur region; see especially pp. 301 ff. and 418. Unfortunately, the documents presented do not carry the story all the way to 1689, but further information can be found in H. B. Morse, *International Relations of the Chinese Empire* (London and New York, 1910), pp. 59-62, 472-77. The final blow to the Ch'ing sable tribute did not come until the Treaty of Aigun in 1858, when China lost the left bank of the Amur and control of the Maritime Province, leaving the best fur regions in Russian hands.

Historical documents tell us that the Manchus used court robes before their conquest of China.[6] Therefore, these—like the Early Ch'ing dragon robes—must have been made either from Chinese figured robes, specifically the Ming dragon robes, or from local Manchurian copies of them. This inference is confirmed by the presence of the four-lobed pattern or the looping dragon pattern on the upper robe, together with the horizontal band on the skirt, all of which were characteristic of the Later Ming dragon robes.

As the Manchu idea of a formal costume demanded a two-piece robe, they apparently cut the Ming dragon robes in half at the waist. Then they took the upper half and cut it in at the sides to fit the body rather snugly. Since this trimming reduced the width of the upper sleeves, they lopped off the dragon-figured lower sleeves at the elbows, as they did for their dragon robes, to avoid leaving an incomplete pattern. After which they must have added an extra strip of figured material below the waist to make the bottom of the jacket, so that it would overlap the skirt. Lastly, lower sleeves, ornamental cuffs, and a spreading collar, made from other materials, would be added to complete the jacket.

Meanwhile, for the skirt, they apparently took the lower half of the Ming dragon robe and merely pleated it at the top, so that it would fit tightly at the waist, while leaving the bottom section full to display the horizontal band of decoration to best advantage. As this costume was to be used solely for court and ceremonial functions, it was not necessary to split the skirts for riding.

For the winter court robes, the Manchus must have followed the same general process. They used the upper half of the Ming-style dragon robe for the jacket, added a fur collar and cuffs instead of cloth ones, and after pleating the upper skirt, simply faced the lower half of it in sables. In the case of the type pictured in the Metropolitan portrait, however, they must have cut out the horizontal band

---

[6] To cite but one instance, the *Tung-hua lu* (T'ien-ming 3.15b) mentions that in January, 1620, Nurhachi bestowed a sable-faced (winter) court costume on one of his Mongol vassals.

from the skirt to add to the bottom of the jacket and then made a new skirt entirely from sable skins.

Since these Manchu court robes were for ceremonial use, they were inevitably controlled by a much stronger, conservative tradition than were the dragon robes, which were only semiformal. This would inevitably have acted for a long time to restrain any experimentation and changes in the basic pattern, such as we found in the Early Ch'ing dragon robes. In fact, the form and pattern remained essentially the same until 1759, except for a few slight additions to the pattern, shown on the robes of the Emperors in their portraits. Thus, for over a century after the Conquest had given them control of the silk-weaving areas of China, the Manchu courtiers and high officials were wearing robes made in the same fashion as those of their ancestors, which had been cut from painfully acquired Ming robes. Even after 1759, until the end of the dynasty, in fact—although the decoration had changed somewhat, both the pattern and the general cut would have indicated a makeshift origin to anyone who thought to look for it.

Having traced the beginnings of the Ch'ing court robes, let us turn back to the Imperial portraits to note the further slight changes in the patterns of the Emperors' robes, before discussing in detail the laws of 1759.

The two later portraits of the K'ang-hsi Emperor which are authentic,[7] as well as that of the Yung-chêng Emperor,[8] show minor additions in the form of four small dragon medallions on the front and back of the lower jacket, between the base of the upper decoration and the strip of ornamentation on the lower border. In addition, they have nine small dragon medallions on the pleated section, on the front and back of the upper skirt. As further distinguishing features, the principal dragons on the jacket are gripping the pearls in their right foreclaws, and the lower sleeves are of separate black material.

[7] *CTTHH* 1, pls. 13, 14. We have already pointed out that the third portrait (pl. 11) was a forgery; see *JAOS,* Vol. 66, p. 296.
[8] *CTTHH* 1, p. 23.

The Imperial portraits fail to show us the Yung-chêng Emperor wearing a special type which he introduced under the name of "sacrificial robe," *chì-fu,* in the first year of his reign (1723).[9] This applied the currently popular dragon medallions to the *ch'ao-fu* form of robe. The upper portion was to have large dragon medallions on breast and back and on each shoulder, and two more on the front and back of the skirt, with a ninth presumably on the inner flap of the upper robe—nine in all. (This is the first reference to a nine-dragon pattern, and perhaps the ninth dragon on the dragon robes was an innovation of this reign.) In addition, the Yung-chêng sacrificial robes had nine small dragon medallions on the strip at the bottom of the upper section at the waist. It is possible that these robes—of which there were four in all, with different colors for the appropriate sacrifices—were used for a time as sacrificial robes distinct from the court robes proper. However, by 1759, if not sooner, a form of court robe was again used for each sacrifice and there was no distinction between court and sacrificial robes. Perhaps the new type was abandoned as untraditional.

We should also mention here that a few pictures of Manchu nobles from the Late K'ang-hsi and Early Yung-chêng periods begin to show four dragons on the upper robe in a four-lobed pattern like the Emperor's. However, they differ from those on the Imperial robes by having the dragons on the shoulders in profile, both facing the front of the robe, like those on the contemporary dragon robes but unlike anything seen later.

In the Palace Museum portrait of the Ch'ien-lung Emperor as a young man, the extra medallions on the lower jacket, shown in the portraits of the K'ang-hsi and Yung-chêng Emperors, have been discarded, though the eighteen on the pleated part of the skirt still remain.[10] Later portraits of the Ch'ien-lung Emperor as an older man show him wearing the final type of court robe as prescribed in the laws of 1759.[11] This has the Twelve Symbols—which appear for

[9] *Hui-tien tsê-li* 65.1b. See Note 2, above, for comment on this pattern as found on forged portraits of earlier Ch'ing rulers.
[10] *CTTHH* 2, pl. 5.
[11] *Ibid.,* 2, pls. 26, 30.

the first time—and it shows the principal dragons (on chest and back) coiled around an elaborate lucky medallion containing the *shou* symbol and the symbols of the Eight Immortals, like the one on the fragment of his dragon robe now in London. His later robes also have great curling waves in the strip of sea below the dragons in the horizontal band across the skirt, recalling the waves on the dragon robes of the Ch'ien-lung period. Lastly, the lower sleeves are now yellow.

The portraits of the rest of the Ch'ing Emperors show them in court robes of practically the same pattern, and it looks as though all were painted at the same time, near the end of the dynasty.[12] The only difference is that all but one, the Tao-kuang Emperor, have only twelve dragon medallions across the upper skirt instead of eighteen; and there is no trace of slight stylistic changes such as one would expect to find from one reign to another.

· · · · · ·

As in the case of the later dragon robes, the laws of 1759 were very specific about the different types of court robes and the patterns on them. For the Emperor, they specified two distinct forms of ceremonial robes, the second of which was made in two styles, making three types in all.

The Emperor's winter court robes (Type 1) were of bright yellow, except that the ones worn at the Altar of Heaven and at the Grain Sacrifice were blue. The broad collar, lapel, and lower skirt were all faced with red (undyed) sable, *tzŭ-tiao p'i*, while the cuffs were of smoked sable, *hsün-tiao p'i*.[13] The usual horizontal band of six dragons was lifted to cover the pleated portion of the upper skirt, in place of the small medallions, which were omitted on this type, and all the Twelve Symbols were confined within the lobed pattern of the upper jacket. (See Plate 19, left.)

[12] *Ibid.*, Vols. 3 and 4. Perhaps these were painted in the first years of the present century to replace a set stolen or destroyed during the Boxer troubles.
[13] *LCTS* 4.7-8.

The Emperor's winter court robes (Type 2)—actually worn in late autumn—were of the usual form shown in the portraits described earlier in this section, except that their edges were trimmed in otter fur, *hai-lung p'i*. They, too, were usually of bright yellow, except that the one worn for the sacrifice at the Altar of the Sun was red.[14] The Twelve Symbols were displayed in substantially the same way as on the dragon robes. The first eight were in the same relative positions, and the last four were placed below the dragons on the horizontal band across the skirt. The illustration of the collar in the *Huang-ch'ao li-ch'i t'u-shih* shows that it was figured with two dragons confronting a flaming pearl (see Plate 20, bottom).

The Emperor's summer court robes were exactly like the preceding in appearance except that they were edged in black and gold brocade, instead of fur.[15] These also were yellow, except that the one worn at the Rain Sacrifice was blue, and the one worn at the Altar to the Moon was green-white. They were made of satin or gauze, in single thickness. (See Plate 19, right.)

The Heir Apparent had the same three types of robes as the Emperor, but all were of orange yellow, and the second and third types had only seven small medallions across the front and back of the pleated upper skirt.[16] (No medallions at all are specified for the robes of the lesser nobles and the officials. However, in the Later Ch'ing many others seem to have appropriated them, for a number of nineteenth-century court robes made for lesser folk, now in our American museums, have ten or twelve medallions on the skirts.)

Imperial princes, the sons of the Emperor, all had the same three types of Court robes. These differed from the Emperor's robes by being golden yellow in color, and by having minor distinctions in the decoration of the skirts. On the second and third types the horizontal band across the skirt contained four profile dragons at front and back, instead of one facing and two in profile, and all three

[14] *Ibid.*, 4.9-10. The robes worn by the later Ch'ing Emperors at the annual Sun Sacrifice apparently constituted the only exception to the Manchus' dislike of red robes. But here the color was required by ritual. See Chapter 2, Note 41.
[15] *Ibid.*, 4.11-12.
[16] *Ibid.*, 4.30-35.

types (officially) lacked the medallions on the upper part of the skirt.[17]

First- and second-degree princes, and sons of the former, had the same three types of court robes, but they were of blue, blue-black, or other colors, unless the Emperor gave them golden yellow. Third- and fourth-degree princes and Imperial dukes had the same three types of court robes, of the same colors—except golden yellow—but these robes had only four-clawed *mang* dragons, unless their wearers had been specifically awarded an extra claw.[18] (See Plate 20, top.)

Chinese dukes and other nobles, civil officials down to the third rank, and military officials of the first and second ranks, also had three types of court robes with four-clawed dragons. The only difference was that the first type had only two dragons across the front and back of the skirt instead of four. The third-rank civil officials and third- and fourth-rank military officials were not permitted to wear the first type (the sable-trimmed winter robe), but could wear the other two.[19]

Civil and military officials of the fifth, sixth, and seventh ranks had only one type of court robe, quite different from any of the preceding. It was made of cloud-figured blue-black satin, with a large square on chest and back, each of which displayed a four-clawed *mang* dragon in profile. (See Plate 20, center.) Imperial Guardsmen of the second and third class also had court robes with these *mang* squares, but they differed in having the collar, lapels, cuffs, and lower robe faced in dark, crinkled satin, while the second-class Guardsmen had an additional strip of decoration on what would correspond to the lower edge of the jacket, though these robes were made in one piece.[20] The court robes of officials and lesser dignitaries below the seventh rank had no dragons at all, so they do not concern us here.

Even after 1759, when these new types were created with the intention of indicating more clearly the distinctions between ranks,

[17] *Ibid.*, 4.46-8.
[18] *Ibid.*, 4.55-7 (first and second degree princes); 4.71-3 (third and fourth degree princes, and Imperial dukes).
[19] *Ibid.*, 5.5-7. See comment in résumé of court robe regulations, in Appendix D.
[20] *Ibid.*, 5.68 (fifth, sixth, and seventh rank officials); 5.62 (second-class Guardsmen); 5.76 (third-class Guardsmen).

the basic form of the *ch'ao-fu* remained essentially the same. As a minor difference, the strip at the bottom of the jacket now tended to become a mere waistband, linking the upper portion to the skirt in what was actually a single garment. Even the pattern remained much the same for those above the fourth rank, though new, unfamiliar types were invented for those below that rank. It is true that the old type with the two main dragons was now permanently discarded, but the four-lobed field of design was maintained on the upper jacket, and the horizontal band of dragons (now increased in number) still decorated the skirts below.

It was only in the later nineteenth century that the pattern tended to get out of hand, at about the same time that deteriorating workmanship was robbing these robes of their proper dignity. The jacket design then broke out of its lower bounds and came down to the waistband, destroying the four-lobed effect, while the horizontal pattern at the knees spread so much to provide for additional lucky symbols that it covered most of the skirt and could no longer be called a band.[21] At about the same time, many of the lesser nobles and officials did not even bother to have complete court robes made for them. They merely wore their ordinary dragon robes with a makeshift court skirt around the lower portion, and a *p'u-fu* jacket concealing the upper robe, topped by a spreading collar over the shoulders (see Plate 20, bottom).[22] These late, wrap-around skirts were usually of deplorably bad workmanship, badly woven and crudely embroidered. Once more the breakdown of tradition in costume was a symptom of decay, foreshadowing the fall of the dynasty.

[21] See *Chinese Court Costumes,* pl. 12.
[22] Miss Rachel Dowd of New Haven, Conn., has one of these late Ch'ing makeshift court costumes, consisting of an ordinary robe, with separate collar and skirt, over which the wearer would have worn his *p'u-fu* jacket.

12

Women's Court Robes and Court Vests

EARLY Ch'ing portraits of the wives and daughters of nobles and officials show an enormous variety of court robes, differing mainly in pattern. A few of the earliest ones show wives of officials wearing a *ch'ao-fu* exactly like their husbands', with the separate jacket and the full skirt pleated at the top.[1] These seem to have soon gone out of fashion, however, and a new type of court robe was developed, solely for women.

This was a long, straight robe like the dragon robe, but it differed from the latter in having the spreading collar, as well as projections above the shoulders, like small epaulettes. These projected beyond the sleeveless court vest, which was worn over the robe, making a very distinguishing feature. The Manchu noblewoman's court robe also had extra bands of decoration just above the elbows, generally containing dragons, like those on the Empress' dragon robes.

The patterns on these earlier women's court robes are often difficult to make out in portraits, because the court vests covered so much of them. However, enough is visible for us to see that they had the same patterns as those on the K'ang-hsi dragon robes: either the two principal dragons looping over the shoulders with a pair of ascending dragons below; or large dragons extending down the front and back and smaller ones on the shoulders; or three dragons in front and three in back, with profile dragons on the shoulders. A few merely had the robe covered with small dragon medallions. (See Plate 18, right, for an example.)

In the absence of laws dictating the patterns, variations were numerous. The significant thing is that all these patterns are those of the Early Ch'ing dragon robes, after the Manchus had begun to

[1] See "The Development of the Mandarin Square," fig. 3.

146

develop their own, and do not carry on the archaic Ming patterns. Thus we can see that this type of woman's court robe must have originated well after the Conquest, probably in the K'ang-hsi period.

Unfortunately, we know almost nothing about the early court costumes of the Empresses and Imperial consorts. The Dynastic Statutes give little information, and the earliest life-portrait of a Ch'ing Empress in the Palace Museum Collection is that of the Ch'ien-lung Emperor's mother, painted in her old age, during the reign of her son.[2] In this mid-eighteenth century portrait of the Empress Hsiao-shêng, the court vest hides most of the pattern. Enough of it shows, however, to indicate that the decoration is essentially the same as that on the contemporary dragon robes (Type 4), except that it has only waves and no *li shui* at all.

In 1759, the patterns of women's court robes were standardized along with all the other elements in Ch'ing costume. At this time the Empress and the Empress-Dowager were given five types of court robes, consisting of variations on two distinct styles, but all colored yellow.

The first style is illustrated by the robe worn by the Ch'ien-lung Emperor's mother. These robes had an allover pattern of nine golden dragons (the ninth under the front flap) as on the dragon robes. However, the pattern differed from that on the dragon robes by having *p'ing shui* instead of *li shui* (that is, it had no deep sea stripes), until very late in the dynasty, when traditions began to break down. It also had the spreading collar with two more (profile) dragons, and the extra pair of dragons on the band around the sleeve above each elbow. Although on the dragon robes these sleeve bands were worn only by the Empress and the highest noblewomen, on the court robes they were supposed to be worn by women of all ranks.

Within this first style, the Empress had three types of robes. The first type was a winter robe with collar, lapel, and cuffs edged in

[2] *CTTHH* 2, pl. 3. The portraits of the previous Empresses are useless for evidence, having all been painted at the same time, early in the Ch'ien-lung reign.

148 CHINA'S DRAGON ROBES

sable; it was slit only at the sides. The second, also a winter robe, was trimmed with otter fur, and the skirt was slit at the back as well. The third was a summer robe, like the second, but was made of lighter material, satin or gauze, and edged in gold brocade instead of fur.[3]

The Empress' second style of court robe resembled the second type of court robe worn by the Emperor as shown in Plate 19, right, in that it had the four lobes of decoration on the upper jacket, and the full skirt with pleats and a horizontal band of decoration. It differed, however, in having the women's epaulettes and extra sleeve-bands, and in lacking the medallions on the pleats and the small projecting flap on the right side. Moreover, the strip across the skirt was somewhat narrower than that on the Emperor's court robes, and had four dragons instead of three—all in profile. A final distinction was the absence of the Twelve Symbols on the Empress' robes, unless these were added in the nineteenth century, as they were on the dragon robes. The Toronto Museum has an Empress' summer court robe of the previous style, with only four symbols. This second style of Empress' court robe was also subdivided. The first type, for winter use, was trimmed with otter fur; the second, a summer court robe, was made of satin or gauze and was edged in gold brocade.[4]

The Imperial consorts and the wife of the Heir-Apparent had the same five types of court robes, but the colors differed according to their rank. Consorts of the first degree had yellow robes like the Empress', those of the second and third degree had golden yellow, those of the fourth degree tawny yellow, while the Heir Apparent's wife had orange-yellow.[5] Below them, the next group had only two types of court robes, both of the first style worn by the Empress. The pattern was much like that on their dragon robes

[3] LCTS 6.13-14 (style 1, first winter type); 6.17-18 (style 1, second winter type, here called Empress' winter court robe No. 3); 6.21-2 (style 1, summer robe, here called Empress' summer court robe No. 2).
[4] Ibid., 6.15-16 (style 2, winter type, here called Empress' winter court robe No. 2); 6.17-18 (style 2, summer robe, here called Empress' summer court robe No. 1).
[5] Ibid., 6.13-22 (first degree consorts); 6.54-63 (second and third degree consorts); 6.81-90 (fourth degree consorts); 6.96-105 (Heir Apparent's wife).

but differed in thickness and in trimming, having otter skin edging for winter and black and gold brocade for summer.

Wives and daughters of first- and second-degree princes had these two types in tawny yellow with five-clawed dragons. Wives and daughters of third- and fourth-degree princes and Imperial dukes, and wives of Chinese nobles, and civil and military officials down to the third rank, had the same two types in blue, blue-black, or other colors, with four-clawed dragons.[6] Lastly, wives of fourth to seventh rank officials had only a single type of court robe, in blue, blue-black, or other colors, with two confronting, profile dragons extending down the front and back—four in all—and none on the shoulders or collar.[7] Wives of officials below the seventh rank did not wear court robes.

Court Vests

It was the court vests, *ch'ao-kua,* worn over these court robes that gave the women's court dress its distinctive patterns (see Plate 18, right). Hence, these cannot be ignored, especially if one wants to study and analyze Ch'ing portraits. All were blue-black in background, though their rich decoration made them more colorful than this might sound.

From portraits we can see that the original type was essentially a woman's dragon robe or dragon jacket, without sleeves, which fastened down the front like the latter. Those for the Empresses and noblewomen of high rank had single dragons on chest and back, and a pair on the front and rear of the skirt—six in all (see Plate 18, right). Those for the lesser noblewomen and wives of officials had only a pair of dragons at front and back.

By the laws of 1759, the Empress(es) and the Imperial consorts had three types of court vests, of which the first two were apparently new types, and the third a continuation of the old one, with a few

[6] *Ibid.,* 6.116-19 (wives and daughters of first- and second-degree princes); 6.140-41 (wives and daughters of third- and fourth-rank princes); 7.6-7 (wives and daughters of Chinese nobles, and first- to third-rank officials). Though the last two references are found in different places, the robes described are essentially the same.

[7] *Ibid.,* 7.30.

changes in decoration. The first had five horizontal panels of decoration. At the top were two "vertical dragons" (*li lung*), in profile, and below them were four alternating bands of horizontal facing dragons and lucky symbols—*shou* characters, swastikas, and bats. The second type of vest was decorated like the second style of court robe—the one like the Emperor's—but it lacked sleeves. It had single large dragons on breast and back, a strip at the waist with two small dragons on front and back, then a row of pleats, and a horizontal strip of dragons across the skirt below. The third type had two ascending vertical dragons at front and back.[8]

Princesses, wives of princes, and wives of Manchu nobles had court vests with four dragons on the front; the upper two facing, and the two lower ones in profile. By contrast, the backs of these garments had three dragons, the upper one facing and the lower two in profile. (At least, they are pictured this way in the illustrations for the Statutes; but the laws simply say, "four profile dragons in front, three profile dragons in back.") Lastly, wives of Chinese dukes and lesser nobles, and the wives of officials down to the seventh rank, had two ascending profile dragons on the front of the vest, and a single large profile dragon on the back.[9]

Judging from the portraits of the Empresses, their third type of vest—which is the only one depicted—apparently underwent a marked evolution in the last century. A broad strip of circular *shou* characters alternating with bats on clouds was introduced to ornament either side of the front opening. And in addition, the lower part of the skirt between the upper waves and the "deep sea" had a broad band of *li shui* with much larger *shou* medallions that appear to have been worked in pearls. Meanwhile, the width of the ornamental strips down the front, and the *li shui* below, so crowded the two front dragons that they could only occupy the space between waist and knees, whereas they had formerly extended almost the

---

[8] *Ibid.*, 6.7-8 (first type of court vest); 6.9-10 (second type); 6.11-12 (third type).
[9] *Ibid.*, 6.104-5 (court vest for princesses, wives of princes, etc.); 7.5 (court vest for wives of Chinese nobles, and of officials down to the seventh rank). The Minneapolis Institute of Arts has handsome examples of both types.

length of the garment. These overelaborate vests may have been spectacular, but the total effect of excess fancy decoration, with grotesquely large lucky symbols, expressed extreme decadence rather than Imperial splendor.[10]

[10] For the development of Type 3 court vests see the Empresses' portraits in *CTTHH* (2, pl. 4; 3, pl. 15; 4, pl. 27). Types 1 and 2 are not shown in this series.

13

The Robes of the Taiping Rebels

IF the mid-nineteenth century Chinese robes were beginning to express the decay of the Ch'ing Dynasty, an even more obvious indication of failing power was the series of violent rebellions that broke out in the 1850's. Among these, the Revolt of the Taipings (1850-66) had several unique features, not the least of which was the theatrical splendor of its ragamuffin court at Nanking.

The unofficial history of the Taipings' "Celestial Kingdom of Peace," which comprised most of Central and Southern China for about fourteen years, devotes part of one chapter to an account of their Court costumes, including dragon robes.[1] At first, it tells us, the rebels dressed quite simply, but after the capture of Wuchang in 1853, when they seized and looted the Imperial storehouses, they decked themselves out in sable jackets (this was wintertime) and in all manner of rich fabrics, with no regard for rank or taste.[2] About this time, their peasant leader, Hung Hsiu-ch'üan, who called himself T'ien Wang or "Celestial King," took to wearing yellow dragon robes.[3]

A few months later the rebels captured Kiangning (Nanking), which became their "Celestial Capital," and obtained control of the factories where the Imperial satins and brocades had been woven. Taking advantage of this, the rebel Court soon issued elaborate laws for official costumes, to be made in the Imperial factories. These laws stressed dragon symbols for the higher nobles, dragons with "phoenixes" on their hats, and dragons on their robes and outer

[1] *T'ai-p'ing-t'ien-kuo yeh-shih* 5.7-12.
[2] *Ibid.*, 5.7-8.
[3] *Ibid.*, 5.8. Hung Hsiu-ch'üan's biography is given in *Eminent Chinese of the Ch'ing Period*, Vol. 1, pp. 361 ff.

jackets.[4] It is especially interesting to see that in spite of all their emphasis on pseudo-Christianity, the peasant rulers turned back to the old Imperial symbols rather than taking new ones from their professed faith. Although, as far as we know, none of the Taiping dragon robes has survived, even in Chinese museums, it is worth while to glance at the descriptions of them and see how they differed from the contemporary Ch'ing costume.

The Taiping hierarchy was divided into sixteen grades, of which the first five were nobles: four ranks of princes or "kings," and the marquises. Below these were the "Ministers of State," and descending ranks of officials, mostly military. The first six ranks had robes of yellow satin.

The T'ien Wang himself had one embroidered with nine dragons; his Prime Minister and Commander-in-chief, "the Eastern King" (first rank), had eight dragons; "The King of the North" (second rank) had seven; "The Assistant King" (third rank) had six; and the "Kings of Yen and Yü" (fourth rank) had five;[5] while the marquises and Ministers (fifth and sixth rank) had four dragons.[6]

Over these robes, the Taiping nobles and officials wore riding jackets, called *ma-kua*, corresponding to the Manchu *p'u-fu*, with circular medallions for insignia. All the nobles and highest officials had jackets of yellow. The T'ien Wang had one embroidered with eight dragon medallions, but the front center medallion held two dragons, giving him nine in all. The "Eastern King" (first rank) had eight medallions, all with single dragons; the other four "kings" (second to fourth rank) had four dragon medallions; and the nobles

[4] *T'ai-p'ing-t'ien-kuo yeh-shih* 5.8-10 (laws for hats); 5.10 (laws for robes and jackets). The text does not give any precise date for these laws, merely saying that after the Taiping rebels extended their rule to Kiangning, where brocaded robes and satins were produced, they changed their laws for costume (p. 10). Since the conquest of Kiangning was in 1853, we can assume that they were issued in that year.

[5] The" Eastern King," or *Tung Wang*, was Yang Hsiu-ch'ing; the "King of the North," or *Pei Wang*, was Wei Ch'ang-hui; the "Assistant King," or *I Wang*, was Shih Ta-k'ai; the "King of Yen," or *Yen Wang*, was Ch'in Jih-kang; and the "King of Yü," or *Yü Wang*, was Hu I-kuang.

[6] *T'ai-p'ing-t'ien-kuo yeh-shih* 5.10. Below these dragon robe wearers, the Supervisors (seventh grade) had plain yellow robes, while officials of the eighth to the sixteenth grade all had plain red robes.

and officials from marquis down to military commanders (fifth to eighth grade), had only two dragon medallions. All these jackets, even that of the T'ien Wang himself, had the characters for their wearer's rank or title inscribed in the center of the breast medallion, thus distinguishing them from any insignia worn by the Manchu nobles or officials.[7]

The "National Relatives," brothers and male cousins of the first four leaders, and the father of the "Assistant King" were to dress like the princes, presumably the one to whom each was related.[8] The women officials—of which the Taipings, as revolutionaries, had a considerable number—were to dress like male officials of the corresponding ranks.[9] None of the latter, however, held positions above the fifth or sixth grade, so very few of them could have had dragon robes.[10]

Ironically enough, so violent was the rivalry and discord among the parvenu nobles in "the Celestial Kingdom of Peace" that only about three years after these laws were made—by the end of 1856— four of the sub-kings had met violent deaths, and the fifth, "the Assistant King," was disgraced and in exile from Nanking.[11] To replace them, the T'ien Wang made his two chief generals princes of the first rank, with the titles "Brave King" and "Loyal King"; raised several members of his family who had been "National Relatives" to princes of the second rank; and created princes of the third and fourth rank in such numbers that the very titles became meaningless.[12] By the fall of Nanking in 1864, there are supposed to have

[7] *Ibid.* The officials below the rank of Commander were divided into three groups. The first group (ninth to eleventh grade) had yellow jackets with embroidered peony medallions on breast and back; the second group (twelfth to fourteenth grade) had red jackets with the embroidered peony medallions. In each case, the front medallion also had the characters for their titles, while the last group (fifteenth and sixteenth grades) merely had circles on the front and back of red jackets, with characters in them. Further distinctions were made by having the characters for the titles in gold, red, or black, depending on the rank of the wearer.

[8] Called *Kuo-tsung,* their names are given in *ibid.,* ch. 14, which presents their biographies.

[9] *Ibid.,* 5.11.

[10] *Ibid.,* 2.26-7 lists the posts that women would occupy.

[11] See *Eminent Chinese* 1.364, 367; 2.656, for accounts of the "kings'" fates.

[12] *T'ai-p'ing-t'ien-kuo yeh-shih* 2.2-6, lists a few of these appointments.

been some 2,700 of these princes, only four of whom had any real ability.[13]   There is no record to tell whether or not all of these wore the dragon robes prescribed by the laws of 1853, but if they did, the Kiangning factory must have been hard-pressed to provide them all.

Since we have only the descriptions of the patterns on the Taiping robes, but no known examples still in existence, we cannot be sure exactly how they looked. A French engraving of the T'ien Wang, first published in 1853, is sometimes reproduced as his "portrait."[14] But, as both his hat and the pattern on his robe are totally unlike those we know he actually wore in Nanking, they must have been products of the foreign artist's imagination, like most Western pictures of the Oriental scene at that period. In the absence of any definite evidence, we can only guess about the appearance of the Taiping dragon robes. We can be sure that they did not have the Manchu horsehoof cuffs, as the rebels tried to be as different from the Manchus as possible, even to the extent of cutting off their queues and letting their hair grow long. On the other hand, they could not have had excessively wide sleeves, like those of the Ming robes, as it would have been impossible to slip on the riding jackets over them. Probably these robes were cut fairly close-fitting, like the modern Chinese "long gowns," without the characteristic Manchu slits at front and rear.

Incidentally, the use of yellow, and the circular badges of rank for officials instead of squares, were apparently also adopted in defiance of the Manchus. For the Ch'ing Court, as we have seen, strictly

[13] See W. J. Hail, *Tseng Kuo-fan and the Taiping Rebellion* (New Haven and London, 1927), p. 134.

[14] This picture was originally the frontispiece of Callery and Yüan's sensational book, *L'Insurrection en Chine*, published in Paris in 1853, and later issued in English translation in London. Its most recent appearance was in P. C. Fitzgerald's *China, A Short Cultural History* (London, 1935), fig. 64, p. 575. I have been unable to find any evidence for the statement in the latter (p. 574), which says that this was "the picture of the Heavenly King circulated among his followers," and I feel that this is impossible. Quite apart from the anachronisms in the costume—particularly the hat—the characters under the portrait say *"T'ien Tê,"* and the *T'ien-Tê Wang*, or "King of Celestial Virtue," was Hung Ta-ch'üan who was another of the early Taiping leaders. Thus, even in the unlikely case that this engraving was made from an actual Chinese woodcut, it would still be the picture of another man.

limited the use of yellow, and permitted circular badges only to princes of the Imperial House.

Even though the Rebellion was crushed, and the Taipings virtually exterminated by 1866, the resentment against anything Manchu remained strong among all Chinese, except those members of the official class who were working with the alien rulers for their own interests. Although the Ch'ing Dynasty was artificially maintained —with foreign help—for half a century more, it finally collapsed in 1911. By then, the anti-Manchu feeling was so great that, outside of Peking, the revolutionaries did away with everything the Manchus had brought to China, including their elaborate costume system. From this time, the dragon robes passed out of the Chinese scene.

14

Dragon Robes in Other Lands

THE history of the use of dragon robes outside of China proper is rather difficult to trace, because of the many scattered references that must be pieced together. But it is especially interesting, if only because of the light it sheds on little-known diplomatic contacts and cultural developments in Eastern Asia during the last few hundred years.

We have seen in discussing the Ming robes that the Chinese Court during the Ming regarded the presentation of dragon robes as an instrument of diplomacy in both trade and politics. By bestowing dragon robes on friendly rulers and potential enemies, it caused their wide diffusion throughout the Oriental world. In spite of the fact that many of these gifts were never recorded in the Ming annals, we find records of their dragon robes going as far afield as Java and Arabia.[1]

Most of these robes given to foreign rulers and chieftains were probably never worn; or if they were used they must have been retailored to conform to local traditions, the way the Manchus treated the Ming robes that they obtained before the Conquest. For example, the Mongol princes probably reduced the width of the sleeves on those they received, as the Manchus did, though the horsehoof cuffs of the Manchus and their split skirts were not part of the Mongol tradition at that time.

The only historical references to the actual use of Ming robes outside of China are preserved in the annals of Liu Ch'iu and Korea.

---

[1] A dragon robe was given to the "King of Java" in 1452, at his own request (*MHT* 111.2366). But, as Java had not yet been reunited since the fall of the Kingdom of Madjapahit in 1389, this must have been merely a petty rajah assuming a big title to lend weight to his demand. The dragon robe that went to Arabia was sent to the Sherif of Mecca in 1518 (*Ming shih* 332.14).

Yet, so sketchy are the Ming records that they make no direct mention of dragon robes ever having been given to the kings of these two countries.

The King of the Liu Ch'iu Islands, reigning from the island now called Okinawa, may have been among the first of the alien rulers to get a Ming dragon robe. A somewhat vague reference in a description of gifts from the Chinese Emperor to the King of Liu Ch'iu in 1442 suggests that they probably included dragon robes woven with gold.[2] At any rate, some such robes must have been presented before 1471, for, in that year, when the leader of the tribute mission from Liu Ch'iu was apprehended and tried for wearing a robe of serge woven with *mang* dragons in gold, he "obstinately insisted" that this was a present received by the King of his country in a former reign.[3]

It is interesting to see that a Ch'ing sketch of the King of Liu Ch'iu receiving an embassy from the K'ang-hsi Emperor, in the following dynasty, pictures him wearing a full-sleeved robe of Ming cut, with large dragons on breast and back looping over the shoulders, and a pair of smaller dragons flanking the mountain below.[4] A passage in a Chinese history of Liu Ch'iu written in 1774 explains that the King wore these Ming-style robes only when receiving envoys from China; on other occasions he wore the national dress of Liu Ch'iu, in which the type and quality of jeweled hairpins and cloth belts marked the chief distinctions in rank.[5]

We would naturally infer from the last passage that dragon robes were essentially alien to the Liu Ch'iu culture. However, a late seventeenth-century native portrait of a Crown Prince of Liu Ch'iu named Shang Ch'un suggests that the highest members of the royal family sometimes recut the Ch'ing dragon robes, or retailored the dragon satins, to make a new style of dragon robe. This portrait shows him

[2] *Liu-ch'iu-kuo chih-lüeh* (1774) 3.19b. As in other records of Ming tribute gifts, it seems possible that *hsi* (Giles, no. 4142) has here been miswritten for *lung-i* (Giles, nos. 7479, 5385).

[3] *Ibid.*, 3.24.

[4] *Chung-shan ch'uan-hsin lu* 2.28.

[5] *Liu-ch'iu-kuo chih-lüeh* 4b.17.

wearing a cloud-figured robe bordered in gold brocade, with a white shawl collar, and very full sleeves. The upper decoration, contained in a four-lobed field, has a large *mang* dragon extending across each shoulder, while a band of profile dragons ornaments each sleeve, and a similar band crosses the skirt below the knees. On the whole, this pattern is unlike anything we know from contemporary China. The Prince wears a Liu Ch'iu ceremonial hat, and his attendants carry Japanese pikes as symbols of power, while a pair of Japanese curtains sets off the picture. In short, the portrait gives an excellent example of the synthesis of cultures in this small island kingdom under the influence of two powerful neighbors.[6]

We do not know how early the Ming Emperors began giving dragon robes to the Kings of Korea. The first references to a Ming presentation robe in the Korean annals date from the later sixteenth century, but there may have been previous gifts. These particular records are especially interesting because they illustrate the excessive veneration of a tributary king for a gift from the Emperor of China, therefore we shall quote from them here.

In a letter to the Wan-li Emperor written in 1588, the Korean king wrote:

> The Rites declare that when a sovereign bestows clothing, one must wear it in order to do homage for the gift, thereby honoring the sovereign's favor. Last year [you] the Ming Emperor bestowed on me a mang robe. I placed it on the sleeping couch, and morning and evening I raised my hands and worshipped it. But I was afraid, and did not dare to wear it. Now I am preparing to venerate the former Kings, and I am about to wear it in order to honor my ancestors.

The annals add: "Thereupon he put on the dragon robe and went to pray at the Temple of [his] Ancestors."[7]

The sentiments expressed in this letter were apparently not mere rhetorical expressions of abasement from a lesser Oriental ruler to his overlord, if we may judge from the king's subsequent attitude toward this robe. Four years later, when the Japanese under Hide-

---

[6] This portrait is reproduced in the *Dai hyakka jiten* (Tokyo, 1934), plate facing p. 241, fig. 1.

[7] *TPMHPK* 174.24b-25. (79.8b has slightly different wording.)

yoshi invaded his kingdom, forcing him to flee into Manchuria, it was the only thing he took with him. In another letter to the Ming Emperor, written in 1596, he tells about it, saying:

> When I hurriedly fled westward [in 1592] the things in the Palace were all abandoned. I left empty-handed except for the imperially-conferred dragon robe, for I decided that at the time of my death I must put on this robe to die. I still have it, and sometimes when I spread it out to look at it, I cannot help letting the tears fall.[8]

As far as we know, this is the first specific mention of a dragon robe in Korean history, although as long ago as 1043 A.D. a King of Korea had forbidden his subjects to wear clothes with golden dragon patterns, indicating that robes with dragons must have been in use at that time, and that he wished to keep them a royal monopoly.[9]

The Manchu relations with Korea antedated their conquest of China, and also involved dragon robes. Early in the seventeenth century, when Nurhachi began the custom of presenting dragon robes and dragon satins, he first gave them to the friendly Mongol chieftains who were his allies, but his first gift of Manchu dragon robes to foreigners was made to Koreans.

This was in 1627, when the younger brother of the King of Korea, who had been brought back to Manchuria after the Manchu invasion of his country, was about to return home. Among the gifts presented to him—for himself, for the other members of the party, and for the King, his brother—were a pair of red satin *mang* robes for the Prince and a Korean Minister of State who was with him. The Manchus requested them to put on their newly bestowed dragon robes to express their gratitude to Nurhachi.[10]

This resulted in a minor diplomatic incident. The Prince and the Minister replied, "Dragon robes are for our King to wear. There are regulations that officials cannot wear them. We would be overstepping the bounds of duty to dress in them." And they refused to put them on.

---

[8] *Ibid.*, 79.8b-9.

[9] *Ibid.*, 80.3. See Chapter 1, Note 13, for more details.

[10] The *Man-chou mi-tang*, p. 125, describes these presents along with the other gifts.

Several of the Manchu officers became angry and taunted them with having a fear of Ming China and insufficient respect for their "Emperor's" gifts. Finally, when one had threatened them that they probably would not be allowed to leave unless they complied, the two Koreans obeyed, and put on their newly-given dragon robes and fur jackets to go and express their gratitude for the presents.[11]

The memory of this humiliation may have combined with the Koreans' deep veneration for Chinese civilization and their contempt for the "barbarian usurpers," in reinforcing their decision to retain their Chinese type of dress rather than change to Manchu styles. In the Yüan their ancestors had worn the Mongol costume, and as vassals of the Ming they had felt compelled to change back to Chinese styles. Now, as vassals of the Manchus, they might have been expected to adopt the Manchu dress. However, the Manchus did not insist on this, as they did in the case of the Chinese, being content to accept Korea as a "younger brother nation" with its own laws and customs.

Though they clung to their hats and robes of Ming cut, the Koreans made some alterations from time to time. For example, beginning in the mid-seventeenth century, we read of a distinctly Korean form of dragon robe called *ryong-po*. Although the words are the same as the Ch'ing expression *lung-p'ao,* these robes were very different from the dragon robes of Ming or Ch'ing. They were full-cut like the Ming robes, yet had very small badges of rank, like the Later Ch'ing insignia. For this reason, we shall use the term "dragon robe" in quotes when referring to them. The first reference to these is in a law of 1649, which says that the King's grandsons should wear "dragon robes" with square dragon plaques, omitting those on the shoulders.[12] From this we can infer that the King and his sons had robes with dragon badges,—probably circular—on their shoulders, as well as on breast and back.

When the Korean statutes were re-issued in 1751, they said that the King's "dragon robe" should be of dark red satin, having

[11] This episode is described in *ibid.,* pp. 125-27, and in the *Tung-hua lu, T'ien-ts'ung* 2.12b.
[12] *TPMHPK* 79.9.

circular plaques with five-clawed dragons in gold on the front and back of the robe and on the shoulders; while those of his sons should be of black satin, having four circular plaques with four-clawed dragons in gold; and those of his grandsons should be of black satin with two rectangular plaques having three-clawed dragons in gold.[13] The consorts of the above had the same types of dragon plaques as their respective husbands, but their robes had other plaques as well, figured with pheasants.[14]

Finally, in 1896, when the King of Korea proclaimed himself "Emperor" to announce his country's break with both China and Japan, he followed the regulations in the Ming *Hui-tien,* and decreed for his ordinary costume a yellow robe with coiled dragons woven in gold on shoulders, breast, and back; while his son, the Heir Apparent, was to have the same kind of robe in red.[15]

Let us return to the subject of Ch'ing presentations. Soon after the Manchus entered China they broadened their tribute system to include most of the nations that had brought gifts to the Ming Court, as well as their pre-Conquest vassals, among whom were the Koreans. Like the Ming Emperors, the Manchu sovereigns rewarded the rulers of tribute-bearing nations with rich silks, and later bestowed such gifts on the envoys as well. However, they usually presented bolts of satin, including "dragon satins," rather than actual robes, probably so that they could be made up in the style of the recipients' country.

The Ch'ing records say that in 1649 the Court began the custom of presenting the rulers of tribute-bearing states with bolts of *mang* satin—along with many other gifts, of course. The first presents went to the King and Queen of Korea; two bolts of "large *mang*

---

[13] *Ibid.,* 79.15 (King), 16 (his sons), 17 (his grandsons). J. H. Longford's book, *The Story of Korea* (London, 1911), frontispiece, shows the next to last king with his son, wearing such robes. It shows that the dragon medallions were smaller than the Chinese type, and had a scalloped border.

[14] *TPMHPK* 79.15b, 16.17. This form of robe was an attempt at synthesis, combining the Ming usages of plaques for insignia and "pheasant robes" (*ti-i*) for noblewomen. In the Ming, these were never worn together.

[15] *Ibid.,* 79.18 (the "Emperor," who also adopted the use of the Twelve Symbols at this time, as mentioned in Chapter 8); 79.20 (the Heir Apparent).

satin" and one bolt of "small *mang* satin" apiece.[16] The "large *mang* satin" sounds like material for an Early Ch'ing robe with bold dragon patterns, while the latter may have had merely dragon medallions.

In the succeeding years of the seventeenth century, similar gifts of dragon satins were bestowed on embassies from the Kings of Liu Ch'iu, Annam, Holland, Portugal, etc.[17] In the eighteenth century they were given to the Pope, the King of England, the Sultan of Sulu, the Prince of Vientiane (modern Laos), and the Kings of Siam and Burma, as well as to the rulers previously honored.[18] In fact, until far into the nineteenth century, dragon satins were still regularly presented to the Kings of Korea, Liu Ch'iu, Annam, Vientiane, Siam, and Burma.[19] The last gift of *mang* satin to the King of Annam was bestowed in 1877,[20] and the last to the King of Korea was given in 1886.[21]

Rarely do we find the mention of an actual robe. In 1736, the Ch'ien-lung Emperor gave the King of Siam robes with large *mang* and *lung* dragons.[22] In 1790, he gave the (usurping) King of Annam, who had come to Jehol for the Emperor's eightieth birthday, several "robes of *mang* satin" and at least three *mang-p'ao,* one of which was golden yellow, in addition to the usual gifts of *mang* satins.[23] On the same occasion, the young Crown Prince of Annam and other high Annamese envoys also received several *mang-p'ao* each.[24]

---

[16] *KHHTSL* 506.2.

[17] *Ibid.*, 506.2b, 4b, 8b, to Liu Ch'iu (in 1654, 1664); 4b, to Annam (in 1661, 1664); 3, 5, 5b, to Holland (in 1656, 1664, 1667); 6, 6b, to Portugal, simply called "The Western Nation," *Hsi-yang Kuo* (in 1670, 1678).

[18] *Ibid.*, 506.10b, 11, to the Pope (Benedict XIII, in 1725); 12b, to Sulu (in 1727); 14b, etc., to Vientiane (in 1729, etc.); 507.1, etc., to Siam (1736, etc.); 12, etc., to Burma (in 1788, etc.); 25-29b to England (1793).

[19] *Ibid.*, 509, *passim*.

[20] *Ibid.*, 509.24b. It is interesting to note that Annam was still sending tribute to China in 1877, in spite of the fact that, three years before, she had signed a treaty with France that amounted in effect to a transfer of allegiance from China to France.

[21] *Ibid.*, 509. 25.

[22] *Ibid.*, 507.1.

[23] *Ibid.*, 507.14 ff.

[24] *Ibid.*, 507.15b ff.

Along with these dragon robes, the Annamese ruler and the courtiers who accompanied him in 1790 were also given Manchu official hats, belts, *p'u-fu* jackets, and other accessories of dress, perhaps in an effort to persuade the court of Annam to adopt the Ch'ing costume.[25] But we have no evidence that the Indo-Chinese ever actually wore these Manchu-style dragon robes. Ever since the Annamese adopted traditional Chinese court dress in 1744, they had considered themselves as being the cultural heirs of Ming, or pre-Manchu China,[26] and this tradition remained strong. Accordingly, even though the dragon robes given them in 1790 apparently did induce the Annamese to borrow the custom of wearing dragon robes (unless perhaps they already had such robes of their own), the patterns on them were by no means slavish copies of the Ch'ing styles—nor were they characteristic of the Ming, either. In fact, the patterns of the Annamese dragon robes were so distinctly unlike those used in China that it seems obvious that these people must have woven and embroidered their own satins, and, for these robes at least, did not utilize the satins given to them in exchange for tribute.[27] This is what we might expect, for in all their copying of things Chinese, the Annamese never seem to have been slavish imitators. Whatever they borrowed from their great Northern neighbor was usually soon altered to conform to their own national genius and was expressed in a more ornate yet delicate style, which may have been due to the influence of the tropical environment.

We cannot tell precisely how early dragon robes came to be an integral part of the Annamese costume tradition, as we have no native records from eighteenth-century Annam. The first detailed laws for costume available to us are those which were issued by the Gia-long "Emperor" at the beginning of the nineteenth century,

[25] In "Development of the Mandarin Square" (p. 118), the date of these presentations was wrongly given as 1786, instead of 1790. The occasion was the eightieth birthday of the Ch'ien-lung Emperor.
[26] In "Development of the Mandarin Square" (p. 118), because of a misprint, the date of the Annamese adoption of Chinese court dress was wrongly given as 1774, instead of 1744.
[27] For an account of Annamese embroidery techniques, see the *Revue Indochinoise,* Vol. 5 (1907), pp. 634-36.

after he had driven out the usurping royal family with French aid, and had founded a new dynasty, the Nguyen.[28]

According to these regulations, the "Emperor" of Annam had a number of robes with five-clawed dragon patterns. No one of these is specifically called a dragon robe, however, and from the descriptions given it is difficult to determine which of these were true dragon robes, with bold dragon patterns. One which seems to refer to a dragon robe speaks of a robe made of "true yellow" gauze or satin, embroidered with large and small dragons, clouds, waves, and *fu* and *shou* characters.[29] Photographs of Annamese "Emperors" of this dynasty show yellow robes with twelve five-clawed dragons; one apiece on chest and back and on each shoulder, two at the front and two at the back of the skirt, and a pair on each sleeve. The base of these robes had the world-mountain jutting from the waves, which sweep outward in rolling curves.[30]

As a rule, Indo-Chinese dragon robes have little or no *li shui* striping, but photographs of recent "Emperors" show exceptions, with a considerable band of stripes along the lower border. These photographs also show very large *shou* medallions on the "Emperor's" robes,[31] and as *shou* characters are not mentioned in descriptions of robes below the rank of "Emperor" and "Empress," it would appear that the use of this symbol may have been an imperial prerogative in Annam, as it seems to have been in China, during the later Ch'ing.

By a law of 1816, the Crown Prince of Annam was to wear a dragon robe of scarlet with five-clawed *lung* dragons.[32] A photo-

[28] These laws are recorded in Chapter 78 of the *Dai-nam hoi-dien siek-le,* a copy of which is in the Bibliothèque Nationale in Paris. The writer is very grateful to M. Jean-Pierre Dubosc, who arranged to have this chapter microfilmed for him and sent to this country. This source will hereafter be abbreviated as *DNHDSL.*

[29] *DNHDSL* 78.2.

[30] *BAVH* Vol. 9 (1922), p. 312.

[31] See the photograph of Emperor Dong-Khanh (1885-86) in *BAVH,* Vol. 28 (1941), pl. 61, facing p. 308; and the much better one of Khai-Dinh, at his coronation in 1916, in *Revue Indo-chinoise,* Vol. 19 (1916), facing p. 10. Note the large *shou* characters on the breasts of their robes and the smaller ones on each sleeve. These robes do not appear to be yellow, but—as in China—the "Emperor" could and did use other colors.

[32] *DNHDSL* 78.9b.

graph of a later Crown Prince shows him wearing two less dragons than the "Emperor," since the main ones on chest and back curled over the shoulders in Ming style, leaving no room for separate shoulder dragons.[33]

The "Emperor's" other sons, and other princes who were his immediate relatives, had scarlet dragon robes with four-clawed *mang* dragons.[34] A photograph of the Prince Regent of Annam, taken in this century, shows him in a robe with two very large, and four smaller dragons on the body of the robe, but none on the sleeves, making six in all.[35] This was probably the usual type of robe for royal princes.

Still lesser princes, and dukes of upper and middle ranks, had "Four Spirits" dragon robes, which, in addition to two large dragons, had the "phoenix," the *ch'i-lin,* and the tortoise.[36] This type of robe was a characteristically Annamese development, not found elsewhere as far as we know, and as such it will be described at greater length below. Variations in rank were indicated by color.[37]

Dukes of the lowest ranks and upper-rank marquises wore dragon robes with *chiao* dragons.[38] In China, the *chiao* was traditionally a young dragon, usually represented with a single horn. Unfortunately, we have never seen an Annamese example and do not know what special distinguishing features it had, besides its smaller size, to differentiate it from the *lung* and *mang* varieties.

By the laws of 1806, Annamese officials of the first three ranks, civil and military, all had purple robes with *mang* dragons,[39] while the military officials of the fourth rank, principal grade, had robes

[33] *BAVH* Vol. 9 (1922), p. 312, and pl. 79 (opposite).

[34] *DNHDSL* 78.10.

[35] *BAVH,* Vol. 18 (1931), pl. 24, facing p. 118.

[36] *DNHDSL* 78.13b-14b.

[37] The robes of the lesser princes were "true orchid", those of upper-rank dukes were "great scarlet," and those of middle-rank dukes were "the color of purple sandalwood."

[38] *DNHDSL* 78.15-15b. The dragon robes of the lowest-rank dukes and highest-rank marquises were of a shade of gold ("sparrow gold"), and those of middle-rank marquises were of "crimson red". Marquises of lesser rank merely had robes with floral patterns.

[39] *Ibid.,* 21 ff.

with *chiao* dragons.[40] However, a decree of 1831 indicates that by then, if not earlier, officials of the first three ranks were also wearing "Four Spirits" robes.[41] By the revised laws for official dress issued in 1845, officials of the first three ranks were formally required to wear "Four Spirits" robes, with different colors to distinguish not only between ranks but also between the principal and subordinate grades within each rank.[42] These colors have very poetic names which are difficult to translate, and do not give any very clear idea of what the colors actually were.[43]

The use of nuances of color on dragon robes to distinguish not only the ranks of nobles and officials, but their subdivisions as well, was an un-Chinese, purely Annamese contribution. It reached its height of development at a time when the Nguyen Dynasty was already showing symptoms of the decay that was to cause Annam to fall so easily under French domination. As in China during the Ch'ien-lung period, the vigor of the dynasty had dissipated, and the more effete descendants of the illustrious founders were content

[40] *Ibid.*, 22b. Officials below the third civil rank, or the fourth military rank, principal grade, could not wear dragon robes. The officials immediately below these ranks, for example, had robes with floral patterns, and those still lower had plain robes.

[41] *Ibid.*, 25b.

[42] *Ibid.*, 27b-28.

[43] The variations in color on the Annamese officials' dragon robes are discussed by Nguyen Don in "Costumes de Cour des Mandarins civils et militaires," *BAVH,* Vol. 3 (1916), pp. 321-23. This work leaves much to be desired, especially in his rendering of Chinese and Annamese terms into French. For example, when he tries to give the names of the birds and animals worn on the mandarin squares, he reaches heights of inaccuracy and confusion, which are only partially resolved by the presence of Chinese characters accompanying one of his plates. However, in the case of colors of robes which he has actually seen, it would seem safe to trust his descriptions.

The first rank, principal grade, had "antique bronze", which he describes as an iridescent golden brown with a greenish tinge; while the first rank, subordinate grade, had "heavenly black," which he describes as a shade of dark purple (probably it was the equivalent of the Ch'ing "stone black," *shih-ch'ing*). The second rank, principal, had "violet jade," which he describes as a reddish blue; while the second rank, subordinate, had "official green." The third rank, principal, had "sapphire blue"; while the third rank, subordinate, had "jade blue," which he describes as a light greenish blue.

Note that this distinction of dress between principal and subordinate grades is peculiar to Annam. In China, all the officials of a given rank always wore the same costume, with no means of distinguishing their principal or subordinate status.

to occupy themselves with minute details of protocol and court etiquette.

An equally distinctive native development in Annam was the "Four Spirits" robe. This displayed a group of four creatures from Chinese folklore—the dragon and "phoenix," *ch'i-lin*, and tortoise. Collectively known in China as the *szŭ ling*, they are called *tu linh* in Annamese. Although the dragons on these were very large and continued on over the shoulders like those on the Ming robes, they resembled the Ming imperial dragons rather than those of Ming officials, having their heads shown fullface instead of in profile. The "phoenixes" were shown in pairs on the very full sleeves, with the peony flowers usually associated with them in later Chinese art, one on the front and one on the back. A pair of confronted *ch'i-lins* was placed just below the waist at the front and rear of the robe, where the Ming robes had had the smaller dragons on a horizontal band. Lower yet, just above the waves at the bottom of the skirt, stood a pair of tortoises, each exhaling a puff of vapor, in which was materialized a sword and a book.

The sword and book, along with the tortoise, form a distinctive symbol combination which distinguishes Annamese dragon robes from any made in China proper.[44] As such, they deserve special mention. The book alone is commonly associated with the tortoise in Indo-Chinese art to symbolize the wisdom supposed to have been gained from this animal by China's legendary Yellow Emperor,[45] but the sword could have no place in this legend. Again, a sword and book were both included in the Indo-Chinese version of the Eight Precious Things (*bat buu*).[46] However, as no other of these eight was worn—in fact, no lucky symbols at all—this is probably not the explanation, either. Very likely the sword and book merely symbolized literary arts and martial skill, the respective functions of the two main classes of officials who wore these robes. Shown with

[44] Illustrated in Nguyen Don's article; but a more accessible example is in Boudet and Masson, *Iconographie de l'Indo-chine française* (Paris, 1931), pl. 76.
[45] See L. Cadière, "L'Art à Hué," *BAVH*, Vol. 6 (1919), p. 98 and pl. 176 (opposite).
[46] *Ibid.*, p. 62.

the tortoise, they could have signified wisdom in these two fields of endeavor.

The pattern on the Annamese "Four Spirits" robes is completed by the sacred flaming pearl that is always associated with the dragon in China.[47] It occupies the center of the robe, at front and back, just below the main dragons, and above the *ch'i-lins* who stare up at it.[48]

By a law of 1838, the costume of an official's wife should conform to her husband's rank, while the dress of father, mother, and sons of an official should correspond to the rank below his.[49] As far as the women were concerned, this law did not affect the wearing of drag-on robes or "Four Spirits" robes, as such robes were apparently never worn by women in Annam. For example, the "Empress" and all noblewomen had robes with "phoenixes" or floral patterns,[50] and the wives and mothers of officials seem to have worn the latter. But the father and sons of a first- or second-rank official presumably could legally wear the dragon robes or "Four Spirits" robes of second- and third-rank officials, respectively.

All the Annamese dragon robes, including the "Four Spirits" variety, originally had very full sleeves and broad skirts slit at the sides, like the robes of Ming China. However, in the twentieth century at least, the skirts have been cut much shorter, about knee length, and changes have been made in the military robes to make them trimmer looking. For example, while the robes of the civil officials retained the simple, round collar, the full sleeves, and the wide, hoop belt of the old tradition, the robes of the military officials were given high collars, close-fitting sleeves, and tight belts, so that

[47] In Indo-China, the meaning of the flaming pearl seems rather confused. Though shown with a complete aura of flames (instead of a mere flame wisp as in China), which gives it the appearance of a solar symbol, it is usually said to be identified with the moon in Annam (*ibid.*, p. 61). Possibly the active flames behind the passive moon disc are combined to suggest the sun and moon in conjunction, an ancient and elemental *yin-yang* concept.

[48] The patterns for the civil and military officials were the same throughout, except for the sleeves. The narrow sleeves on the later military robes did not leave room to show the "phoenixes," so they had simple cloud motifs instead.

[49] *DNHDSL* 78.30.

[50] *BAVH*, Vol. 11 (1924), pl. 72, facing p. 202 (portrait of the Empress-Dowager Nguyen-Huu-Do); and Vol. 21 (1934), pl. 63, facing p. 166 (portrait of an Annamese Princess).

in form, if not in pattern and colors, they bore a closer resemblance to European military tunics.[51]

On all ceremonial occasions, the officials were supposed to wear outer coats over these dragon robes, like the *p'u-fu* jackets of Ch'ing China. For solemn Court functions, they wore red outer robes, and for less formal occasions, robes of blue with their squares of rank (copied after the Ch'ing mandarin squares, but with a slightly different sequence of birds and animals). In this century, however, courtiers at Hué and many of the military officials have often appeared at outdoor ceremonies without their outer robes, possibly because they found that their French overlords were more impressed by the greater splendor in the patterns of the dragon robes themselves.

As we have said, it seems probable that the Ch'ing Court usually presented bolts of dragon satin to foreign rulers and their envoys, rather than the made-up robes, because they realized that other countries had other styles of dress. Perhaps it was also because they had no idea of the size of the recipients. In this way they at least avoided unpleasant situations such as the time when the Ming Court sent the King of Korea a set of sacrificial robes that were too large for him to wear.[52]

However, it was also customary in the Ch'ing to give actual robes as well as bolts of dragon satin to important vassals within the Empire, such as the Mongol nobles of Inner and Outer Mongolia and Chinese Turkistan, when they came to Peking for special audiences with the Emperor, or on tribute missions. While all the Mongol tribes of the regions mentioned were not subjugated by the Manchus until the latter part of the eighteenth century, a goodly

[51] For the older, full-skirted type, see *BAVH,* Vol. 17 (1930), pl. 32. For the more modern, short-skirted type, see *BAVH,* Vol. 26 (1939), pls. 30b and 31 (facing pp. 138, 140), and *National Geographic Magazine,* Vol. 60 (1931), No. 2, pl. 11. The last shows the official on the left, in the right-hand picture, wearing what appears to be a recut Ch'ing dragon robe; but its distinctive collar and narrow sleeves would prevent it from being mistaken for a Chinese robe. See also Note 48, above.

[52] *TPMHPK* 79.8b. This was in 1596, after the Ming Emperor had sent a new set of sacrificial robes to replace those lost in the Japanese invasion of Korea.

number of them had been allies and vassals of the Manchus for some time before the conquest of China. In token of this, the Ch'ing Court decreed in 1661 that Mongol princes and *beiles* (lesser princes) should have clothing and insignia corresponding to the Manchu princes of the same ranks,[53] and from that time this became the recognized custom.[54]

As a rule, the Mongol princes were expected to obtain their own robes, as were the Manchu courtiers, but we find records of many bestowals. In 1691, for example, when a prince of the Khalkas from Outer Mongolia first paid tribute to Peking, he was given a fine robe made of dragon satin and fox skins.[55] In 1723, four principal Mongol princes were presented with five-clawed dragon robes of satin, among other gifts.[56] In 1754, the Court made definite laws for bestowing Imperial *mang* satins on princes of the frontier,[57] but this did not end the giving of actual robes, and in the early nineteenth century (in the reign of Chia-ch'ing) especially, we find several instances of the bestowal of *mang* dragon robes as well as dragon satins on the Mongol princes of Turkistan.[58]

In addition to these gifts on the occasion of visits to Peking or on tribute missions, many of the Mongol nobles, in their role as fathers-in-law of members of the Manchu ruling house, were given court robes for part of the official dowry,[59] while dragon robes and

---

[53] *KHHTSL* 992.6. In Inner Mongolia, the nobles of the highest rank had the title of *Jassak,* of which there were six degrees, corresponding to Manchu princes of the first, second, third, and fourth degrees, and first and second degree Imperial dukes. In practice, the first and second degree jassaks were usually called *wang* like the highest Manchu princes, and sometimes lesser ones were also given this title by courtesy. The second group of Inner Mongolian nobles had the title of *Taiji* (or *Tabnang*), of which there were four degrees, equivalent in rank to Chinese and Manchu officials of the first and fourth ranks. (See the Kuang-hsü *Hui-tien,* 64.1b-2b.) In Outer Mongolia (and Turkistan), the higher nobles had the titles of *Khan* (superior prince), *Beile* or *Beitze* (lesser princes), *Kung* (duke), and *Taiji* (*ibid.,* 66.3).

[54] *KHHTSL* 992.5b, and Kuang-hsü *Hui-tien* 64.9.

[55] *KHHTSL* 990.15-15b.

[56] *Ibid.,* 990.6b-7.

[57] *Ibid.,* 990.8b-9.

[58] *Ibid.,* 990.6, 10b, 12b.

[59] *KHHT* 49.10b, 13.

dragon jackets were given to the (Mongol) mothers-in-law of first-
or second-degree Manchu princesses.[60]

It is important to note that the conservatism of the Mongol
nobles, together with the absence of a silk industry in Mongolia,
and their inability to get new robes from Peking with any great
frequency, led them to wear dragon robes of older types long after
they had gone out of style in China.[61] The same conservative
spirit also caused the persistence of dragon robes in Mongolia after
they had died out in China. Whereas dragon robes disappeared
from the Chinese scene (except in Peking) after the Revolution of
1911, the Mongols of rank continued to wear them, and the princes
of the Inner Mongolian banners who were under the rule of the
Japanese during the recent war still donned dragon robes with
p'u-fu jackets for special occasions.[62]

Not only did the secular nobles of Mongolia wear dragon robes,
but the dignitaries of the Lama Church were also permitted to wear
them. By a law of 1655, the higher lamas of Mongolia and Tibet
who had the title of *Gelung* were allowed to wear yellow robes, but
unless they were especially granted the right to wear five-clawed
dragons by the Emperor of China, they had to wear the four-clawed
mang.[63] As far as we know, the only lamas who were permitted
to wear the five-clawed dragon, when it was still a highly restricted
privilege to do so, were the Dalai and Panchen Lamas of Tibet,
and the Jebtsun-dampa Hutukhtu, the Grand Lama of Urga. In
1694 the Court decided that these three heads of the Lama Church
should be permitted to receive Imperial five-clawed dragon satins
in return for their tribute.[64]

Tibet was not conquered by the Manchus until 1720, and did not
come firmly under their control until 1793. As early as 1648, how-

[60] *Ibid.,* 49.10b, 12.
[61] Kozlov, *Mongoliya i Amdo,* has two photographs of Living Buddhas, taken
about 1908, showing them wearing rather archaic dragon robes (pp. 397, 449).
[62] See Tokuhiro Keihin, *Mōko no jittai wo saguru* (Hsinking, Manchuria, 1938),
p. 3, top and right. For other post-1912 photographs of Mongols wearing dragon
robes, see *National Geographic Magazine,* Vol. 39 (1921), pp. 512, 515.
[63] *KHHT* 48.15.
[64] *KHHTSL* 1213.13b-14.

ever, long before the physical conquest, Tibetan dignitaries had sent tribute missions to the Manchu Court and had received dragon satins among other presents.[65] We have already seen that the Dalai and Panchen Lamas were sent five-clawed dragon satins in return for tribute, and when further details of tribute protocol were worked out in 1713, it was decided that the Panchen Lama's envoy should receive a piece of golden yellow *mang* satin, while the Dalai Lama's vice-envoy, and the principal ambassador of the Living Buddha of Chamdo in Eastern Tibet, were each to get a piece of "third grade *mang* satin."[66] In this way a limited amount of dragon satins entered Tibet each year, and the Tibetan nobles—both princes of the Church and the lay nobles, their relatives—came to acquire a taste for dragon-figured robes, and proudly wore them for special occasions.

The recipients of the satins apparently had them made up locally in their own national style, for the dragon robes worn by the Tibetans differed from those of Ch'ing China in cut. They featured a plain shawl collar and long narrow sleeves without cuffs, extending a foot or so beyond the hands of the wearer, and had unslit skirts. In short, they resembled the robes worn by the Mongols of the Yüan, suggesting a survival from the long period of Mongol domination over Tibet, which was not terminated until 1720.

Dragon robes, especially yellow ones, are still highly prized in Tibet. A modern book on that country, citing the sumptuary laws that regulate the quality, material, and color of the clothing worn by each class of Tibetans, remarks: "All lamas may wear some yellow in their robes. Indeed, the Dalai and Tashi Lamas' entire dress is often of this color; but among all the laymen only those with the titles of *Kung* (duke) or *Shap-pé* (Chief Minister) may wear this royal yellow. The pattern is also regulated, the only

[65] *KHHT* 74.12.
[66] Kuang-hsü *Hui-tien* 67.13b, and *KHHTSL* 990.16-16b. The latter says that the Panchen's envoy received a golden yellow *mang* robe. However, the last word seems to be a mistake here, as it was not customary to give the actual robes to Tibetans, much less to lesser dignitaries such as this, and golden yellow robes were a prerogative of high Manchu nobles.

persons being permitted to wear robes with dragon designs being of these two ranks." [67]

Modern photographs of the highest Tibetan nobles in Lhasa show them wearing magnificent robes of surprisingly archaic pattern.[68] One in particular is outstanding, not only because it is unusual, but also because it provides evidence for another type of Early Ch'ing pattern. The front of the robe has two large facing dragons, with their heads on either side of the wearer's chest, extending down the robe on either side. Two smaller dragons ornament the shoulders, and two very small dragons flank the five-peaked mountain at the bottom of the skirt. The waves are bold but not curling, and there is no sign of *li shui*. The lapels and lower sleeves show parts of other dragons, apparently having been made from pieces of another robe.[69] It seems certain that the pattern on the robe proper must date back to the K'ang-hsi period.

We have also seen two pictures of robes with the Early Ch'ing pattern of Type 3, having single large dragons extending down the front and back, and slightly smaller ones reaching down each sleeve.[70] It seems quite probable that when these and other archaic patterns went out of style in China, some robes that were not yet made up were sold or given to the Tibetans and were finished in the Tibetan fashion.

Both in Tibet and Mongolia the prohibition against the wearing of dragon patterns by all except the nobles and highest churchmen was apparently waived or ignored for certain religious ceremonies, notably the "Devil Dances." For the latter, the Mongol and Tibetan lamas frequently wore modified Chinese dragon robes.[71] These had the usual eight dragons on the body of the robe, which was sometimes even of yellow. But they differed in the addition of very wide, triangular sleeves, usually ending in broad strips of red and

[67] D. Macdonald, *The Land of the Lama* (London, 1929), p. 156.
[68] F. Spencer Chapman, *Lhasa the Holy City* (London, 1938), plate facing p. 300.
[69] Liu Man-ch'ing, *K'ang-Tsang yao-chên* (Shanghai, 1933), pl. 17.
[70] *National Geographic Magazine*, Vol. 90 (1946), p. 197, shows a good example.
[71] See Sven Hedin's report of the Sino-Swedish Expedition, *History of the Expedition in Asia*, Vol. 4 (Stockholm, 1945), pl. 18, facing p. 401, and pl. 21, facing p. 412.

blue silk that swung out brightly as the lamas gyrated in the faster measures of the dance.[72] Over these robes the officiants generally wore elaborately decorated cloud collars.[73] This custom of wearing dragon robes with cloud collars is undoubtedly a survival from the Tartar costume of the Mongol Dynasty and earlier, and it recalls to us the origin of the dragon robe in Mediaeval Asia.

[72] Old Chinese court robes as well as dragon robes were sometimes remade for lama dance-robes by the addition of these triangular sleeves. The Minneapolis Institute of Arts has a good example.

[73] Examples of these lama cloud collars are illustrated in the *National Geographic Magazine,* Vol. 54 (1928), No. 5, pls. 4, 10, 11, 12, 14; and the plain photographs on pp. 608-9, 612. Most of these modern cloud collars have tended to lose the archaic scalloped form, but a good example of the traditional type, as it still persists, is shown being worn over an Early Ch'ing robe on p. 605.

Ibid., Vol. 60 (1931), No. 1, pl. 11, shows other examples of the Lama's dancing dress including dragon robes, with some good examples of the aprons often worn over them. Note that, in two cases, the aprons are decorated with mandarin squares, showing one typical fate of these badges of rank after they became obsolete in China.

15

Summary

W E began by defining a "dragon robe" as a robe on which the principal design consisted of dragons. This automatically excluded the traditional sacrificial robe of the Chinese Emperors, which has been inaccurately described by Western writers as a "dragon robe" or a "dragon-figured robe," because on the latter small dragons occupied only a minor place in the pattern, among a number of other traditional symbols.

Dragon patterns may have been used on Imperial robes during the T'ang Dynasty. This is very doubtful, however, since the only mention of them from this period merely speaks of the presence of dragon medallions on a set of robes given to princes in 694 A.D.

In the Sung, dragon-figured robes seem to have been an Imperial prerogative, at least after the year 1111. Unfortunately, however, we have no idea what they looked like, except that the dragons must have been the older, three-clawed type, and that the patterns were probably small and subtle in keeping with the spirit of the over-cultivated Court of that time. We have only one recorded instance of the presentation of a dragon robe in the Sung. This had coiled dragons worked in pearls.

Probably it was one of the contemporary Tartar dynasties in the North that developed the use of large, bold dragon patterns. The Khitan rulers of the Liao Dynasty kept dragon patterns as an Imperial monopoly, while the Ju-chên rulers of the Chin apparently had robes with dragon patterns and with cloud collars. It seems to have been the influence of this cloud collar motif that caused so many of the later robes—Yüan, Ming, and Early Ch'ing dragon robes, and Ch'ing court robes—to have the pattern on the upper robe, around the neck, in four lobes of design, extending down on the breast and back and out on the shoulders.

The Mongols of the Yüan, as heirs to the Sung and the Chin, took over the use of robes with dragon patterns as a definite institution. This was so firmly established that, even though the Ming Chinese—in reaction to foreign rule—tried to reject all Yüan innovations, the dragon robe was retained as an unofficial court costume throughout that dynasty. The earliest occurrence of the arrangement of the two main dragons on chest and back with their bodies looping back over the shoulders is shown in a Yüan Dynasty portrait, and this convention might have been a Yüan innovation. If so, it was a significant contribution, as it persisted for centuries, and has survived to the present time in Indo-China.

The Ming had several forms of robes with dragons. The principal types were: the Emperor's semiformal robes which at first had four dragon medallions, and later had twelve (eight on the outer robe, proper) along with the Twelve Symbols; the common form with the two large dragons above, and the smaller ones on the band across the skirt and on the sleeves; and the simplest type which merely had dragon squares on chest and back. All these carried over into the Early Ch'ing in somewhat altered forms, even though the style and cut of the Ch'ing dragon robes were utterly different from the traditional Chinese ones of the Ming.

An interesting feature of the dragon robe institution in the Ming was the Court's effort to keep them as an exclusive monopoly, awarding them as a mark of favor at home, while using them as an instrument of diplomacy abroad. The Ming Emperors sent them to the rulers of the spice-producing regions south of China to promote good relations for trade, and conferred them on rebellious border chieftains in the North to keep them pacified when the Chinese armies proved ineffective. So greatly were these robes prized that Chinese officials went to great lengths to have the robes conferred upon them, and foreign rulers sent in "begging letters" asking for them as gifts.

The continuation of dragon robes by the Manchus, after their conquest of China in 1644, was no real exception to their rejection of the Ming costume tradition. Dragon robes as such were not new for the Manchus, as they had been obtaining and wearing Ming dragon robes as part of their own costume for some time before they came into China. However, they altered these before wearing them, to make their own style. They cut them down to give them slimmer lines and tighter sleeves, in order to carry out their own traditions for a practical warrior's costume, and in so doing they cut off the lower sleeves of the original robes and added new ones. In short, the style of the Manchu robes, if not their patterns, was a pronounced innovation in China, and this Manchu costume tradition was imposed on the conquered Chinese along with the queue.

As the Ch'ing dragon robes were only intended for semiformal use, no laws were issued about them until the dynastic costume was formalized and made rigid as the first symptom of dynastic degeneration in the mid-eighteenth century. In spite of this, the Early Ch'ing statutes contain other laws that tell what forms of decoration could or could not be worn by different ranks. With these, together with the orders to the Imperial silk factories and the evidence provided by existing robes and portraits, we can see that at this period of great experimentation in patterns certain elements were characteristic. The use of three-clawed dragons, two principal dragons looping over the shoulders, huge giant dragons on the front and back of a robe, all the dragons in profile, and dragons that are bold and vigorous with exceptionally long jaws: any of these conventions is a reliable indication of Early Ch'ing date.

All these variants—except the three-clawed dragons—are shown in existing portraits, but only two or three actual Early Ch'ing robes, from the late seventeenth or early eighteenth centuries, are represented in our American collections. We have more robes that date from the transitional period between 1722 and 1759. During these years the new spirit of sophistication among the Manchus was causing them to lose their enthusiasm for the older, excessively bold patterns, and was creating a new interest in more subtle designs, especially of the medallion type.

The Later Ch'ing robes date from after 1759, when the Ch'ien-lung Emperor had the Board of Rites issue an illustrated book of sumptuary laws. The laws dealing with clothing dogmatically specified distinctions in patterns that made the dragon robes better indications of rank than they had previously been, while at the same time they rigidly fixed the patterns so that henceforth the only changes could be minor stylistic ones within the basic pattern. The laws of 1759 are also significant because they include the first mention of the Twelve Symbols on Ch'ing robes, indicating that these traditional Chinese emblems were introduced at this time by the Ch'ien-lung Emperor. This concession to Chinese tradition, like the fixing of the patterns against change, was a clear symptom of the decay of Manchu culture, a decay that began when to outward appearance the Ch'ing Dynasty was at the height of its power.

In time, some of the Ch'ien-lung laws were flagrantly disobeyed, notably the ones that specified the number of claws on the dragons. But the basic patterns as such were strictly maintained, without any possibility of further experimentation, until the fall of the Dynasty in 1911. As the cut of the robes was not involved in the laws, some latitude was taken in the later nineteenth century, when the cuffs were widened so that they could be turned back, but even then they retained the old horsehoof shape. Meanwhile, the succeeding issues of the Dynastic Statutes repeated the laws of 1759 almost without change. They even illustrated them with copies of the same cuts, although the latter were long out of date as regards minor stylistic details.

The majority of the robes in our American collections fall within this Late Ch'ing period from 1759 to 1912, and of course all the Twelve-Symbol robes do. We have seen that these Twelve-Symbol robes may be roughly sorted into groups and ascribed to certain emperors. However, it is not yet possible to do this with exact precision. One of the problems is the confusion between the robes of emperors and empresses, since several of the Late Ch'ing empresses also wore the Twelve Symbols; and incomplete imperial robes have been carelessly made up to sell to foreigners.

By Manchu custom, the dragon robes for women were almost the same as those for the men, made from identical materials. Except for the robes of the later empresses and highest noblewomen, who had extra bands of ornamentation on the sleeves, the only differences were in the position of the slits in the skirts. Men's dragon robes had the skirts slit front and rear for horseback riding and, in the case of nobles, at the sides as well. The women's robes, by contrast, were merely slit at the sides.

Noblewomen by the laws of 1759 wore "dragon jackets" over their dragon robes. These jackets were patterned after the robes, but had short sleeves. They seem to have been derived from an earlier garment by the same name, which was worn by noblewomen and wives of officials in Early Ch'ing; but the earlier ones differed by opening down the front, and by having long sleeves without the horsehoof cuffs. The Early Ch'ing dragon jackets are especially important in studying the evolution of the dragon robes, for they preserve evidence of several patterns that were probably used on the robes but have otherwise been lost.

Considerable space has been devoted to the symbols on the dragon robes. The comparative scarcity of extraneous symbols on the Early Ch'ing robes placed emphasis on the dragons themselves and on the elements in the background that formed a picture of the Universe, thus indicating a period of strength and purpose. Then in the mid-eighteenth century the tradition-loving Ch'ien-lung Emperor revived the use of the Twelve Symbols, showing that the Manchus were gradually succumbing to Chinese cultural influence. Ironically enough, he did this at the very time when he was urging his Manchu people to retain their national costume and resist the temptation of adopting the time-honored Chinese styles. At the same period, the Ch'ien-lung Emperor condoned, if he did not actively encourage, the development of more delicate background patterns, including an excessive number of symbols of wealth and good fortune. The latter trend seems to indicate a growing superstition among the sophisticated Manchus, who were no longer so sure of themselves. Finally, the greater sophistication and weakness in the later nineteenth century led to the development of even more elaborate symbols of luck, many of which were based on complicated puns. Some of the punning symbols are especially worth noting, because, although they are common as art motifs, they have rarely been explained.

The study of textile techniques might seem quite far removed from our historical interests; however, while briefly tracing the methods used in making the robes, we came across several items that seem to be historically significant. For example, the great variety of elaborate techniques mentioned in the Sung records suggests that the textile arts of China reached their peak in that period. Again, the little-known fact that the Manchus attempted silk-raising in the North, in the early seventeenth century, is an interesting example of their pre-Conquest assimilation of Chinese culture. Lastly, the great complexity of the Ch'ing system for manufacturing the court textiles—with its Weaving and Dyeing Office in Peking, and its factories at Hangchow, Soochow, and Kiangning (Nanking) —helps to explain why the decay of the Ch'ing bureaucracy hastened the decline of dragon robes and other textiles.

It is possible to trace the progress of the Ch'ing Dynasty as reflected in the technical execution of the dragon robes. The Early Ch'ing dragon robes show strength rather than complexity, with simple patterns strongly woven in bright colors. By contrast, those of the Ch'ien-lung period display a great variety of techniques, meticulously rendered in subtle shades. Then, after a brief period of no further progress, the later nineteenth-century robes show a rapid deterioration in weaving and embroidery, coloring, and design. The ultimate decline seems to have begun with the economic collapse that followed the foreign invasions in the middle of the century, and it was accelerated by the Taiping Rebellion.

In Part Two we have discussed a number of kinds of dragon-figured garments that were related to the official dragon robes but

actually belonged in other categories, because of being differently
made or differently used, or because they belonged to other cultures.
First among these were the "dragon coats" which were generally
worn by the wives and mothers of Chinese officials in the Ch'ing
in place of the (Manchu) women's dragon robes, and were used by
Chinese women of lower degree as part of their wedding and burial
costume. For a time, actual Ming dragon robes seem to have been
worn or else copied, but these dragon coats were generally shortened
to display the ornamental pleated skirt that was an integral part of
the costume and which assumed greater prominence towards the end
of the dynasty. The patterns tended to preserve the Ming style
quite late, only gradually changing in the absence of laws to fix
their details. Thus we find the two main dragons curling over the
shoulders and the band of smaller dragons across the skirt long
after these features had disappeared from the official Ch'ing dragon
robes.

Another kind of unofficial dragon-figured robe comprises those
worn in the Chinese dramas. We have seen that the Chinese
theater has had no tradition of historical research such as has rather
lately been developed in the West, and that, as a result, although the
costumes are vivid and colorful, they are invariably anachronistic.
Probably it is because the modern Chinese are accustomed to seeing
ancient heroes portrayed on the stage in dragon robes with recently
developed patterns that they tend to believe that such robes are of
very ancient origin, dating back to earliest Chinese history. Very
like the theatrical dragon robes, because of their similar cut and
patterns, were the dragon robes specially made to clothe images in
the temples. But these were of widely differing sizes and often had
special sleeves to facilitate attaching them to the statues.

The Manchu court robes have a dual significance in a study of
the evolution of the Ch'ing dragon robes. Not only did they have
dragon patterns too, but they also had a similar origin in the Ming
dragon robes. In spite of the latter fact, the Ch'ing court robes for
men—especially in their final form after 1759—do not appear to
bear any resemblance to the contemporary dragon robes, either in

cut or in pattern. In cut, they differed by having flaring collars and in being made in two sections, with separate jacket and skirt. In pattern, they preserved many elements from the original pre-Conquest court robes that were retailored from the Ming dragon robes, although some of the more archaic ones passed out with the change of laws in 1759. This persistence of old patterns on the court robes was due to the fact that conservative forces were much stronger in the ceremonial dress, holding them more rigidly to established forms. Meanwhile, the less formal dragon robes—especially in the Early Ch'ing period of experimentation—had been evolving new and varied patterns, which took them further and further away from the Ming prototypes. As a result, by Middle Ch'ing we find two utterly different types of robes with all traces of the original connection lost.

The Ch'ing court robes for women were apparently a later invention. They were long, one-piece gowns, with patterns conforming closely to those on the Middle Ch'ing dragon robes from which they seem to have been derived. The only exception was one type worn by the Empress and the Imperial consorts that resembled the Emperor's court robes, and this was apparently a survival from a time when Manchu noblewomen dressed like their husbands. In spite of the similarity of pattern between the women's court robes and the Middle Ch'ing dragon robes, they differed from all dragon robes in having spreading collars like those on the men's court robes, as well as projecting epaulettes. Handsomely ornamented, sleeveless "court vests" were worn over these robes to complete the women's court costume. The latter seem to have been derived from the Early Ch'ing dragon jackets and, like them, fastened down the front.

Having seen how the Late Ch'ing dragon robes and court dress expressed the decline of the dynasty in their unaltered but deteriorating patterns, their excess display of lucky symbols, and their increasingly bad workmanship, we went on to consider the Taiping Rebellion, which was a political expression of the same dynastic decay, in order to see its effect in the history of dragon robes. The Taiping rebels, by seizing the Southern industrial centers where the

Imperial silks were woven, contributed to the disintegration of the Ch'ing court and official robes, which now had to be made in the North by overtaxed workers. At the same time, the Taiping Court had its own styles of dragon robes, which are interesting for the student because they were so unlike those of the contemporary Ch'ing nobles and officials.

Lastly, we considered the subject of dragon robes worn outside of China. In spite of the rather extensive presentation of Ming dragon robes to the rulers of other nations, we have only two records of their actual use, from the annals of Liu Ch'iu and Korea. If others were used, they were probably recut, just as the Manchus altered theirs, to conform to other traditions of dress. Perhaps it was because they were aware of this that the Ch'ing Emperors usually presented bolts of dragon satin rather than the actual robes, so that the recipients could have them made up in their own fashion. During the Ch'ing period, the Koreans used "dragon robes" that were not really dragon robes in the Chinese sense but conformed more to the Ch'ing jackets with insignia; while the Court of Annam in Indo-China devised an independent tradition with distinctive dragon robes of their own design. Meanwhile, the temporal and spiritual rulers of Mongolia and Tibet cultivated a fondness for Ch'ing dragon robes that has persisted to the present time. Thus, though the tradition of dragon robes died out in China in 1911, it was still preserved in remote parts of Asia.

· · · · · ·

In looking back over the long history of the dragon robe in China, which covers nearly a thousand years from the first recorded dragon robe of the Sung to the last Manchu one, one striking thing emerges: the strength and continuity of the dragon-robe tradition. No matter whether the dynasties that ruled during this period were native or foreign, they all took to the use of dragon robes, even though these did not become part of the Chinese official costume until the seventeenth century.

In the meantime, dragon robes made a deep impression on the surrounding peoples, beyond China's borders. This is particularly vividly illustrated by the developments in the last two dynasties. Though the Ming Chinese hated the Mongols whom they supplanted, they carried on the dragon-robe tradition which their predecessors seem to have greatly developed. And again, when the Manchus took over China after the fall of the Ming, even though they proclaimed the unique national character of their own institutions, the Ming dragon-robe tradition had already pervaded their whole costume. Although the Manchus gradually modified the Ming patterns, developing some distinctive features of their own, their robes preserved vestiges of the Ming elements to the very end of their dynasty, until the impact of new forces from without changed China's old culture, wiping out the dragon-robe tradition.

BIBLIOGRAPHY OF THE PRINCIPAL
ORIENTAL SOURCES

1. *The Twenty-four Histories* (Chi'en-lung ed.) I have consulted the various dynastic histories in this collection for the pre-Ming period, and have made especial use of the *Ming shih* (ch. 67) for material on the Ming.
2. Shên Tê-fu, *Yeh-huo pien* (1606). Interesting contemporary comments on Ming costume, especially dragon robes, among essays on other topics of an antiquarian nature.
3. *Ming Hui-tien,* the Ming Dynastic Statutes *(MHT).* I have used the Commercial Press' fine modern reprint of the Wan-li edition (1587), published in the *Wan-yu wên-k'u* Collection (Shanghai, 1934).
4. *Chung-kuo li-tai ti-hou-hsiang* (Shanghai, no date), no pagination. An album of photographs of the portraits of Emperors and Empresses of the Ming and earlier dynasties, in the Palace Museum, Peking. Poor reproductions, but they still show most details.
5. *Shan-yin-chou-shan Wu-shih chih-p'u* (1919). The Wu Family History, containing interesting Ming portraits and Court scenes, etc., showing nobles and officials, eunuchs, and attendants.
6. *Ch'i-yang Wang-shih-chia wên-wu t'u-hsiang* (Peiping, 1937). The Li Family History, containing fine portraits of Ming and Early Ch'ing nobles and officials in various types of costume.
7. *Ch'ing-shih kao,* Draft History of the Ch'ing Dynasty. Ch. 109 contains information on costume, drawn from many sources.
8. *Ta Ch'ing hui-tien,* the Ch'ing Dynastic Statutes, issued in five editions (K'ang-hsi, 1690; Yung-chêng, 1732; Ch'ien-lung, 1764; Chia-ch'ing, 1818; and Kuang-hsü, 1899). The last two editions had supplements of related material, *Hui-tien shih-li,* and illustrated supplements, *Hui-tien t'u.* We have drawn most frequently from the K'ang-hsi ed. of the *Hui-tien* *(KHHT),* and the Kuang-hsü ed. of the *Hui-tien shih-li* *(KHHTSL).*
9. *Huang-ch'ao li-ch'i t'u-shih* of 1759 *(LCTS).* Invaluable for its pictorial presentation of the costume laws, with innovations made during the reign of Ch'ien-lung. Its illustrations were merely copied directly for the two editions of the *Hui-tien t'u,* mentioned above, so the latter are actually useless for studying the later developments in Ch'ing costume.
10. *Ch'ing-tai ti-hou-hsiang* (Peiping, 1934). Portraits of the Ch'ing Emperors and Empresses *(CTTHH).* Many of these portraits from the Palace Museum Collection are obvious forgeries (see Chapters 13 and 14), but the presumably authentic ones offer invaluable evidence for costume study.
11. Wang Kan, *Huang-ch'ao kuan-fu chih,* in the *Pa-shan ch'i-chung ts'ung-shu* (1865). At first glance this would seem a valuable source for material on Ch'ing costume. But it merely discusses official costume of the nineteenth century, with little more information than is given in the Chia-ch'ing *Hui-tien* and its supplements. As the author apparently lacked historical

background, it gives the false impression that these Late Ch'ing styles were characteristic of the whole dynasty, ignoring the long evolutionary development before 1759.

12. Sung Ying-hsing, *T'ien-kung k'ai-wu* (1637). A book on techniques of manufacture. It has long sections on weaving, with a description of the making of Imperial dragon robes, and on dye-making.

13. Li Shih-chên, *Pên-ts'ao kang-mu* (preface, 1590) (*PTKM*). Another valuable source on dyestuffs. In discussing medicinal plants, this source generally mentions whether they were also used for dyeing, with some description of the way in which they were employed. To find the equivalent Latin names for the Chinese trees and plants used in making dyes we have consulted the *Tz'ŭ-hai* dictionary, and the Commercial Press' splendid "Dictionary of Botanical Terms" *Chih-wu-hsüeh ta tz'ŭ-tien* (2d ed., 1923).

14. Wu Hsing and Ling Shan-ch'ing, *T'ai-p'ing-t'ien-kuo yeh-shih* (4th ed., Shanghai, 1928) (*TPYS*). Among other items concerning the Taipings is a detailed description of their official costume, including their form of dragon robes.

15. *Tsung-po mun-hön pi-ko* (Seoul, 1906), the revised edition of the Collected Statutes of Korea (*TPMHPK*). This has valuable material on Korean costume for more than a thousand years.

16. *Dai-nam hoi-dien siek-le* (place and date of publication unknown) (*DNHDSL*). The Supplement to the Collected Statutes of Annam, in Indo-China. This has a complete listing of the regulations for Annamese official dress from the founding of the last dynasty until Annam was taken over by the French. The copy of this in the Bibliothèque Nationale in Paris is the only source for Indo-Chinese court regulations in the Occident, as far as is known.

APPENDICES

Appendix A

RÉSUMÉ OF EARLY CH'ING CONVENTIONS FOR DRAGON ROBES
(BEFORE 1759)

Emperor	bright yellow, tawny yellow, blue, etc.	5-clawed or 3-clawed dragons
Heir Apparent (1676-1712)	tawny yellow	5-clawed or 3-clawed dragons
First degree princes and their sons, Second degree princes	any colors except yellow (unless that was especially conferred)	5-clawed dragons
Third and fourth degree princes, Imperial dukes, and Chinese nobles, Officials, first to fourth rank, Officers of the Imperial Guards	any colors except yellow (unless that was especially conferred)	4-clawed dragons (unless the right to use a fifth claw was conferred)
Empress	bright yellow, tawny yellow, etc.	5-clawed dragons
Imperial Consorts	any colors except yellow	5-clawed dragons

Appendix B

THE SIX BASIC TYPES OF EARLY
CH'ING DRAGON ROBES

Type 1. *Six Dragons:* two very large, with heads in profile, bodies arching over shoulders of robe; four smaller ones on skirts. Waves below.

    1a. A subtype, had the heads of the two large dragons shown fullface.

Type 2. *Two Giant Dragons:* with heads in profile, extending down the front and back of the robe. Waves below.

    2a. A subtype, had two smaller dragons down the sleeves.

    2b & c. (?) Probably these also had subtypes with the heads fullface.

Type 3. *Four Giant Dragons:* two dragons in profile extending down the front of the robe, and two more down the back, both pairs confronting. Waves below.

    3a. A subtype, had two smaller dragons down the sleeves.

Type 4. *Eight Dragons in Two Sizes:* four large ones fullface on the upper robe; four smaller profile dragons below. Waves and beginning of *li-shui*. Decorated lapel and cuffs.

    4a. A subtype, had all the dragons in profile.
    4b. The main dragons on breast and back shown fullface; the ones on the shoulders, like those on the skirts, are shown in profile.

Type 5. *Eight Dragon Medallions:* on a severely plain dark robe; four upper dragons facing, four lower ones in profile.

    5a. An early subtype, had all eight dragons in profile.
    5b. The same eight medallions against a figured background.
    5c. A later subtype, had waves added at the bottom of the robe.
    5d. The eight medallions against a cloud-filled background with waves below.

Type 6. *Eight Dragons of Approximately Same Size:* usually with a ninth under front flap of robe. Broad strip of *li-shui* below waves. Many lucky symbols in background. Decorated lapel and cuffs. This was the only type after 1759.

Appendix C

RÉSUMÉ OF LATE CH'ING LAWS FOR DRAGON ROBES (AFTER 1759)

			4 slits in skirt
Emperor	bright yellow (or other colors)	Nine 5-clawed dragons	Twelve Symbols
Heir Apparent	orange yellow	"	"
Imperial princes	golden yellow	"	"
First and second degree princes	blue or blue-black (golden yellow if specially conferred)	"	"
Third and fourth degree princes, Imperial dukes, and other nobles	blue, etc.	Nine 4-clawed dragons (unless right to fifth claw was conferred)	"
Chinese nobles, First, second, third rank officials	"	"	2 slits (front and back)
Fourth, fifth, sixth rank officials	"	Eight 4-clawed dragons	"
Seventh, eighth, ninth rank	"	Five 4-clawed dragons (officially). In practice, they apparently did not wear dragon robes.	"

Except for the Empress and Imperial Consorts (see Chapter 8), women wore dragon robes of their husband's rank, or their father's, if unmarried. But women's dragon robes differed in being slit only at the sides.

193

Appendix D

RÉSUMÉ OF MEN'S COURT ROBES AFTER 1759

These were distinguished from the "dragon robes" by flaring collars and semidetached, pleated skirts, as well as by their distinctive patterns.

Emperor

Winter 1, faced in sable, pattern on bright yellow,* 4 dragons on jackets, 6 on skirt, Twelve Symbols.

Winter 2, bright yellow,* 4 dragons on jacket, 4 on strip at waist, 6 on skirt panel, dragon medallions on pleats at top of skirt, Twelve Symbols. Trimmed in otter.

Summer, same as winter 2, but edged in gold brocade.

Heir Apparent

Same three types, but in orange yellow; 6 dragons on skirt panels of winter 1, 8 on winter 2, and eight on summer robe.

Emperor's sons

Same three types, but in golden yellow.

First and second degree princes

Same three types, but blue, blue-black, or other colors, unless bestowed golden yellow.

Third and fourth degree princes, and Imperial dukes

Same three types, blue, blue-black, or other colors, 4-clawed dragons, unless bestowed the five-clawed variety.

Chinese dukes and other nobles, first to third degree civil officials, first and second degree military officials, and first degree Imperial Guardsmen

Same three types, same rules as last, but *Hui-tien t'u* shows only 4 dragons, instead of 6, on skirt of winter robe 1.

Fourth degree civil, and third and fourth degree military officials

Only two types: winter 2, and summer robes.

Fifth, sixth, and seventh degree officials

Only one type: cloud-figured satin, with 4-clawed profile dragons in squares on breast and back.

Second degree Imperial Guardsmen

Same, except that collar and lapel, cuffs, and lower robe, are faced in dark satin, and has additional strip, with dragons, at waist.

Third degree Imperial Guardsmen

Same as second degree, except that it lacks strip of decoration at waist.

Appendix E

RÉSUMÉ OF WOMEN'S COURT ROBES AFTER 1759

These also had flaring collars, but differed from the men's in having epaulettes that projected beyond the court vests which were worn over them. In addition, they were distinguished by the extra bands of decoration on the sleeves, and (except for a few cases) different patterns.

Empress, Empress-Dowager, first degree Consorts

- Winter 1, pattern like dragon robe 1, bright yellow, 5-clawed dragons, edged in sable.
- Winter 2, patterns much like Emperor's style 2, bright yellow, 5-clawed dragons, edged in otter.
- Winter 3, like winter 1, but skirt split in rear, bright yellow, 5-clawed dragons, edged in otter.
- Summer 1, like winter 2, bright yellow, 5-clawed dragons, edged in brocade.
- Summer 2, like winter 3 (skirt split in rear), bright yellow, 5-clawed dragons, edged in brocade.

Second and third degree Consorts
- Same five styles, but golden yellow, with 5-clawed dragons.

Fourth degree Consorts
- Same five styles, but tawny yellow, with 5-clawed dragons.

Heir-Apparent's Consort
- Same five styles, but orange yellow, with 5-clawed dragons.

Wives and daughters of first and second degree princes
- Two robes: winter robe like Empress' winter 3, but of tawny yellow. Summer robe (like Empress' summer robe 2) but tawny yellow.

Wives and daughters of third and fourth degree princes and imperial dukes; wives of Chinese nobles and first, second, and third rank officials
- Same two types, but blue, blue-black, or other colors, with 4-clawed dragons.

Wives of fourth to seventh rank officials
- One type of court robe: blue, blue-black, or other colors, with two confronting, profile dragons on front and back, respectively, edged in brocade; plain collar.

195

Appendix F

LAWS FOR MANDARIN SQUARES

1. Civil Officials

Rank	Early Ming China (1391-1527)	Later Ming (1527-1644)	Ch'ing (1652-1911)	Annam (19th century)
First	crane or golden pheasant	crane	crane	crane
Second		golden pheasant	golden pheasant	crane
Third	peacock or wild goose	peacock	peacock	golden pheasant
Fourth		goose	goose	peacock
Fifth	silver pheasant	silver pheasant	silver pheasant	wild goose
Sixth	egret or mandarin duck	egret	egret	silver pheasant
Seventh		mandarin duck	mandarin duck	egret
Eighth	oriole or quail	oriole	quail	mandarin duck
Ninth		quail	paradise flycatcher	quail
Unclassed officials	paradise flycatcher	paradise flycatcher	—	—

2. MILITARY OFFICIALS

Rank	Ming China (1391-1644)	Early Ch'ing (1652-)	Later Ch'ing (-1911)	Annam (19th century)
First	lion	lion	chʻi-lin (after 1662)	chʻi-lin
Second	lion	lion	lion	pai-tse [1]
Third	tiger and/or leopard	tiger	leopard (after 1664)	lion
Fourth	tiger and/or leopard	leopard	tiger (after 1664)	tiger
Fifth	bear	bear	bear	leopard
Sixth	panther [2]	panther	panther	bear
Seventh	panther	panther	rhinoceros (after 1759)	panther
Eighth	rhinoceros	rhinoceros	rhinoceros	sea horse
Ninth	sea horse [3]	sea horse	sea horse	rhinoceros

[1] This was a mythical horned lionlike animal that had been used in the Ming for nobles' squares. See "The Development of the Mandarin Square," p. 108.

[2] On previous occasions the writer has followed Occidental custom in calling this animal a "tiger cat." This name is misleading and incorrect.

[3] This is actually a horse. See "Development," p. 110 and fig. 11b.

197

Appendix G

WOMEN'S STOLES AS INDICATIONS OF RANK

The Ming stoles for ladies of rank had carefully prescribed patterns. By the Early Ming laws:

The Empress' stole had a pattern of dragons

Imperial concubines, wives of princes, and princesses had "phoenixes"

Wives of dukes, marquises, earls, and of first and second rank officials had tartar pheasants

Wives of third and fourth rank officials had peacocks

Wives of fifth rank officials had mandarin ducks

Wives of sixth and seventh rank officials had paradise flycatchers

Wives of eighth and ninth rank officials had flowers

Late Ming portraits show the birds on the stole the same as those on the squares of rank, though they still served as indications of rank in themselves. In the Ch'ing, on the other hand, the stoles seem never to have had any relation to the rank of the wearer. The stoles of Chinese officials' wives in Early Ch'ing often had gold medallions enclosing various flowers or birds. Later, the stoles often had dragons (de Groot, *Religious System* 1, pl. 5), and sometimes they bore all nine birds of the civil ranks (see Appendix F, Part 1, Col. 3).

GLOSSARY

GLOSSARY

ORIENTAL BOOK TITLES: CHINESE, JAPANESE, ANNAMESE, AND KOREAN

ien shuo by Chou Tun-i, 周敦頤, 愛蓮說.

-kiang mi-chüan chang-ch'êng 浙江來捐章程.

i-yang Wang-shih-chia wên-wu t'u-hsiang 歧陽王世家文物圖像.

h-chin-chai ts'ung-shu 尽進齋叢書.

h-wu-hsüeh ta tz'ǔ-tien 植物學大辭典.

n shih 金史.

ing-ch'ao ch'ien-chi by Mêng Sên, 孟森, 清朝前妃.

ing-shih kao 清史稿.

ing shih-lu 清實錄.

ing-tai ti-hou-hsiang 清代帝后像.

u T'ang-shu 舊唐書.

-tsêng ch'ang-li 酌增常例.

ou-chi pien by Yang Ching-jen, 楊景仁, 籌濟編.

ou li 周禮.

Chou-li chu-su （欽定）周禮注疏.

Chung-kuo li-tai ti-hou-hsiang 中國歷代帝后像.

Chung-shan ch'uan-hsin lu 中山傳信錄.

Dai hyakka jiten (J) 大百科事典.

Dai-nam hoi-dien siek-le (A) （欽定）大南會典事例.

Erh-ya i, 王符, 爾雅翼.

Hou-Han shu 後漢書.

Huang-ch'ao kuan-fu chih by Wang Kan, 王侃, 皇朝冠服志

Huang-ch'ao li-ch'i t'u-shih 皇朝禮器圖式.

Hsin Yüan-shih 新元史.

Kan-Rikuchō no fukushoku (J) by Yoshito Harada, 原田淑人
漢六朝の服飾.

K'ang-Tsang yao-chên by Liu Man-ch'ing, 劉曼卿,
康藏軺征.

Kisshō zuan kaidai (J) by Seikin Nozaki, 野崎誠近,
吉祥圖案解題.

Ko-chih ching-yüan 格致鏡原.

Ku-kung chou-k'an 故宮週刊.

ang-ch'ün fang-p'u 廣群芳譜.

o shih 遼史.

-ch'iu-kuo chih-lüeh 琉球國志略.

n-chou mi-tang 滿洲秘檔.

n-chou shih-lu t'u 滿洲實錄圖.

ng hui-tien 明會典.

ng Hui-yao 明會要.

ng kung shih 明宮史.

ng shih 明史.

ng shih-lu 明實錄

ko no jittai wo saguru (J) by Tokuhiro Keihin, 桂濱德廣,
蒙古の實態を探了.

n-Ch'i shu 南齊書.

hon Kiryaku (J) 日本紀略.

shan ch'i-chung ts'ung-shu 巴山七種叢書.

-ts'ao kang-mu by Li Shih-chêng, 李時珍, 本草綱目.

ya by Lu Tien, 陸佃, 埤雅.

-tsai t'u-hui 三才圖會.

Shan-hai ching   山海經.

Shan-t'ang szŭ-k'ao   山堂肆考.

Shan-yin-chou-shan Wu-shih chih-p'u   山陰州山吳氏支譜

Shên-i ching, attributed to Tung-fang Shuo,   東方朔, 神異經

Shih chi   史記.

Shih-lin kuang-chi   事林廣記.

Shih-tsu Chang-huang-ti shih-lu   世祖章皇帝實錄.

Shina minzoku-shi (J) by Ryōzō Nagao,   永尾龍造,

       支那民俗志.

Shu-ching chi-ch'uan by Ts'ai Shên,   蔡沈, 書經集傳.

Sung shih   宋史.

Sung shu   宋書.

Szŭ-pu ts'ung-k'an   四部叢刊.

Ta-Ch'ing hui-tien   大清會典.

Ta-Ch'ing hui-tien shih-li   大清會典事例.

Ta-Ch'ing hui-tien t'u   大清會典圖.

Ta-fa sung by Liang Chien-wên-ti,   梁簡文帝, 大法頌(序

Ta-hsüeh yen-i-pu by Ch'iu Hsün,   邱濬, 大學衍義補

yün-shan-fang shih-erh-chang t'u shuo by Yün Ching,

惲歉, 火雲山房十二章圖說.

i-p'ing-t'ien-kuo yeh-shih, by Wu Hsing and Ling Shan-ch'ing,

吳興, 凌善清, 太平天國野史.

i-tsung Wên-huang-ti shih-lu 太宗文皇帝實錄.

ng hui-yao 唐會要.

ng Yen Li-pên ti-wang-t'u chên-chi 唐閻立本帝王圖

真蹟.

n-kung k'ai-wu by Sung Ying-hsing, 宋應星, 天工開物.

ng-hsiu ch'ou-hsiang shih-li t'iao-k'uan 增修籌餉事例

條欵.

ng-po mun-hön pi-ko (K) 增補文獻備考.

shu chi-ch'êng 圖書集成.

g-hua lu 東華錄.

an sansai zue (J) 和漢三才圖會.

-shou ch'êng-tien 萬壽盛典.

huo pien by Shên Tê-fu, 沈德符, 野獲編.

n shih 元史.

n tien-chang 元典章.

2. PERSONAL NAMES

Chang Tsan 張瓚

Ch'in Jih-kang 秦日綱

Hu I-kuang 胡以晃

Hsia Yen 夏言

Hung Hsiu-ch'üan 洪秀全

Hung Ta-ch'üan 洪大全

Kuo Ch'ing-Wang 果親王

Li Chên 李真

Ning Wan-wo 寧完我

Shang Ch'un 伺純

Shih Ta-k'ai 石達開

Sung Ying-hsing 宋應星

Tung Ch'iu-hui 董通海

Wang Chi 王驥

Wei Ch'ang-hui 韋昌輝

Wên-hui T'ai-tzŭ 文惠太子

Yang Hsiu-ch'ing 楊秀清

3. ROBES AND COSTUME ACCESSORIES

ch'ang-fu 常服

ch'ao-fu 朝服

ch'ao-kua 朝褂

ch'ao-tai 朝帶

ch'êng-yü-fu 乘輿服

chi-fu 吉服

chì-fu 祭服

chüeh-tai 角帶

chung-ching-fu 忠靜服

fêng-kuan 鳳冠

hsi-lan 膝襴

hsia-p'ei 霞帔

hsüan-tuan-fu 玄端服

hua-fu 花服

ku-ha 賈哈

kun 袞

kun-fu 袞服

jên 社

li-fu 禮服

ling-t'ou 領頭

lung-i 龍衣

lung-p'ao 龍袍

ma-kua 馬褂

ma-ti hsiu 馬蹄袖

mang-ao 蟒襖

mang-ch'ün 蟒裙

mang-fu 蟒服

mang-i 蟒衣

mang-p'ao 蟒袍

mang-p'u 蟒補

mien 冕

pao-ho-fu 保和服

p'i-chien 披肩

p'i-ling 披領

pien-fu 便服

p'u-fu 補服

ryong-po (K) 龍袍

ts'ai-fu 彩服

ti-i 翟衣

yü chên-chu pan-lung i 御真珠盤龍衣

yä-fu 輿服

yün-chien 雲肩

4. Materials and Fabrics

an-hua chih tuan 暗花之緞

chin-hua tuan 金花緞

chuang tuan 粧緞

hai-lung p'i 海龍皮

hsün-tiao p'i 熏貂皮

hua su tuan 花素緞

k'o-ssŭ 緙絲 [刻絲]

lo 羅

mang tuan 蟒緞

na-ch'i-shih 納奇寶 [納石失]

pien-chin 片金

su-pu-tu (*na-ch'i-shih*) 速不都

ta-na-tu (*na-ch'i-shih*) 苔納都

tuan 緞

tzŭ-tiao p'i 紫貂皮

Wo tuan 倭緞

5. Colors, Dyes, and Dye Plants

chê　柘

chê-huang　赫黄

chiang　絳

ch'ien-ts'ao　茜草

chin-huang　金黄

ch'iu-hsiang-sê　秋香色

hsiang-sê　香色

hsiang-wan-tzŭ　橡椀子

hsing-huang　杏黄

hsüan　玄

hung-hua　紅花

huang-po　黄蘗

huang-lu　黄櫨

huang-chih　黄梔

huai　槐

i-p'in se　一品色

lan-tien　藍澱 [靛]

liao-lan 蓼藍

lu-mu 蘆木

ming-huang 明黃

shih-ch'ing 石青

su-mu 蘇木

ta-hung 大紅

tzŭ-ts'ao 紫草

wu-pei-tzŭ 五棓子

yang-mei p'i 楊梅皮

yüeh-pai 月白

6. Symbols and Decorative Motifs Used on the Robes

ch'ang-ch'un-hua 長春花

chêng lung 正龍

chi 戟 [吉]

chi ch'ing ju i 戟磬如意 [吉慶如意]

chi ch'ing ho p'ing 戟磬合瓶 [吉慶和平]

chiao 蛟

ch'i-lin 麒麟

ch'i-lin sung tzŭ 麒麟送子

Chih-ch'êng-kung 芝成宫

ch'ih-mu 尺木

ch'ing 磬 [慶]

ch'ing yün 慶雲

chüeh lu ch'ung kao 爵祿 [祿] 崇高

chung kuei (for Chung K'uei) 鐘圭 [鍾馗]

Fang-chang 方丈

fang shêng 方勝

fei-yu 飛魚

fên-mi 粉米

fu 蝠 [福]

fu 黻

fu 黼

fu-kuei-hua 富貴花

hai-shih shên-lou 海市蜃樓

hsing-ch'ên 星辰

hsing lung 行龍

hua-ch'ung 華蟲

hung fu chih t'ien 紅蝠至天 [洪福致天]

i ting shêng san kuei-chi 一錠生三貴戟 [一定升三貴級]

ju-i 如意

kuan tai ch'uan liu 冠帶船榴 [官代傳流]

k'uei-lung 夔龍

K'un-lun Shan 崑崙山

li lung 立龍

li shui 立水

ling-chih 靈芝

lu 鹿 [祿]

lung 龍

lung chung 龍種

mang 蟒

Miao-kao Shan 妙高山

nien 鮎 [年]

nien nien wan fu 鮎鮎乐蝠 [年年萬福]

pa chi-hsiang 八吉祥

pa pao 八寶

P'êng-lai Shan 蓬萊山

pi chung 筆中 [必中]

pi ting ju i 筆錠如意 [必定如意]

p'ing shêng san chi 瓶生(笙)三戟 [平升三級]

p'ing shui 平水

Po Shan 博山

san-chao lung 三爪龍

shên (also pronounced *ch'ên*) 蜃

shên-ch'i lou-t'ai 蜃氣樓臺

shên-shih 蠶市 [勝事]

shêng 勝

shih-erh chang 十二章

shou 壽

shou-shan fu-hai 壽山福海

shuang-hsi 囍

szŭ ling 四靈

tan mang 單蟒

tieh 蝶 [耋]

tieh shang liang chüeh 碟 [送] 上兩爵

tou-niu 斗牛

tsao 藻

tso mang 坐蟒

tsung-i 宗彝

wan nien ju i 卍鮎如意 [萬年如意]

wan nien lien fu 卍鮎蓮蝠 [萬年連福]

wan-shou-chü 萬壽菊

wan wan nien hung fu 卍卍鮎紅蝠 [萬萬年洪福]

wu fu p'êng shou 五福捧壽

wu-chao lung 五爪龍

Ying-chou 瀛州

yü 魚 [餘]

yüan shêng 圓勝

7. Titles and Official Terms

An-ch'a-shih   按察使

Hu-pu   戶部

I-k'u   衣庫

Kuan chih-jan-chü ta-ch'ên   管織染局大臣

Kuo-tsung   國宗

Nei chih-jan-chu   內織染局

Nieh-t'ai   臬台

Shang-i   尚衣

Ssŭ-fu   司服

Tuan-k'u   緞庫

INDEX

Abahai, 20 note 1, 51, 136.
acorns for dyeing, 114.
Aigun, Treaty of, 138 note 5.
allover patterns, 8, 9, 61, 100, 106, 120.
Altan Khan, 14.
Altar of Heaven, 53-54, 86, 142.
Altar of the Sun, 19 note 41, 143.
alterations on robes 19, 24-25, 138-140, 157, 158.
alum for dyeing, 114.
Amur River, 138.
Amur cork tree, 113.
An-ch'a shih, 32 note 31.
an-hua chih tuan, 118.
an-hua patterns, 45, 118.
aniline dyes, 62-63, 123-124, 134.
animal symbols, 77-81, 83-84, 87, 88, 89, 91, 99-100, 101-102, 106.
Annam, 86, 163, 164-170, 184; King of, *see under* King.
Arabia, 157, text and note 1.
aspiration symbols, 103, 105-106, 129.
autumn robes, 56, 137.
axe symbol, 12, 53, 88-89, 90, 91, 93.

bamboo symbols, 96, 97.
Banners, 127, 172.
basket symbols, 97, 98.
bat symbols, 40, 98, 99, 101-102, (104), 106-107, 130, 150.
Beck Collection, 31, 122.
bell symbols, 38, 75, 103-104.
belts: Yüan Mongol, (8), 10; Ming, 10, 127-128, 169; Manchu, 21, 27, 29, 164; Liu Ch'iu, 158; Annamese, 169; as a symbol, 129.
bird symbols, 75, 83, 88, 91, 98-99, 127, 129, 130, 196, 198.
birthday of Emperor, 28, 74, 163.
black, 14, 114.
bleached silk, 114.
blue, 24 note 7, 25, 53-54, 114, 119, 123, 131, 142, 143, 144, 149, 170.
blue-black, 52, 54-55, 72, 114, 144, 149.

Board of Revenue, 30 note 27, 45 note 20.
Board of Rites, 10, 50, 56, 179.
boat symbol, 129.
bolt silk, 24, 64 note 20, 116-117, 124, 162-163, 170, 184.
book symbols, 95, 168-169.
Boston Museum of Fine Arts, 43, 85 note 22, 132.
Boxer Rebellion, 64, 65.
bridal robes, Chinese, 36, 99, 127-130, 131, 182.
bright yellow; *see* yellow: Imperial.
brocade, gold, 5, 7, 8, 52, 109, 110, text and note 2, 112, 117, 119, 122, 137, 152.
brocading, 5, 31, 112, 117, 122, 123.
brown, 115.
brush, writing, 102, 122.
Buddha's hand citron, 98.
bureaucracy, 121, 181.
burial robes, 19, 38, 45-47, 83, 127, 182.
Burma, 163.
butterfly symbol, 102.

Caesalpinia sappan, 113.
canopy, royal, 96.
carp symbol, 77, 78, 106.
Carthamus tinctorius, 113.
cassia, 87, 129.
castanets, 96.
catfish symbol, 106-107.
"Celestial Kingdom of Peace," 152, 154.
ceremonial robes, 22, 25, 51 note 4, 53, 114, 136, 142.
Chamdo, 173.
ch'ang-ch'un-hua, 98.
ch'ang-fu, robes, 22.
Chang Tsan, 17 note 36.
ch'ao-fu, robes, 22, (74), 135-145, 146-151.
ch'ao-kua, vests, 146, 149-151.
ch'ao-tai, belts, 21.
Chavannes, E., 101.
chê, tree, 113.

chê-huang, color, 110.
Ch'êng Huang, 133.
chêng lung, 81; *see also* facing dragons.
Chêng-tê Emperor, the, 17.
ch'êng-yü fu, robe, 5, text and note 10.
chestnut oak, 114.
chi, halberd; *see* halberd symbols.
chi ch'ing ho p'ing, 106.
chi ch'ing ju i, 104-105.
chi-fu, robes, 22.
chi-fu, robes, 141.
ch'i-lin, 38, 77, 99, 166, 168, 169.
ch'i-lin sung tzŭ, 99.
Chia-ching Emperor, the, 13, 17-18.
Chia-ch'ing Emperor, the, 60-61, 80, text and note 17.
Chia-ch'ing reign period, 39, 58, 60-61, 65, 121.
chiang, color, 109.
chiao dragons, 166.
Chicago Art Institute, 105 note 69.
Chicago Natural History Museum, 67, 71, 82.
Ch'ien-lung Emperor, the, 22 note 4, 23 note 5, 24 note 7, 33 note 32, 40, 45 note 20, 48, 50-53, 59, 61, 80 note 7, 92, 93-94, 96, 119, 141-142, 163, 179, 180.
Ch'ien-lung reign period, 39, 41, 46-48, 58-59, 60-61, 65, 75, 80, 85, 87, 94, 101, 119, 121, 124, 128-129, 142, 167.
ch'ien-ts'ao, 113.
Chih-ch'êng-kung, 83.
ch'ih-mu, 77-78.
Chin Dynasty, 6, 50, 86, 92, 176.
chin-hua tuan, 117.
chin huang, color, 54, 113.
Ch'in Jih-kang, 153 note 5.
China: general, 3, 6, 7, 10, 21, 25, 29, 32, 63, 78, 86-87, 102, 103, 108, 109, 124, 128, 139, 165, 167, 172, 174, 178, 185, *et passim;* North, 6, 84, 184; South, 25, 30, 66, 102, 116, 117, 152, 183.
Ch'ing Court, the, 24, 25, 28, 31, 33, 74, 87, 116-117, 121, 122, 123, 127, 138, 155, 162, 170, 173.
Ch'ing Dynasty, 3, 19, 20-22, 25-34, 35-49, 50-57, 58-68, 69-76, 103, 107, 113,

116-117, 124, 127, 131, 132, 135-145, 146-151, 152, 156, 162-163, 170-173, 178-185, *et passim.*
ch'iu-hsiang sê, 25; *see also* yellow: tawny.
Chou Dynasty, 85, 92.
chrysanthemum symbol, 97.
chuang tuan, 117.
chüeh lu ch'ung kao, 103.
chüeh-tai, belt, 127-128.
chung-ching-fu, robe, 13.
Chung K'uei, 103, 104 note 64.
claws of dragons, 4-5, 7-8, 18, 24, 25, 29, 31-32, 56, 77, 78, 79, 132, 179.
Cleveland Museum of Art, 120.
cloud collar, 6-7, 9, 14, 16, 130, 135 note 1, (136), 175, 176-177.
cloud patterns, 5, 13, 22, 112, 118, 119.
cloud symbols, 40, 47, 49, 52, 57, 60, 69, 71, 81-82, 84-85, 97, 103.
cochineal, 123.
coins, 3, 95.
collars, on dragon robes, 5, 37, 41, 43, 47, 52, 72, 108, 117, 169; *see also* cloud collars; court collars; *ku-ha;* and *ling-t'ou.*
colors: general, 16, 26, 39, 61, 85, text and note 19, 91, 109, 114, 123, 131, 132, 166-167, 181, 191, 193; *see also* yellow; red; blue; blue-black; purple; green; black; white; brown.
conch symbols, 84, 96, 100.
consorts, *see* Imperial consorts; Heir Apparent's consort.
"consort robes": false, 39, 41; true, 41, text and note 13, 119.
constellation, 12, text and note 8, 53, 88; *see also* stars.
copperas, for dyeing, 114.
coral beads, 71, 122.
coral symbol, 94.
Corea, *see* Korea.
Cossacks, 138.
cotton, 57.
couching, 118, 119, 121.
Court, the: Ming, 10, 14, 16, 18, 23, 157, 170, 177; Ch'ing, 24, 25, 28, 31, 33, 74, 87, 116, 117, 121, 122, 123, 127, 138, 155, 162, 170, 173.

court collars, 22, 34, 109, 135, 137, 139, 142, 143, 145, 146, 147, 183.

court robes, Ch'ing: general, 3, 19, 22, 40, 53, 109, 117, 127, 135-151, 176-177, 182-183, 184; Imperial, 87, 136, 140-143, 147-148; for men, 22, 135-145, 182-183, 194; for women, 39, 73, 74, 146-151, 183, 195.

court vests, 146, 149-151.

courtiers, 11, 15, 17, 65, 134, 140, 170, 171.

crane symbols, 75, 83, 98-99, 120.

cuffs, 21, 24, 34, 37, 43, 44-45, 47, 52, 70, 71, 108, 117, 137, 139, 147, 179.

cup symbols, 12, 53, 89, 90, 91, 103.

Customs, Chinese Maritime, 62-63, 124.

Dalai Lama, 45 note 20, 172, 173.

damask, 112, 118.

dating, 35-49, 58-68, 71.

Dayton Art Institute, 42.

David, Lady, 70-71.

deer symbols, 4, 75, 99, 102.

"Devil Dances," 174-175.

diaper patterns, 9, 61, 120.

double pun symbols, 105-109.

Dragon, the: as a symbol, 3, 53, 77-78, 88, 90, 91; three-clawed *lung,* 4, 5, 8, 25, 26, 27, 78, 79, 116, 117, 162, 178, 191; five-clawed *lung,* 3 note 1, 7-8, 14-16, 17, 24-25, 27, 29, 30-32, 54, 56, 78-79, 116-117, 149, 162, 165, 172; four-clawed *mang,* 3 note 1, 5, 7-8, 13, 14, 15-17, 27-29, 54, 56, 78-79, 81, 117, 132, 133, 144, 166, 172; five-clawed *mang,* 15, 17, 31-32; coiled, 4, 11, 13, 22, 162; hoofed, 129; *see also* facing dragons; profile dragons; vertical dragons; *tou-niu; fei-yü; chiao; k'uei-lung.*

dragon coats, 19, 99, 127-130, 182.

dragon jackets, 33, 72-76, 81, 102, 104, 109, 149, 172, 180, 183.

dragon patterns: general, 3, 6-7, 11-14, 16-17, 27-28, 35-49, 52, 129-130, 135, 136-137, 141-142, 144, 146-149, 153-154, 161-162, 165-167, 174, 176, 177, 178-179, 180, 192; two dragons, 9, 16, 37, 130, 168; four dragons, 11, 37-38, 74, 130, 153, 174; five dragons, 55; six

dragons, 35-37, 39, 74, 166, (174); eight dragons, 17, 39-42, 43-49, 55, 74, 75, 128, 153, 174; nine dragons, 52-54, 141, 147, 153; ten dragons, 129, 166, 174; twelve dragons, 12, 74, 165; many dragons, 9, 13, 37, 41; dragon medallions, 4, 11-12, 27, 42-47, 71-73, 116-117, 118, 141, 143, 146, 161-162, 163, 192; confronting dragons, 39, 149, 174; giant dragons, 37-39, 146, 149, 174, 178; dragons looping over shoulders of robe, 9-11, 14-18, 35, 37, 55, 128-129, 133, 136-137, 139, 146, 158, 166, 168, 177-178, 182; profile dragons on shoulders, 38, 42-43, 132-133, 141, 146.

dragon robes: general, 3, 7, 9, 10, 13, 19, 176, 191-193, *et passim;* Imperial, 5, 6, 7, 10-13, 25-26, 53-54, 58-67, 87, 109, 110, 119, 121; Yüan, 7-9, 10, 21, 109-110, 136; Ming, 9-19, 20-21, 23, 24, 35-36, 38, 39, 43, 113-114, 115-116, 128, 136, 139, 157, 158, 178, 182, 183, 184; Manchu, 20-21, 22, 26-30, 33-34, 35-49, 50, 52-57, 58-68, 69-72, 95, 102, 118, 127, 129, 131, 140, 146, 158, 163, 172, 178; theatrical, 130-131, 182; for images, 43, 132-134, 182; Korean, 161-162, 184; Indo-Chinese, 165-170, 184; Taiping, 152-156, 184.

dragon satins, 23, 24, 110, 115, 116-117, 118, 162-163, 170, 172, 173, 184.

dragon skirts, 127, 130.

dragon squares, 9, 13, 16, 112, 144, 161-162.

draw looms, 110, 111.

ducks, 99 note 53, 130, 196, 198.

Dukes, 26, (54), 144, 166, 171 note 53, 173; Duke's wives, 149.

dye plants, 113-115.

dyes, 62-63, 109, 110-115, 123-124, 134.

Dynastic Statutes, 5, 56, 59, 179.

Early Ch'ing period (1644-1722), 22, 25-28, 30, 31, 32, 35, 37-38, 39, 40, 42-44, 76, 79, 81, 99, 104, 118, 120 note 31, 135-140, 146, 174, 176, 178, 180, 183, 191.

Earth, symbolized, 81, 88 note 32, 91.

Eight Buddhist Symbols, the, 96-97, 100, 102, 104 note 64.
Eight Jewels, the, see Eight Precious Things.
Eight Precious Things, the, 52, 70, 71, 94-97, 102, 104, 168.
Eight Symbols of the Taoist Immortals, the, 59, 94, 96-97, 142.
embroidering, 14, 32, 37, 45, 71, 91, 92-93, 108-109, 112, 118, 119-121, 123, 130, 131, 133, 153, 164, 181.
Emperors of China: general, 3 note 1, 12, 92, 93, 176; T'ang, 4-5; Sung, 4-6, 109; Ming, 10, 11, 24 note 7, 43-44, 52, 86, 157, 162, 177; Ch'ing, 25, 26, 31, 32, 33, 38, 41 note 13, 43, 52, 53, 58-68, 72, 79, 84, 87, 92, 134, 135, 140, 162, 172, 180, 184; see also (for Ming): Hung-wu, Hsüan-tê, Ying-tsung, Hung-chih, Chêng-tê, Chia-ching, Wan-li; (for Ch'ing): Shun-chih, K'ang-hsi, Yung-chêng, Ch'ien-lung, Chia-ch'ing, Tao-kuang, Hsien-fêng, T'ung-chih, Kuang-hsü, Hsüan-t'ung.
Emperors' secondary wives, or concubines; see Imperial consorts.
Empresses: Sung, 5; Ming, 15 note 23; Ch'ing, 26, 66-67, 69-72, 75, 84, 93, 99, 105 note 68, 120, 146, 147-148, 149, 150, 180, 183; see also Hsiao-chên, Hsiao-ch'in, Hsiao-ho, Hsiao-shêng, Hsiao-ting.
Empress-Dowagers, Ch'ing, 66, 70, 71, 147; the last: see Hsiao-ch'in.
endless knot symbol, 96.
England, 163.
epaulettes, 146, 148, 183.
eunuchs, 14, 15, 16, 18, 37 note 4, 112.
Europe, 62-63, 123.
exhibitions, 58, 66, 71.

facing dragons, 11, 15, 18, 42-43, 44, 52, 78, 80, 81, 133, 168.
factories, silk; see silk factories, Imperial.
fan symbol, 96.
Fang-chang Island, 83.
fang shêng symbol, 94.
fei yü, 17.

fêng-huang; see "phoenix."
fêng-kuan, hat, 127-128.
Fêng Yu-hsiang, General, 64.
ferrous sulphate, for dyeing, 115.
fertility symbols, 99.
fire symbols, 12, 53, 89, 90, 91.
fish symbols, 78, 96, 100, 102, 106.
Five Colors, the, 84-85 note 19, 91, 114, 119.
Five Elements, the, 91.
Five Symbol robes, 93.
flames, 12, 53, 89, 90, 91.
Florentine stitch, 120, 121.
floss silk, 120.
flower patterns, 22, 73, 117-118, 166 note 38, 169.
flower symbols, 96, 97-98, 168.
"flowery bird," the, 88; see also pheasant symbol.
flute symbol, 97.
flying fish, the, 17, text and note 36.
formal jacket, Ch'ing; see p'u-fu.
Four Spirits, the, (77), 166-168.
Four Spirits robes, 166, 167, 168-169.
Four Symbol robes, (70), 73, 148.
France, 163 note 20.
French, the, 66 note 25, 165, 167, 170.
frog symbol, 84.
fruit symbols, 94, 98.
fú symbol, the, 12, 53, 88, 90, 91, 93.
fu-kuei hua, 97-98.
fungus symbol, 98.
fur, 21, 33, 56, 137-138, 139-140, 142-143, 144, 148, 152, 161, 171.
fur jackets, 21, 33, 138, 152, 161.

gall nuts, 114.
Gardenia florida, 113.
gardenias, 113.
gauze, 45, 56-57, 71, 105 note 69, 117, 120, 143.
Gelung lamas, 172.
giant dragons, 37-39, 146, 149, 174, 178.
gods, 132-133.
gold (color), 5, 7, 11, 14, 22, 118.
gold foil, 119, 122.
gold clothing ornaments, 109, 117.
gold threads, 45, 118-119, 122, 124, 134, (158).

golden yellow; *see under* yellow.
goldfish symbol, 106.
Gordon, General Charles, 33 note 33.
gourd and crutch symbol, 96.
grain symbols, 12, 53, 89, 90, 91.
Grand Council, Ming, 16, 18.
Grand Lama of Urga, 172.
grass orchids, 97.
green, 37 note 4, 103, 114, 123, 132, 133.
gromwell, 115.
Guards, Imperial, officers of, 26, 54, 55, 144.

hai-lung p'i, 143.
hai-shih shên-lou, 84 note 17.
halberd symbols, 38, 104-106, 129.
Han Dynasty, 10, 20, 85, 92, (131).
Hangchow, 63, 110, 116, 181.
happiness symbols, 83, 85, 98, 101-102, 106-107, 150.
hare, 87.
hat, 50, 87, 92, 127-128, 129, 152, 159, 161, 164.
hat jewels, 21, 27, 29, 44, 67 note 32.
hat symbol, 129.
Heaven, 91, 92.
Heir Apparent, 11, 26, 54, 79, 84, 143, 148.
Heir Apparent's consort, 69, 72, 73.
hemp, 113.
"hidden pattern," 118.
Hideyoshi, 159-160.
Holland, 163.
Hong Kong, 63.
hoop belts, 10, 127-128, 169.
horizontal band on skirt, 9, 10, 14, 128, 136, 137, 139, 142, 145.
horns on dragons, 5, 7, 17, 77, 78, 79, 99, 166.
horsehoof cuffs, 21, 24, 70, 74, 155, 157, 179.
hsi-lan 16; *see also* horizontal band on skirt.
Hsi Tsung, Emperor, 13 note 10.
hsia-p'ei stole, 128, 198.
Hsia Yen, 17 note 36.
hsiang sê, 72; *see also* yellow: tawny.
hsiang-wan tzǔ, 114.
Hsiao-chên, Empress, 71.

Hsiao-ch'in, Empress, 64, 70, 71, 73, 121.
Hsiao-ho, Empress, 70.
Hsiao-shêng, Empress, 147.
Hsiao-ting, Empress, 71.
Hsien-fêng Emperor, the, 62, 63, 66.
hsing huang, 54.
hsing lung, 81; *see also* profile dragon.
hsüan, color, 114.
Hsüan-tê Emperor, the, 11-12.
hsüan-tuan-fu, 13.
Hsüan-t'ung Emperor, the, 65 note 24; *see also* P'u-yi.
hsün-tiao p'i, 142.
Hu I-kuang, 153 note 5.
Hu pu, 30 note 27.
hua-fu robes, 22.
hua su tuan, 118.
huai, tree, 113.
Huang-ch'ao li-ch'i t'u-shih, 50, 51, 143, 187 no. 9.
huang chih, 113.
huang lu, 113.
huang po, 113.
Huang Ti, the Yellow Emperor, 85, 132, 168.
Hué, 170.
Hui-tien tsê-li, Ta Ch'ing, 51.
Hunan Province, 102.
Hundred Antiques, the, 38.
Hung-chih Emperor, the, 16.
hung fu chih t'ien, 102.
Hung Hsiu-ch'üan, 152; *see also* T'ien Wang.
hung hua, 113.
Hung Ta-ch'üan, 155 note 14.
Hung-wu Emperor, the, 10-11, 14.

i-k'u, 116 note 16.
i ting shêng san kuei-chi, 129.
image robes, 43, 132-134, 182.
Immortals, Eight, symbols of the, 59, 94, 96-97, 142.
Immortals, Isles of the, 83, 98.
Imperial consorts, 26, 69, 72, 73, 84, 147-148, 183.
Imperial Family, the, 6, 26, 64, 79, 100.
Imperial Weaving and Dyeing Office, 63, 116, 121, 181.
Imperial yellow; *see under* yellow.

imported dyes, 62-63, 123-124, 134.
indigo, 114, 124.
Indo-China, 164-170, 177, 184.
ingot symbols, 95, 102, 129.
Inner Mongolia, 170, 172.
Inspectors, Official Silk, 64, 108, 121.
International Exhibition of Chinese Art, London, 71.
Isles of the Immortals, 83, 98.
ivory tusk symbols, 94.

jackets, formal, 21, 28, 29, 30, 33, 37, 72, 153, 155, 170.
jade, 46 note 21, 129.
jade musical stone, 94, 102, 104, 105-106.
Japan, 78, 79, 86, 159-160, 162, 172.
Japan pagoda tree, 113.
"Japanese satin," 117.
Java, 157, text and note 1.
Jehol, 163 note 20.
jên, flap, on court robes, 135.
jewel symbols, 83, 84, 94, 95.
Ju-chên tribe, 6, 8, 176.
ju-i: scepter, 95, 102, 104-105; jewel, 94, 95.

K'ang-hsi Emperor, the, 25-26, 28, 36, 43, 59 note 8, 74, 136, 140, 141, 158.
K'ang-hsi reign period, 29, 32, 37, 39, 42, 58, 74, 78 note 4, 135, 146, 174.
Khalkha Mongols, 171.
Khitan tribe, 6, 8, 86, 176.
Khubilai Khan, 7, 9.
Kiangning (Nanking), 63, 116, 117, 152, 153 note 4, 155, 181.
Kings: Annamese, 86, 159, 163, 165-166; Korean, 86, 159-160, 161-162, 163, 170; of Liu Ch'iu, 158, 163.
kingfisher feathers, 109.
Korea, 6 note 13, 79, 86, 157, 159-162, 163, 170, 184.
k'o-ssŭ, 25, 32 note 31, 71, 79, 117, 119, 122, 124.
ku-ha, collar, 135.
Kuan chih-jan-chü ta-ch'ên, 116 note 16.
kuan tai ch'uan liu, 129.
Kuan Ti, 132, 133.
Kuang-hsü Emperor, the, 65, 71.
Kuang-hsü reign period, 65, 104.

k'uei-lung dragons, 73.
kun robes, 3, text and note 2; 4, text and note 4.
kun-fu, jacket, 28 note 23.
K'un-lun Shan, 82.
Kuo Ch'ing-Wang, 45, text and note 20, 48; tomb of, 45, 46, 47, (75), 83, 104, 119, (120).
Kuo Tsung, 154 note 8.

Lama (Buddhist) Church, the, 64, (97), 172, 173.
lamas, high, 26 note 15, 172-175.
lan-tien, 114.
Laos, 163.
lapels, 41, 52, 67, 72, 80, 108, 147.
Later Ch'ing (1759-1911), 19, 29, 30, 32, 35, 37, 42, 56, 58-68, 69-73, 75-76, 79, 80-81, 92-94, 98-99, 103-104, 108, 120-124, 129-130, 132, 135, 165, 179-181, 183.
laws for costume, general, 4, 5, 6, text and note 13, 7, 10, 11, 17, 20, 25, 26, 27, text and note 17, 29, 45, 50, 51, 52-57, 84, 97, 127, 142-149, 152-154, 155, 161-162, 164, 167, 173, 178, 179-180, 196-197.
Laws of 1759, the, 50-57, 69-70, 72-73, 141-145, 147-150, 193-195.
Lhasa, 38, 174.
Li Chên, 8 note 22.
Li Family History, The, 8 note 22, 18 note 40, 187 no. 6.
li-fu, ceremonial costume, 22, 25, (26).
li lung, 81, 150.
li shui water convention, 40, 47, 48, 52, 57, 60, 61, 65, 70, 71, 72, 75, 81, (84), 130, 131, 147, 150, 165.
Liao Dynasty, 6, 50, 86, 92, 135, 176.
liao-lan, 114.
Liaoyang, 115.
likin taxes, 124.
ling chih, 98.
ling-t'ou, collar, 33-34.
lining of robes, 56-57, 137.
Lithospermum officinale, 115.
Liu Ch'iu, 157-159, 163, 184.
Living Buddha of Chamdo, the, 173.
lo, serge, 112.

longevity symbols, 41, 83, 98, 100, 101-102, 142, 150.
looms, 64, 108, 110, 111, 122.
lotus symbols, 96, 97, 98 note 51, 106.
lu mu, 113.
lucky symbols, general, 40, 49, 57, 70, 85, 97, 120, 122, 130, 145, 150, 180, 181, 183.
lung, 7, 78; *see also* Dragon.
lung chung, 41 note 13.
lung-i, 3 note 1.
lung-p'ao, 3 note 1, 52, 54.
lye, for dyeing, 113.

ma-kua, jacket, 153.
ma-ti hsiu, 21; *see also* horsehoof cuffs.
madder for dyeing, 109, 113.
Malacca, 14.
Malachite Green, 123.
Malaya, 123.
magnolia, 97.
Manchu Dynasty, the; *see* Ch'ing Dynasty.
Manchu Emperors; *see under* Emperors.
Manchus, the, general, 19, 20-27, 50-52, 79, 87, 114, 115-116, 127, 128, 138-139, 155, 156, 157, 160-161, 180, 181, 182-183, 184, *et passim.*
Manchu Conquest, the, 19, 20, 21, (115), 140, 178, 181, (185).
Manchu national tradition for clothing, the, 19, 20-21, 29, 43, 50-52, (135), (139-140), 178-181, 184-185.
Manchu script, 42.
Manchuria, 6, 21, 23-24, 30, 114, 115-116, 138, 139, 160-161.
"mandarin buttons," *see* hat jewels.
mandarin squares, 21, text and note 3, 25, 27, 62, 73, 75, 83, 98, 99, 112, 118, 120 note 31, 128, 167 note 43, 170, 175 note 73, 196-197.
mandarin ducks, 99 note 53, 130, 196, 198.
mang, dragon, 7, 15, 78; *see also under* Dragon.
mang-ao, 127.
mang-ch'ün, skirt, 127.
mang-fu, 28; *see also* mang robes.
mang-i, 3 note 1, 13, 16.

mang-p'ao, 3 note 1, 28, 32, 54, 163.
mang-p'u, 16.
mang robes, 3 note 1, 13-17, 23-24, 28, 38, 54-56, 158, 163, 171, (172).
marigold symbol, 98.
marquises, 18, 153.
marriage robes; *see* bridal robes, Chinese; *and* wedding robes.
marriage symbols, 63, 71, 99, 100, 130.
Martin Collection, 37-38, 99, 104, 120.
Mecca, 157, text and note 1.
merit, rewards for, 15, 28, 31, 107.
metal threads, 118-119, 122-123, 124.
Methyl Violet 2B, 62-63, 123-124.
Metropolitan Museum of Art, New York City, 41, 58 notes 1 and 2, 67 note 31, 73 note 17, 74, 75, 92, 119, 120-121, 128, 137, 139.
Mexico, 123.
Miao-kao Shan, 82.
Middle Ch'ing period (1723-1759), 24 note 7, 31-32, 33, 36, 38, 40, 42, 44-47, 48, (69), 74-75, 79, 80, 81, 85, 96, 102, 108, 121, 141, (163), (178-179), 183.
mien hat, 92.
millet symbols, 12, 53, 89, 90, 91.
Min-ning, Prince, 93.
Ming Court, the, 10, 14, 16, 18, 23, 157, 170, 177.
Ming Dynasty, 4, 9-19, 30, 32, 35, 78, 79, 110-112, 127-128, 136, 157, 161, 164, 176, 177, 184.
ming huang, 25, 52, 113.
Ministers of State, 17 note 36, 31.
Minneapolis Institute of Arts, 48, 58 note 1, 80 note 7, 83, 100 note 56, 106, 120, 121, 150 note 9, 175 note 72.
mirage, the sea monster's, 84, 97.
Mongol Dynasty, *see* Yüan Dynasty.
Mongolia, 170-172, 174, 184.
Mongols of the Yüan, 7-9, 10, 20, 86, 109, 173, 177, 184.
Mongols, post- Yüan, 12, 14, 23, 24, 116, 157, 160, 170-172.
monkey symbols, 89, 129.
monopolies, Imperial, 6, 24, (25), 31, 117, 122, 177.
moon symbols, 6, 7, 12, 13, 53, 70, 73, 87, 90, 91, 92, 93, 133, 169 note 47.

"moon white"; *see* white; green-white.
mordants, 113, 114, 115.
Mount Meru, 82.
mountain symbols, 6, 12, 16, 36, 38, 40, 46, 53, 60, 73, 75, 81-83, 88, 91, 165, 174.
Muhammad Iskander Shah, 14 note 19.
museums; *see* Boston Museum of Fine Arts; Chicago Art Institute; Chicago Natural History Museum; Cleveland Museum of Art; Dayton Art Institute; Metropolitan Museum of Art; Minneapolis Institute of Arts; Nelson Gallery; Palace Museum; Royal Ontario Museum of Archaeology; Seattle Art Museum; Textile Museum of Washington, D.C.; University Museum; Victoria and Albert Museum; Walters Gallery; Yale Gallery.
musical instrument symbols, 94, 97, 102, 104, 105-106.

nachidut, 110.
na-ch'i-shih, 110, text and note 2.
nakhut, 110.
Nanking, 110, 116, 152, 154-155, 181; *see also* Kiangning.
National Museum, U.S., Washington, D.C., 34, 73 note 17.
Nei chih-jan-chü, 116.
Nerchinsk, Treaty of, 138.
Nelson Gallery, Kansas City, 37 note 4, 45, 48, 67, 70, 133.
Nguyen Dynasty, in Annam, 165, 167.
Nieh-t'ai, 32 note 31.
nien nien wan fu, 106.
Nine Symbol robes, 85 note 22, 86, text and note 27.
Ning Wan-wo, 21.
nobles; non-Chinese, 7, 166-167, 170-172, 173; Ming, 11, 15; Ch'ing, general, 22, 26, 32-33, 44, 52, 55, 67, 79, 81, 135, 136-137, 138, 143, 144; Ch'ing, Manchu, 22, 26-27, 43, 44, 45, 54; Ch'ing, Chinese, 26, 54, 129.
Noblewomen: Ch'ing, 42, 46, 47, 66, 146-147, 149, 150, 180, 183; wives of nobles, 27, 73, 150.
Northern Wei Dynasty, 50.

Nozaki, S., 101.
numbers, symbolic, 52, 77-78, 92, 97 note 50.
Nurhachi, 23, 24 note 7, 115, 136, 160.

oak, chestnut, 114.
Officials: general, 3, 4, 7-8, 11, 15, 52, 132, 166-167, 177; Ming, 13, 15, 18; Ch'ing, general, 22, 28, 31, 32, 33-34, 54-56, 67, 79, 129, 135, 137, 138, 140, 143, 144; Ch'ing, Manchu, 21, 27; Ch'ing, Chinese, 21, 27, 51, 87; wives of officials: general, 18, 19, 109, 169; Ch'ing, Manchu, 27, 69, 73, 127, 149, (180); Ch'ing, Chinese, 19, 27, 69, 99, 127-128, 129-130, 182.
Okinawa, 159.
orange yellow, *see under* yellow.
orchids, grass, 97.
ordinary costume, Manchu, 21, 22.
otter skins, 143, 148, 149.
Outer Mongolia, 170, 171.

pa chi-hsiang, (96), 97 note 49.
pa pao, 52, 53, 94, 96.
palaces, 33, 65, 66, 160.
Palace Museum, Peking, 4, 8, 12, 15 note 23, 36, 58 note 5, 70, 135.
Palace Storehouse, 64 note 21, 116 note 16, 117.
palace symbols, 83.
Panchen Lama, 172, 173.
pao-ho-fu, 13.
Parasilurus asotus L., 106.
pavilion symbols, 83-84.
peach symbols, 94, 98, 129.
peacock feathers, 38, 120, text and note 31, 122, 132.
pearls, 5, 70, 109, 110 note 2, 117, 122, 150.
pearl symbols, 40, 77, 95, 140, 169, text and note 47.
Peking, 23, 25, 63, 64, 65, 66, (69), 87, 101 note 59, 116-117, 121, 128, 138, 170-171, 172; *see also* Palace Museum.
Pên-ts'ao kang-mu, 112-113.
P'êng-lai Shan, 83, 99, 105 note 68.
peony symbols, 22, 97-98, 129, 130, 168.
Perkin, W. H., 63.

Persia, 8-9, 109.
petit point, 120.
pheasant symbol, 12, (53), 88, 90, 91, 99 note 53, 162, text and note 14.
Phellodendron Amurense, 113.
"phoenix," or *fêng-huang,* 6 note 13, 26, 77, 88, 99, 127, 129, 130, 152, 166, 168, 169.
"phoenix bonnet," 127-128.
p'i-chien, collar, 135.
pi chung, 102.
p'i-ling, collar, 135.
pi ting ju i, 102.
picric acid, 123.
pien-chin, brocade, 52.
pien-fu, costume, 22.
pine trees, 83, 98.
p'ing shêng san chi, 105-106.
p'ing shui, water convention, 40, 147.
plant symbols, 12, 53, 89, 90, 91, 97, 98.
plum blossoms, 97.
Po Shan, 77-78.
pomegranate symbols, 98, 129.
Pope of Rome, 163.
porcelains, 80, 95.
portraits, 4-5, 7, 8-9, 10-11, 12, 13 note 10, 14, 18, 19, 27, 32, 35, 36, 43, 44, 55, 59, 61 note 12, 70, 127, 128, 135, 137, 140, 142, 155, 158-159, 187 no. 10.
Portugal, 163.
potash for dyeing, 113.
pre-Conquest Manchus, 20-21, 23-24, 51, 115-116, 139, 157, 160-161, 181, 183.
presentation robes, 4, 5, 14-18, 23-24, 28, 39, 109, 157-161, 163, 177, 184.
presentation satins, 116-117, 162-163, 164, 170.
Prince Kuo, *see* Kuo Ch'ing-Wang.
Princes: T'ang, 4, 176; Yüan, 7; Ming, 11, (16); Ch'ing, 26, 30-31, 38, 41 note 13, 54, 143-144, 171; non-Chinese, 14, 158-159, 160-162, 163, 165-166, 171; wives and children of, 26, 73, 149, 150.
princesses, (72), (150), 172.
profile dragons, 11, 15, 42, 43, 44, 52, 81, 168, *et passim.*
p'u-fu, jackets, 21, 28, 33, 56, 73, (75), 145, 164, 172, (184).
pun symbols, 84, 99, 100-107, 129, 181.

punishments, 27 note 17, 121 note 35.
purchase of rank, 29-30, 122.
purple, 62, 114, 115, 123-124, 166.
P'u-yi, 65; *see also* Hsüan-t'ung Emperor.

queues, Manchu, 21, 155, 178.
quilted robes, 56-57.

rebus symbols, 99, 100-107, 129.
red, color, 5, 11, 16-17, 19, 24 note 7, 101-102, 109, 113-114, 123-124, 128-129, 131, 132, 133, 143, 161-162, 165-166, 170.
Republic of China, 86.
Revolution of 1911, (64), 65, 172, 179.
Rhamnus, 114.
rhinoceros horn symbol, 94-95.
Rhus cotinus, 113, 114.
rooster, 87.
rose symbol, 98.
royal canopy, 96.
Royal Ontario Museum of Archaeology, Toronto, 37, 41, 43, 44, (73), (74), 118, 148.
Rubia cordifolia, 113.
rugs, 78 note 4.
Russia, 138, text and note 5.
ryong-po, Korean robes, 161-162.

sable skins, 137-138, 139-140, 142, 144, 148, 152.
Sacrifices, the Annual, 22, 28, 53, 86-87, 93, 141.
sacrificial robes: general, 3-4, 7 note 12, 17, 19 note 41, 53, 86, 170, 176; Ch'ing, 22, 141.
safflower, 113.
sale of ranks, 29-30, 121.
san-chao lung, 79, 117; *see also* Dragon: three-clawed *lung.*
sapan wood, 113, 114, 123.
satin: general, 7, 13, 22, 25, 26, 27, 28, 31, 37 note 4, 38, 39, 112, 116-118, 120, 124, 143-144, 152, 161, 162-163, 171; cloud-figured, 13, 112, 118; "Japanese," 117.
satin stitch, 118, 120.
satins, dragon; *see* dragon satins.

scales on dragons, 77, 78.
scepters: *ju-i*, 95, 102, 104-105, (132); *kuei*, 103.
Sea, the, symbolized, 36, 40, 49, 65, 81, 83, 84, 150, 174; see also *li shui* and *p'ing shui*.
sea monster, *shên*, 77, 83-84, 97, 100.
sea otter skins, 143, 148, 149.
seasons, 56-57, 97.
Seattle Art Museum, 36, 128-129.
Secondary wives of the Emperor; see Imperial consorts.
semiformal robes, 22.
serge, 112, 158.
serpent, 15 note 19, 77.
Shang Ch'un, Prince, 158.
Shang-i, 116 note 17.
Shanghai, 62-63.
Shên monster, the, 77, 84, 100.
shên-ch'i lou-t'ai, 84 note 17.
shên shih, 84.
Shên Tê-fu, 18.
shêng jewel symbols, 84, 94-95, 96.
shêng musical instrument, 105.
shih-ch'ing, color, 52, 114.
shih-erh chang, 3-4, 4 note 3; see also Twelve Symbols.
Shih Ta-k'ai, 153 note 5.
shou symbol, 41, 59, 73, 92, 94, 100, 101 note 60, 142, 150, 165.
shou-shan fu-hai, 83.
shuang-hsi, marriage symbol, 63, 71, 100.
Shun, 85.
Shun-chih Emperor, the, 87, 136.
Shun-chih reign period, 41.
Siam, 123, 163.
silk, general, 7, 33, 162, *et passim*.
silk factories, Imperial, 25, 61, (63-64), 66, 110, 116-117, 123, 152, 155, 178, 181, 183-184.
silk-raising, 115, 181.
Silk Storehouse, the Imperial, 64 note 21, 116 note 16, 117.
silk tapestry, see *k'o-ssu*.
silk thread, 63, 118 note 25, 124.
silk waste, 57.
silk weaving, 24, 115.
silk-weaving areas, the, 110, (115), 116, 140.

Six Boards, the, 18, (45 note 20); see also Board of Rites, *and* Board of Revenue.
skirts: of court robes, 22, 135, 137, 138, 139-140, 142, 143-144, 145, 146, 183; of dragon robes, 10, 21, 27, 39, 44, 52, 54, 66-67, 70, 180; of Chinese brides, 127, 130.
skirt band, horizontal, 9, 10, 14, 16-17, 35, 128, 136, 137, 139, 142, 145, 177.
Sky, the, symbolized, 39, 81, 101.
sleeves, 8, 10, 21, 24-25, 32-33, 37, 39, 42, 70, 72, 108, 127, 128, 132, 138, 139, 140, 142, 157, 159, 169, 173, 174-175, 177, 182.
sleevebands, additional, 42, 47, 66, 69-70, 72, 74, 146, 147-148, 180.
snake, 77, 78.
Soochow, 110, 116, 181.
Sophora Japonica, 113, 114.
South America, 123.
South Kensington Museum, the; see Victoria and Albert Museum.
Spring robes, 56, 137.
square patterns, 9, 13, 16, 112, 144, 161, 170; *see also* mandarin squares.
Ssŭ-fu, 116 note 17.
stars, 12, text and note 8, 53, 70, 73, 79 note 5, 88, 90, 91, 93.
state umbrella, the, 96.
stoles, for women, 15 note 23, 99, 128, 198.
stole-vest, 128, 130.
"stone black," *see* blue-black.
straps for fastening, 131.
su mu, 113.
su-pu-tu (na-ch'i-shih), 110 note 2.
success symbols, 84, 102-103.
Sui Dynasty, 24 note 8.
Sulu, 14, 163.
sumac, 113, 114.
Summer Palace, the Old, 66.
summer robes, 21, 45, 56-57, 120, 137, 143, 148-149.
sun symbols, 6, 7, 12, 13, 48, 53, 70, 73, 87, 90, 91, 92, 93, 133.
sunbird, the, 48, 87.
Sung Dynasty, 5, 7, 9, 22 note 4, (77), 78, 79, 90, 92, 109, 176, 184.

Sung Ying-hsing, 112 note 3.
swastika symbols, 95, 100, 106-107, 150.
sword symbols, 96, 168-169.
symbols, general, 77-107.
szŭ ling, 77, 168.

Ta Ch'ing hui-tien, 26, 187 no. 8.
ta hung, 16, 113.
tail of dragons, 77, 80, 81.
tailoring, 19, 24-25, 64, 67, 80, 108-109, 138-140, 157, 158, 174, 178, 183, 184.
Taiping Rebellion, 30, 66, 115, 116 note 17, 121, 124, 152-156, 181, 183-184.
ta-na-tu (na-ch'i-shih), 110 note 2.
tan mang, 15, 81.
T'ang Dynasty, 4, 9, 10, 20, 78, (89), (131), 176.
tannic acid, 114.
Tao-kuang Emperor, the, 61, text and note 12, 61, 62, 80 note 7, 93, 142.
Tao-kuang reign period, 30, 58, 61, 65, 70.
Taoist symbols; see Eight Symbols of the Taoist Immortals.
tapestry weave; see k'o-ssŭ.
Tartars (Tatars), 6, 7, 78, 175, 176.
tawny or brownish yellow; see under yellow.
taxes, 30, 124.
techniques, textile, 108-124, 181; see also embroidering; weaving.
temples, 64 note 20, 132-134.
tent stitch, 120-121.
Textile Museum of Washington, D.C., 31, 75, 83, 104.
theatrical robes, 130-131, 182.
thistle, 113.
thread, metal, 45, 118-119, 124, 134.
thread, silk, 63, 118 note 25, 124.
ti-i, robes, 162 note 14.
Tibet, 38, 39, 45 note 20, 172-175, 184.
tieh shang liang chüeh, 103.
T'ien-kung k'ai-wu, 110-114, 188 no. 12.
Tientsin, 63.
T'ien Wang, 153, 154, 155.
tiger symbol, 7, 77, 89.
toad symbol, 87 note 31.
Toronto Museum; see Royal Ontario Museum of Archaeology.

tortoise symbol, 166, 168.
tou-niu, 17, 79.
tradition for clothing, Manchu; see Manchu national tradition.
Treasury, Imperial, 30.
treaties, 138, text and note 5.
tree symbols, 83, 97, 98.
tribute, 14, 23, 28 note 21, 138, 162-163, 164, 171, 172, 173.
tribute silk, 110; as symbol, 95.
ts'ai-fu, robes, 22, 46, 73, 74.
tso mang, 15, 18, 81.
tu linh, 168.
tuan, 117; see also satin.
Tuan-k'u, 64 note 21, 116 note 16.
T'ung-chih Emperor, the, 62-63, 64, 80 note 7, (93).
T'ung-chih reign period, 30 note 28, 62-63, 65.
Tung Ch'iu-hui, 5, 109.
Turkistan, 170, 171.
Twelve Symbols, the, 3-4, 4 note 3, 7 note 17, 12-13, 40-41, 43, 48, 52-53, (54), 58-59, 70-71, 73, 85-93, 120, 121, 133, 141-142, 143, 148, 162 note 15, 177, 179-180.
Twelve-Symbol robes: Emperor's, 12-13, 53-54, 58-67, 80, 82, 87, 106, 119, 120, 123, 179-180; Empress', 66-67, 70-71, 75-76, 100 note 56, 148, 179-180.
Tzŭ-hsi, Empress-Dowager; see Hsiao-ch'in.
tzŭ-tiao p'i, 142.
tzŭ-ts'ao, 115.

umbrella, the state, 96.
uncut dragon robes, 37 note 4, 64 note 20, 132, 174.
unicorn, 99.
Universe, symbols of the, 36, 53, 81-82, 84, 91, 180.
University Museum, Philadelphia, 79.
Urga, 172.

vase symbols, 38, 96, 105-106.
velvet, 33.
vertical dragons, 81, 150.
vests: court vests, 146, 149-151; stole-vests, 128, 130.

Victoria and Álbert Museum, South Kensington, London, 47 note 25, 59-60, 94, 133, (142).
Vientiane, Laos, 163.

Walters Gallery, Baltimore, 92, 119.
Wan-li Emperor, the, 159.
wan nien ju i, 106.
wan nien lien fu, 106.
wan-shou-chü, 98.
wan wan nien hung fu, 106-107.
Wang Chi, 15.
Wang Shih-hsiang, 58 note 5.
water weed, 12, 53, 89, 90, 91.
wave patterns, 16, 39, 40, 42, 46, 48, 49, 57, 60, 75, 81, 102, 103, 104, 122, 147, 165, 174.
wax myrtle, 114, 115.
wealth symbols, 94, 95 note 46, 102, 180-181.
weaving, 24, 42, 45, 108, 110-111, 116-119, 121, 122, 133, 164, 181.
Weaving and Dyeing Office, the Imperial, 63, 116, 121, 181.
wedding robes, 36, 63, 64-65, 70-71, 100, 121-122; *see also* bridal robes, Chinese.
Wei Ch'ang-hui, 153 note 5.
Wên-hui, Prince, 120 note 31.
Wheel of the Law, 96, 102.
white, 85 note 19, 114; green-white, 143.
winter robes, 21, 33, 56-57, 137-138, 139-140, 142-143, 147-149.
Wo tuan, 117.
woad, 114.
women's robes, 18, 19, 26, 27, 34, 39, 41-42, 45, 46-47, 69-76, 81, 99, 101 note 59, 121-122, 127-130, 146-151, 169, 180, 182, 183.
World-mountain, the; *see* mountain symbols.

wu-chao lung, 117; *see also* Dragon; five-clawed *lung.*
Wu Family History, The, 14 note 16, 187 no. 5.
wu fu p'êng shou, 101 note 60.
wu-pei-tzŭ, 114.
Wuchang, 152.

Yale Gallery, New Haven, Conn., 75.
yang symbols, 77, 78, 87 note 30, 88.
Yang Ch'iung, 89.
Yang Hsiu-ch'ing, 153 note 5.
yang-mei (p'i), 114, 115.
yellow: Imperial, 6, 11, 16, 24, text and note 7, 25, text and note 10, 26, 40, 52, 53, 64 note 20, 69, 70, 71-72, 75, 92, 110, 113, 120, 123, 132, 136, 142-143, 147, 148, 152, 153, 155, 162, 165, 172, 173; golden, 54, 113, 144, 148, 173; orange, 54, 72, 143, 148; tawny, 25, 26, 72, 116, 148, 149.
Yellow Emperor, the, Huang Ti, 85, 132, 168.
Yin-chên, Prince, 36, 44.
yin symbols, 78, 87 note 31, 88.
Ying-chou Island, 83.
Ying-tsung, Emperor, 12.
Yüan (Mongol) Dynasty, 4, 5 note 12, 7-9, 10, 11, 14, 20, 21, 50, 78, 86, 92, 108, 109-110, 112, 136, 161, 173, 175, 176, 177.
yüan shêng, 94.
Yüan Shih-k'ai, 86.
yüeh pai; see white: green-white.
yün-chien; see cloud collar.
Yung-chêng Emperor, the, 36, 40-41, 44, 45 note 20, 80 note 7, 136 note 2, 140, 141.
Yung-chêng reign period, 38, 39, 42, 46, 58, 74, 80, 101 note 60.
Yung-lo reign period, 13.
Yünnan, 15.